OPERATING SYSTEMS

Nastaran Nazar Zadeh

Toronto Academic Press

Operating Systems

Nastaran Nazar Zadeh

Toronto Academic Press
224 Shoreacres Road
Burlington, ON L7L 2H2
Canada
www.tap-books.com
Email: orders@arclereducation.com

ISBN: 978-1-77469-760-3

ABOUT THE AUTHOR

Nastaran Nazar Zadeh is a highly experienced computer engineer, researcher, and advisor in the fields of robotics, artificial intelligence and computer science. She holds a Master of Science in Computer Engineering from Mapua University of the Philippines and pursed her Ph.D. in Electronic Engineering at the same institution. With over seven years of teaching experience, Nastaran has taught electronic and computer engineering programs at several reputable academic institutions, where she has also led numerous thesis studies. Her research focuses on developing robotics systems with A.I. and machine learning, which enables her to stay up-to-date with the latest advancements in the field and implement cutting-edge technologies.

Contents

3 Structure of Operating Systems 57

4 Processes in Operating Systems 85

5 Memory Management 103

6 File Systems 129

7 Mobile Operating Systems 157

8 Distributed Operating Systems 175

INDEX 193

List of Figures

List of Tables

List of Abbreviations

AOSP	Android Open-Source Project
API	Application Program Interface
ASCII	American Standard Code for Information Interchange
BSD	Berkeley Software Distribution
CDFS	CD-ROM File Systems
CP/M	Control Program for Microcomputers
CPU	Central Processing Unit
DDM	Digital Rights Management
DLL	Dynamic Link Library
EFS	Encrypting File System
FAT	File Allocation Table
FMS	Fortran Monitor System
GPR	General-Purpose Register
GUI	Graphical User Interface
HDDs	Hard Disk Drives
I/O	Input and Output
IPC	Interprocess Communication
JVM	Java Virtual Machine
LFN	Long File Name
LIFO	Last-In, First-Out
LSI	Large Scale Integration

MFT	Master File Table
MMU	Memory Management Unit
MPI	Memory Protection Information
MS-DOS	Microsoft Disk Operating System
MULTICS	MULTiplexed Information and Computing Service
NTFS	New Technology File System
OS	Operating System
PCB	Process Control Block
PCD Data	Program-Controlled Dynamic Data
PCD	Process Control Data
PDA	Personal Digital Assistant
PL	Programming Language
POSIX	Portable Operating System Interface for UNIX
PSW	Program Status Word
RAMAC	RandoM ACcess
ReFS	Resilient File System
SB	Stack Base
SDK	Software Development Kit
SSDs	Solid-State Drives
TB	Terabytes
TOS	Top of the Stack
UDF	Universal Disk Format
UI	User Interface
UID	User Identification
VM OS	Virtual Machine Operating System
VM	Virtual Machine
YB	Yottabyte

PREFACE

Operating systems (OSs) are software that manages computer hardware and software resources, providing services for computer programs. It is the interface between the hardware and the software applications running on a computer. The operating system manages various resources such as the CPU, memory, disk space, input/output devices, and network devices. Operating systems are the backbone of modern computer systems, and they play a critical role in enabling the execution of applications and providing a secure and efficient environment for computing. Understanding the concepts and principles of operating systems is essential for anyone who wants to develop or work with computer systems.

The discussion of the book starts with the fundamentals of operating systems, followed by the different types and history of operating systems. Also, the structure of operating systems and the concept of processes in operating systems are described in detail in this book. The fundamental concept of memory management in operating systems is also explained in detail. Another important concept known as file systems, which facilitates managing, storing, and retrieving crucial data, is described in the book. The basics of mobile operating systems are also part of this book. Lastly, the distributed operating systems are described in detail at the end of this book.

This book comprises of eight-chapters; Chapter 1 discusses the fundamentals of operating systems with an emphasis on different types of operating systems and different concepts related to operating systems. Chapter 2 deals with the history of operating systems and provides an insight into the different generations of operating systems.

Chapter 3 is about the structure of operating systems and describes the monolithic and layered structure of operating systems. Chapter 4 discusses the processes in operating systems and describes the hierarchies of processes and implementation of processes in operating systems.

Chapter 5 describes the concept of memory management in operating systems along with memory hierarchy and static and dynamic allocation of memory in operating systems. Chapter 6 deals with the concepts of file systems in operating systems that facilitate managing, storing, and retrieving crucial data. Chapter 7 is about mobile operating systems and describes the significance, applications, and security concerns related to mobile operating systems, and Chapter 8 is about distributed operating systems and provides insight into features and design issues in operating systems.

This book has been written specifically for students and scholars to meet their needs in terms of knowledge and to provide them with a broad understanding of operating systems. We aim for this book to be a resource for academics in many subjects since we believe it will provide clarity and insight for its readers.

—Author

CHAPTER 1

FUNDAMENTALS OF OPERATING SYSTEM

UNIT INTRODUCTION

A CPU (one or more), including primary memory, a keyboard, disks, a display, printers, a mouse, networking interfaces, and several other I/O devices, make up a contemporary computer. No code would ever be developed if every application programmer had to comprehend how each function in great detail (Dulman & Havinga, 2002). Furthermore, it is a very difficult job to manage all of these components and use them optimally. The operating system (OS) is a software layer built into computers as a result (Goullon et al., 1978). Its role is to provide users with a model of the product that is high quality, simple, clean, and meets all of the requirements listed above. In this book, OSs are the focus.

Although appearances might be deceiving, the majority of per users will definitely have some familiarity with an OS like OS X, Windows, Android, FreeBSD, or Linux. Although it requires the OS to do its tasks, the program that users interact with is not a part of it. It is typically referred to as the shell or command-line interface when it is only text-based and as the graphical user interface (GUI) when it employs icons (Denning & Stone, 1980).

Figure 1.1 briefly summarizes the major elements under discussion here (Davey & Ince, 1999). The underlying hardware is observable here. The hardware comprises microchips, boards, disks, a keyboard, a monitor, and other material items. The software is interfaced on top of the hardware. Most computers have two modes of operation: kernel mode and the user mode. The most basic and fundamental part of the software, the OS, runs in kernel mode, commonly referred to as supervisor mode (Sinha, 1998). It can carry out any instruction the device can carry out in this mode because it has full access to all hardware. The remaining program operates in user mode, where a limited number of machine instructions are available. User-mode applications are specifically prohibited from executing any instructions that change how the machine is controlled or performs input and output (I/O) (Curry, 1984). Throughout this book, they shall revisit the distinction between kernel and user modes several times. It is essential to the operation of OSs.

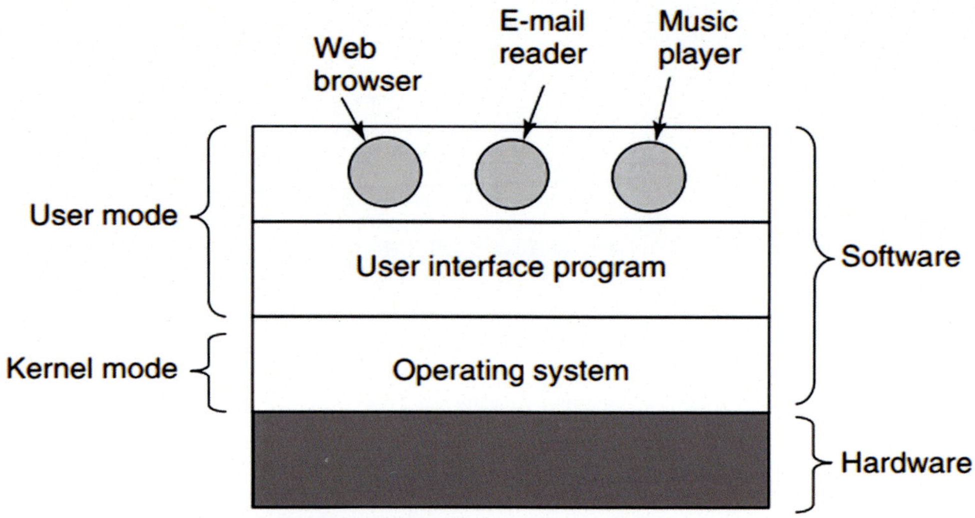

Figure 1.1. Illustration of an operating system.

Source: Andrew S. Tanenbaum, Creative Commons License.

The user can launch additional applications, such as a Web browser, email reader, or music player, from the user interface (UI) program, often known as the shell or GUI, the lowest level of user-mode software (Hughes, 2000). These programs also utilize the OS quite a bit.

Figure 1.1 depicts where the OS should be located (Power & Ford, 2009). It functions on the bare minimum of hardware and is the framework for all other applications.

In many systems, some applications operate in user mode yet support the OS or carry out privileged tasks. For instance, it is common to find a tool that enables users to modify their passwords. Although it is not a component of the OS and does not operate in kernel mode, it performs a sensitive function and has to be specially secured. In certain systems, this notion is taken too far, and components of what is typically thought of as the OS operates in user planetary. It is challenging to define a distinct border in such systems. All software running processes in kernel mode are undoubtedly a component of the OS, but some applications in other modes could also be considered a part of it or, at the very least, intimately related to it (Lister et al., 1993).

Learning Objectives

After the chapter, students will be able to understand the following:

- Basic idea of operating systems;
- Fundamental concept of operating systems as extended machine and as resource manager;
- Different types of operating systems;
- Understanding different concepts related to operating systems.

Key Terms

- Address spaces
- Computer hardware
- Extended machine
- File management
- Mainframe
- Memory management
- Operating systems
- Processes
- Server

1.1. OPERATING SYSTEM (OS)

The only accurate definition of an operating system (OS) that is not always false is that it is the system software that runs in the kernel mode. The fact that the OSs manage these hardware resources and provide programmers who write applications with a clean set of resources rather than the clumsy hardware ones is a contributing factor to the issue. They might hear primarily about one function or the other, depending on who is speaking. Now let's examine both of these.

1.1.1. Operating System (OS) as an Extended Machine

Did you Know?

The first operating system was developed in the early 1950s at MIT for the IBM 701 computer.

The structure of most computers, including their instruction set, memory organization, input/output, and bus topology, is simple and difficult to program (Redell et al., 1980). Consider the contemporary SATA (Serial ATA) hard disks found in most computers to illustrate this idea further. The interface has undergone numerous revisions since then and is now more complex than in 2007. No rational programmer would logically wish to work with this disk at the hardware level; that is obvious. Instead, a program known as a disk driver takes care of the hardware and offers a user interface (UI) for reading and writing disk blocks without diving into the specifics. Many drivers are present in OSs to manage the I/O devices.

This stage is far too cheap for most systems. Because of this, all OS offer files as a further layer of abstraction for using disks. Programs can read, write, and create file(s) using this abstraction without worrying about the complex intricacies of how the hardware is operating (Theimer et al., 1993).

The secret to controlling all of this complexity is one abstraction. An almost difficult task is broken down into two doable ones using effective abstractions. The first step is creating and using abstractions. The second is tackling the issue at hand utilizing these abstractions (Dasgupta et al., 1991). The file, as previously indicated, is one abstraction that practically every computer user is familiar with. As a digital photo, an email message that has been saved, a song, or a Web page, it is a piece of information that is helpful. Dealing with pictures, emails, songs, and websites is considerably simpler than dealing with the specifics of SATA (or other) disks (Silberschatz et al., 1991). The OS's role stands to provide high-quality abstractions, which are used to implement and manage the resulting abstract objects. Abstractions will be a major topic in this book. One of the secrets to comprehending OSs is their use.

It is worthwhile to reiterate this argument in different phrases because it is crucial. Hardware is unsightly, according to the industrial experts who painstakingly developed the Macintosh (Karne et al., 2005). The people who have to build software to leverage real processors, memory, disks, and other devices face challenging, inconvenient, peculiar, and inconsistent UIs. This can sometimes be attributed to the requirement for backward hardware compatibility. Sometimes it's an effort to cut costs. However, frequently the hardware designers are unaware of the problems they are creating for the software. Hiding the hardware and providing programs with pleasant, clean, elegant, consistent abstractions to deal with instead is one of the main goals of the OS. As seen in Figure 1.2, OSs transform the ugly into the beautiful (Anderson et al., 1991).

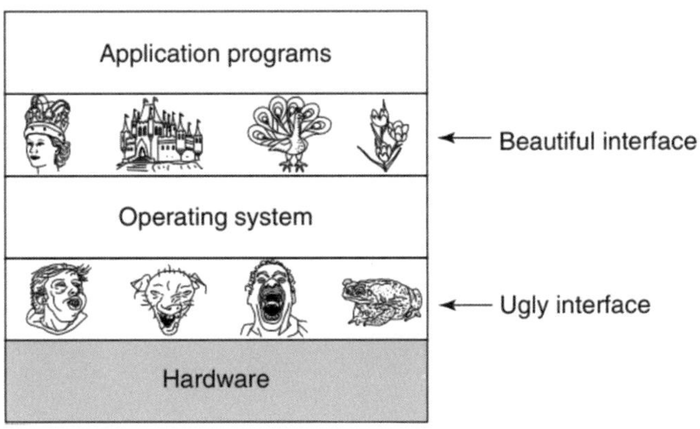

Figure 1.2. Representation of operating systems turning ugly hardware into beautiful abstractions.

Source: Herbert Bos, Creative Commons License.

It should be remembered that the application software, by the application programmers, are the OS's true clients. Application Programmers are the ones who directly interact with the abstractions of the OS (Bardram et al., 2006). In comparison, end users work with the abstractions offered by the UI, which can be a graphical interface or a command-line shell. While there are times when the OS's abstractions and those at the UI are comparable, this is not always the case. Deliberate the standard Windows desktop and the command line interface to understand this idea further. Both are Windows-based programs that make advantage of the abstractions that Windows offers, but they have completely different UI (Doane et al., 1990). However, the underlying OS is the same in these cases. They shall examine the abstractions offered to application programs in considerable detail in this book, but they will say relatively little about UIs. Although it is a broad and significant topic, OSs are only tangentially related.

1.1.2. Operating System (OS) as a Resource Manager

Taking a top-down approach means that the main function of an OS is to provide layers to application programs (Zeng et al., 2016). An alternative viewpoint that takes a bottom-up approach claims that the purpose of the OS is to regulate each and every component of an intricate system. The components that make up modern computers include things like processors, memory, timers, disks, mouse, network interfaces, and printers, among many other things (Silberschatz et al., 2009). Based on the bottom-up approach, it is the role of the OS to ensure that the multiple programs that need memory, processing units, and I/O devices are allocated to them in a methodical and controlled manner (Linden, 1976).

Several programs can run simultaneously in memory thanks to modern OS. Imagine what would happen if three computer programs attempted to print their results to the same printer simultaneously. The printout's initial few lines may come from program 1, the next few lines from program 2, the following few lines from program 3, and so on. Absolute pandemonium would be the outcome (Christopher et al., 1993). By buffering all output for the printer on the disk, the OS can control the potential mayhem. When one program has been running, the OS can copy the output from the disk file saved for printing.

The requirement for controlling and safeguarding the I/O devices, memory, and other resources is increased when a computer has several users since they may otherwise interfere with one another (Cohen, 1993). Additionally, users frequently need to exchange information in addition to the hardware. But, according to this theory of the OS, its main duties include keeping track of which applications are utilizing which resources, approving resource requests, recording consumption, and mediating disputes between programs and users. Multiplexing resources in time and space is a resource management component (Eckert et al., 2016). When a resource is time multiplexed, various users or programs use it alternately. The resource is first used by one of them, then by another, and so forth. For instance, when there is only one CPU available, and several applications compete for its usage, the OS first assigns the CPU to the first program. Once it has had a chance to operate for a while, however, another program is allowed to use it, and finally, the first program is given the CPU once more. The OS is responsible for determining how the resource is time multiplexed, including who goes next and for how long (Agne et al., 2013). The sharing of a printer is another illustration of time multiplexing. A choice must be made regarding which print job will be printed next when several are waiting to print on a single printer. Space multiplexing is the other type of multiplexing (Barak & La'adan, 1998). Each consumer receives a portion of the resource rather than having to wait their turn. For instance, main memory is typically shared among numerous active programs so that each can operate simultaneously. If there is enough memory to accommodate numerous applications, it is more effective to run several of them simultaneously rather than giving one of them access to the entire memory, particularly if it only requires a small portion of the total. Naturally, this causes concerns with justice, protection, and other issues, and the OS must address them. The disk is another resource that uses space multiplexing. A single disk can store files from multiple users at once in numerous systems. A typical OS task is allocating disk space and tracking who is utilizing which disk blocks (Mustafa, 2013).

Did you Know?

The Linux operating system is named after its creator Linus Torvalds.

1.2. OPERATING SYSTEM (OS) ZOO

More than 50 years have passed since the invention of OSs. Many of them have been created throughout this time; however, not all of them are well-known. Nine of them will be discussed in this part.

1.2.1. Mainframe Operating Systems (OSs)

The OS for mainframes, which are extremely large computers that can fill an entire room and can still be found in some of the most important corporate data centers, is the most advanced (Boeckmann et al., 2022). These computers differ from personal computers in that they include an I/O capability. Mainframes are seeing somewhat of a renaissance as a result of their increasing use as high-end web servers for large online retail sites, and administrators for business-to-business operations.

The OS for mainframe computers is largely focused on handling numerous concurrent jobs, most of which require enormous quantities of I/O (Brown et al., 1997). Batch, transaction processing, and timesharing are the three types of services that are generally provided. A batch system performs routine tasks in the absence of an interacting user. Batch mode is frequently used for tasks like processing claims for an insurance business or reporting sales for a network of stores. Many small requests are handled by transaction-processing systems, such as processing bank checks or making airline reservations. Although each work unit is small, the system must be able to process hundreds or thousands of them every second. Multiple remote users can conduct tasks on the computer simultaneously with the help of timesharing technologies, such as searching a sizable database. These tasks are often performed by mainframe OSs since they are all closely related. An ancestor of OS/360 is OS/390, a mainframe OS (Skipper, 1998). However, UNIX derivatives like Linux are progressively displacing main-frame OSs.

1.2.2. Server Operating Systems (OSs)

Server OSs are one level below that. They function on servers, such as mainframes, workstations, or large personal computers (Studiawan et al., 2020). They enable users to collaborate on hardware and software resources while serving several users simultaneously across a network. Print, file, and web services are all available from servers. Websites utilize servers to store the Web pages and respond to incoming requests, and Internet service providers run many server computers to support their users. Windows Server 201x, Solaris, FreeBSD, and Linux are common server OSs (Cole, 2007).

1.2.3. Multiprocessor Operating Systems (OSs)

Connecting many CPUs into a single system is becoming increasingly popular for obtaining major-league computing capacity (Cheong et al., 2020). These systems are called parallel computers, multi-computers, or multiprocessors, depending on how precisely they are coupled and what is shared. They require specialized OSs; however, these are frequently modifications of server computer OSs with unique features for connectivity, consistency, and communication.

Even traditional personal computers and notebooks OS now deals with multiprocessors if only on a limited scale, thanks to the recent introduction of multicore CPUs for personal computers. The number of cores and threads is certain to increase over time (Mondal & Sarddar, 2016). Fortunately, there is a lot of information on multiprocessor OSs that have been gleaned from years of prior research, so applying this information to multicore systems shouldn't be difficult. Utilizing all this computational power will be difficult for apps. Multiprocessors are used to operate several well-known OSs, including Windows and Linux.

1.2.4. Personal Computer Operating Systems (OSs)

The OS for personal computers is the following category. All contemporary ones enable multiprogramming, frequently launching hundreds of programs at boot time. Their responsibility is to give one user excellent service (Salvucci &

Anderson, 2000). For games, Internet access, word processing, and spreadsheets, they are frequently utilized. FreeBSD, Linux, Windows 8, Windows 7, and OS X are typical instances. OSs for personal computers are so well-known that little introduction is likely necessary. A lot of individuals aren't even aware that there are additional varieties.

1.2.5. Handheld Computer Operating Systems (OSs)

They reach tablets, cellphones, and other portable computers and continue to descend to smaller and smaller systems. A portable computer also called a personal digital assistant (PDA), is a little computer that they may operate while holding user mode in their hand (Gu et al., 2011). The most well-known examples are smartphones and tablets. iOS by Apple and Android by Google are currently the industry leaders, as they have already seen, but they are not the only players in the market. Majority of these systems feature multicore CPUs, GPS, cameras, and other sensors, as well as ample memory and advanced OSs. More third-party software (or "apps") is available on all of them than they can shake a (USB) stick at.

1.2.6. Embedded Operating Systems (OSs)

On computers that are not often thought of as computers and that do not accept user-installed software, embedded systems are executed (Bigum, 2005). Microwaves, TVs, automobiles, DVD recorders, conventional phones, and MP3 players are typical examples. The fundamental characteristic that sets embedded systems apart from handheld devices is the assurance that no unreliable software will ever be installed. All the software in their microwave oven is in ROM; therefore, they cannot download new programs (Mugendi et al., 2016). Because of this, there is no requirement for shielding between uses, which simplifies the design. Popular systems in this field include Embedded Linux, QNX, and VxWorks.

1.2.7. Sensor-Node Operating Systems (OSs)

Numerous applications involve the deployment of networks of tiny sensor nodes. These nodes are tiny computers that use wireless communication to connect to a base station and communicate with one another. Sensor networks are employed for various purposes, including perimeter protection for structures, border surveillance, fire detection in forests, temperature, and precipitation measurement for weather forecasting, gathering intelligence on enemy activities on battlegrounds, and much more (Morris et al., 1986). The sensors are tiny computers with radios that run on batteries. They must labor for extended amounts of time outdoors, unaccompanied, and usually in challenging environmental conditions with minimal power (Pfiffer, 1998). As the batteries start to deplete, there will be an increase in the frequency of individual node failures; hence the network must be resilient enough to withstand them.

With RAM, CPU, ROM, and one or more environmental sensors, each sensor node functions as a true computer. It runs a modest but functional OS, typically an event-driven one that reacts to outside events or performs periodic measurements based on an internal clock. The nodes have limited RAM, and battery life is a significant concern; thus, the OS needs to be compact and straightforward (Dongarra et al., 1993). Additionally, like embedded systems, all the programs are loaded beforehand; users do not abruptly launch apps they got from the Internet, simplifying the architecture. An established sensor node OS is called Tiny-OS.

1.2.8. Real-Time Operating Systems (OSs)

The real-time system is a different kind of OS (Brown & Seltzer, 1997). Time is a crucial characteristic in these systems, which is how they are distinguished. For instance, real-time computers must gather data about the manufacturing process and use it to manage the factory's machinery in industrial process-control systems. There are frequent time constraints that must be met. For instance, specific tasks must be performed at specific times when a car is traveling down an assembly line. The car will be destroyed, for instance, if a welding robot welds either too early or too late. There is a hard real-time system if the activity must occur at a specific time (or within a defined window). Numerous are in aviation, military, industrial process control, and related application fields. These systems must offer unwavering assurances that a specific action will take place by a specific time. While occasionally missing a deadline is undesirable, it is acceptable in a soft real-time system and has no negative long-term effects. These include digital audio or multimedia systems.

Since meeting deadlines is critical in real-time systems, the OS may occasionally be reduced to little more than a library linked in with the application programs, with everything being tightly coupled and lacking protection. E-Cos is an illustration of this kind of real-time system (Jackson, 2011).

There is significant overlap between the categories of embedded systems, handhelds, and real-time systems. They all have at least a few soft real-time components. Only the software included by the system designers is used by embedded and real-time systems, which makes protection simpler. Users cannot install their software. Real-time systems are more suited to industrial use, while handhelds and embedded systems are designed for consumers. Nevertheless, there are some things they have in common.

1.2.9. Smart Card Operating Systems (OSs)

The smallest OSs are powered by smart cards and CPU-equipped devices the size of a credit card (Letia et al., 2010). They are severely limited in terms of memory and processing power. Some are powered via the reader's contacts, but contactless smart cards are inductively powered, severely restricting their functionality. Some of them, like those that handle electronic payments, can only do a single function, while others can handle several functions. These are frequently exclusive systems.

Some smart cards are focused on Java. A Java virtual machine (JVM) interpreter is stored in the smart card's ROM. Small programs called Java applets are downloaded to the card and run on the JVM interpreter. Some of these cards can manage numerous Java applets concurrently, resulting in multiprogramming and scheduling requirements (Chen & Zhou, 2021). When two or more applets are active at once, resource management and protection also become a problem. These problems must be handled by the card's OS, which is typically incredibly basic.

1.3. OPERATING SYSTEM (OS) CONCEPTS

Certain fundamental ideas and abstractions, such as processes, address spaces, and files, are provided by most OSs and are essential to comprehending them. As an introduction, a quick look will be given at a few of these fundamental ideas in the following parts. Later in this book, they shall be revisited in great depth.

1.3.1. Processes

The process is a fundamental idea in all OS. A process is essentially software that is being run. Each process has an address space, a list of locations of the memory from 0 to a certain maximum that the process job can read from and write to (Laprie, 1995). The program's data, its executable, and stack are all in the address space region. Each process also has a collection of resources attached to it, which often include registers, a list of open files, a list of ongoing alarms, a list of connected processes, and all the additional data required to operate the program. Fundamentally, a process is a container that houses all the data required to perform a program.

Think about a multiprogramming system when trying to understand a process to have a good intuitive feel. It is possible that the user launched a video editing program, gave it instructions to convert a one-hour video to a specific format (which can take hours), and then left to browse the Internet. A background task periodically checking for new emails may have already begun operating.

Thus, the video editor, web browser, and email receiver are all (at least) active processes. Now and again, the OS chooses to switch from one process to another, possibly because the previous one consumed more CPU time recently than was necessary.

When a process is momentarily halted in this manner, it must be restarted exactly in the same condition as when it was stopped. This implies that during the suspension, all process-related data must be explicitly preserved. For instance, the procedure can have several files open for reading simultaneously. A pointer indicating the current location is connected to each file.

All these pointers must be saved when a process is momentarily halted for a read call made after the process is restarted to read the correct data. In many OSs, the process table, an array of structures with one structure for each running process, is where all the details about each process—aside from the contents of its own address space—are kept (Wulf et al., 2021).

A (suspended) process, therefore, consists of its address space, often known as the core image (in honor of the magnetic core memories used in earlier times), and its process table entry, which stores the information needed to restart the process later as well as the contents of its registers.

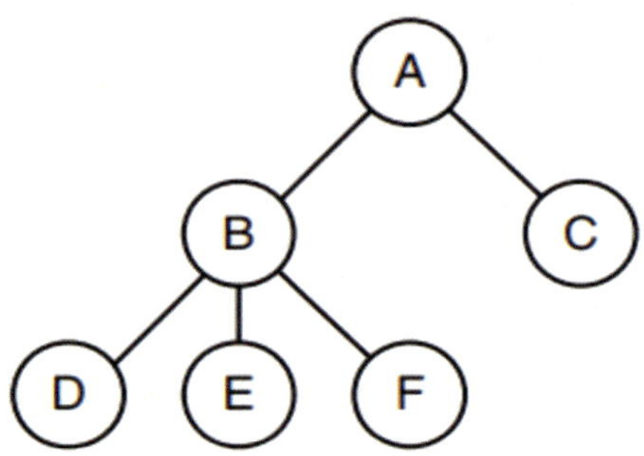

Figure 1.3. Illustration of a process tree.

Source: Andrew S. Tanenbaum, Creative Commons License.

The calls to the process-management system that deal with starting and stopping processes are the most important ones. Think of a common instance. Commands from a terminal are read by a process known as the command interpreter or shell. The user has just entered a command to request the compilation of a program (Borgman & Dalton, 1987). The compiler must now be run via a new process that the shell must create. Once the compilation is complete, that process makes a system call to end itself.

Related processes working together to accomplish a task often need to communicate with each other and synchronize their activities. If the process is capable of executing one or more other processes (called child processes) and this process is also capable of creating child processes, it quickly moves to the process tree structure of Figure 1.3 (Skousen & Miller, 2000). Inter-process communication is the name given to this communication.

Other process system calls can be used to wait for a child process to end, request more memory (or release unneeded memory), and overlay the application running in that process with another (Wang, 2010).

Sometimes, it becomes necessary to deliver information to a process that is already in motion and not waiting for it. For instance, a process might use a computer network to send messages to another process on a different machine to communicate with it. The sender can instruct its OS to alert it after a predetermined time to allow it to resend the message if no acknowledgment has been received, protecting against the potential that a message or its reply would be lost. The software may carry on with other tasks after starting this timer (Zareie & Najaf-Zadeh, 2013).

The OS alerts the process when the predetermined number of seconds has passed. The signal causes the process to briefly stop what it was doing, save its registers on the stack, and begin running a particular signal-handling method, such as resending a message that is thought to have been lost. The operating process is restarted in the same state it was in just before the signal when the signal handler completes (Hermocilla, 2009).

In addition to timers running out, signals, which are the software equivalent of hardware interrupts, can be produced for several reasons. Many traps found by hardware, including using an invalid address or executing an illegal instruction, are also turned into signals for the response process.

The system administrator issues a UID (user identification) to each user granted access to a system (Royce, 1987). Every process that is started contains the UID of the initiator. The UID of a child process matches that of its parent. Users can join groups, and every group has a unique GID.

One UID, referred to as the superuser or root user in UNIX or the Administrator, simply admin in Windows, has exceptional authority and can ignore many of the protective measures. Only the system administrator has access to the password for superusers in large installations, but many regular users spend a lot of time looking for system weaknesses that let them become superusers without the password.

1.3.2. Address Spaces

Each computer has primary memory, which is used to store running programs and applications. A single program runs at a time in memory in a very basic OS. The first program must be removed to launch the second program, which must then be pushed into the memory (Dannenberg & Bencina, 2005).

Multiple programs can run simultaneously in memory thanks to more advanced OSs (O'Brien, 2017). Some protection mechanism is required to prevent them from interacting with one another. Although the OS is in charge, this mechanism must be in the hardware.

The management and security of the computer's main memory are the focus of the aforementioned perspective. Managing the address space of the processes is a different but equally significant memory-related challenge. Each process normally has a range of addresses it can utilize, usually starting at 0 and going up to a certain limit. The simplest scenario is where a process's maximal address space is less than its primary memory. In this manner, a process can utilize its entire address space, and the main memory will have adequate space to accommodate it.

On many systems, however, addresses are either 32 or 64 bits long, resulting in address spaces that are 232 or 264 bytes long, respectively (Çakiroğlu & Öngöz, 2017). What happens if a process wants to use all its available address space, but the computer's main memory is full? Such a technique in the early computers was merely luck. Today, a method known as virtual memory exists, as was previously described, in which the OS retains some of the address space in main memory and some of it on disk and switches between them as necessary. In essence, an address space is created by the OS as a set of addresses that a process may use. The address space is independent of the machine's physical memory and can differ in size from that memory.

1.3.3. Files

The file system is yet another essential idea that is supported by almost all OSs. The OS's primary job, as previously said, is to mask the quirks of the disk drives and or other I/O devices and provide programmers with a beautiful, tidy user-friendly model of device-independent files (Tanenbaum & Woodhull, 1997). System calls are required to add, delete, read, and write files. A file must be located on the disk, opened, and closed before it can be read; thus, calls are supplied to carry out these tasks.

Most computers OS contain the idea of a directory or a catalog as a manner of grouping files to give a place or a to put them. A student might, for instance, have a directory for each course he is enrolled in (for the programs required for that course), another directory for his email, and still another directory for his homepage on the World Wide Web. Then, to create and delete folders, system calls are required. Additionally, calls are supplied to move a file from a directory and to add an existing file to it. Files or other directories can be entries in a directory. As seen in Figure 1.4, this model also generates a hierarchy, the file system (Weber, 2008).

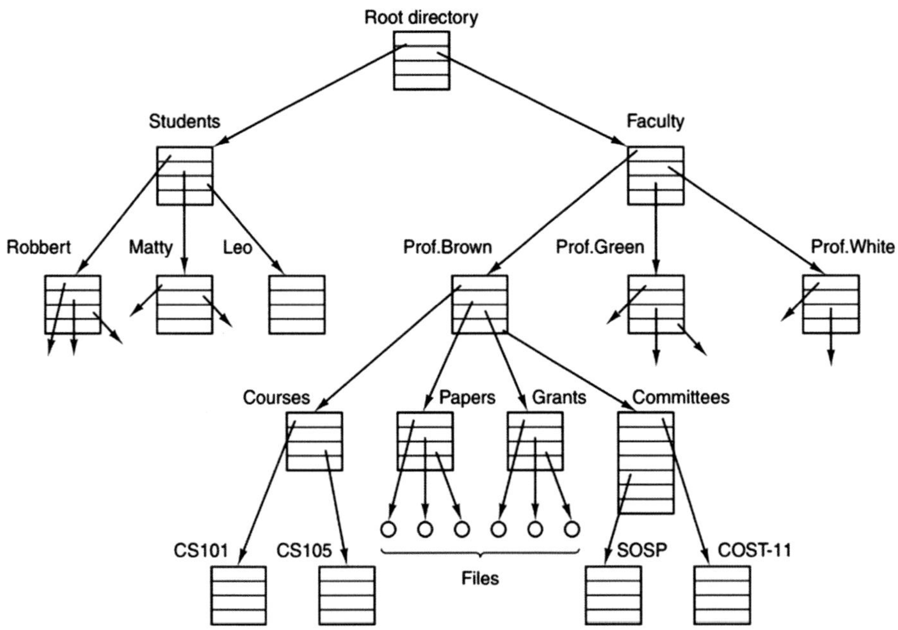

Figure 1.4. Representation of a file system for a university department.

Source: Herbert Bos, Creative Commons License.

Although both the process and file hierarchies are structured as trees, that is where the similarities end. In contrast, to file hierarchies, which can have four, five, or even more levels, process hierarchies are rarely particularly deep (more than three levels). Process hierarchies normally last a few seconds, although directory hierarchies might last many years. Processes and files have different ownership and protection (Hill & Gokhale, 2005). Although mechanisms are almost always there to permit access to files and directories by people other than the owner, only a parent process typically can govern or even access a child process.

The path name from the root directory, which is at the top of the directory hierarchy, can specify any file within it. Slashes are used to delineate the components of such absolute path names, a list of the directories that must be passed through before reaching the file from the root directory. The path to file CS101 in Figure 1.4 is /Faculty/Prof. Brown/Courses/CS101 (Krzyzanowski, 2014). The leading slash denotes an absolute path, starting at the root directory. For historical reasons, Windows uses the backslash () character as the separator rather than the slash (/); therefore, the file path stated above would be written as FacultyProf.BrownCoursesCS101.

Each process has a current working directory where path names without a "/" or "\" slash are searched at any given time. For instance, if /Faculty/Prof. Brown was the working directory in Figure 1.4 (Levy & Silberschatz, 1990). Using the path Courses/CS101 would produce the same file as the above-mentioned absolute path name. By making a system call with the new working directory specified, processes can modify their current working directory.

A file must first be opened, where the permissions are verified before being read or written. The system returns a tiny integer called a file descriptor for further operations if access is allowed. An error code is returned if access is restricted.

The mounted file system is another crucial idea in UNIX. Most Personal Computers have one or more optical drives that can accept CDs, DVDs, and sometimes Blu-ray discs for storage. Most computers include USB ports that can connect USB sticks, which are solid-state disk drives or simply "SSDs," and some also have floppy drives or external HDDs. UNIX permits the file system on the optical disc drive to be merged to the main tree to provide an elegant solution for handling these removable media. Think about the scenario shown in Figure 1.5(a). The root file system on the hard drive and a second file system on a CD-ROM are independent and unrelated before the mount function.

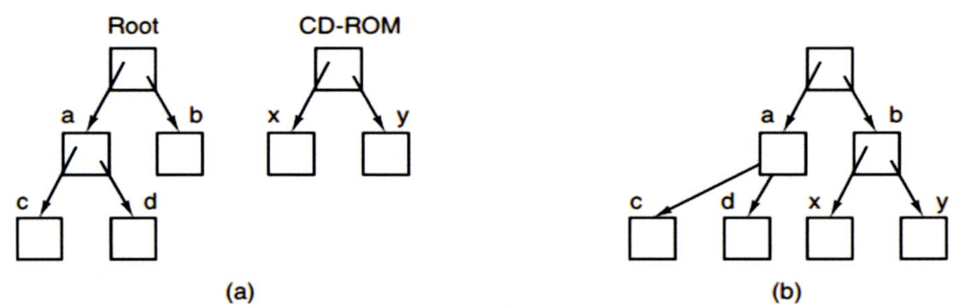

Figure 1.5. Illustration of files on CD-ROM (a) before; and (b) after mounting.

Source: Dave Probert, Creative Commons License.

However, as there is no method to specify path names on the CD-ROM's file system, it cannot be used. Since that would be the exact type of device reliance that OSs should remove, UNIX does not permit the prefixing of path names with a drive name or number. The CD-ROM file system can instead be mounted to the root file system wherever the software desires, thanks to the mount system call (Lamie, 1976). The file system on the CD-ROM has been mounted on directory b in Figure 1.5(b), making it possible to access files /b/x and /b/y (Pinkert & Wear, 1988). Since /b refers to the CD-ROM's root directory, if the directory "b" contained any files, they would not be accessible while the CD-ROM was mounted. (Not having access to these files is not as bad as it initially looks because file systems are often mounted on empty directories.) Multiple hard drives can also be mounted into a single tree if a system has them.

The special file is another crucial idea in UNIX. To make I/O devices appear to be filed, special files are provided (Francis-Mezger & Weaver, 2018). The same system calls used to read and write files can be used to read and write these objects. Block special files and special character files are the two categories of special files. Devices like disks, which are made up of several randomly addressable blocks, are modeled using special block files. The software can directly access the fourth block on the device by opening a special block file and reading, for example, block 4, without considering the file system structure on the device. Similar to how printers, modems, and other devices that accept or output a character stream are modeled, special character files are utilized. The special files are generally kept in the /dev directory (Jeffrey, 1991). For instance, the printer could be /dev/lp.

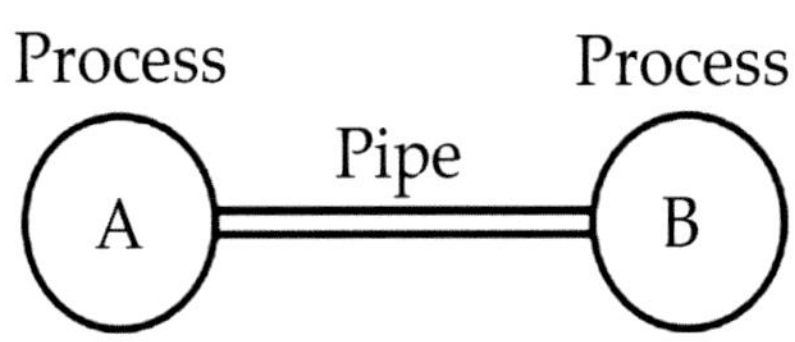

Figure 1.6. Depiction of two processes connected by a pipe.

Source: Ada Gavrilovska, Creative Commons License.

Pipes are the final feature we'll cover in this review, and they apply to both processes and files. As seen in Figure 1.6, a pipe is a type of pseudo-file that can link two processes (Laadan et al., 2011). Processes A and B must prepare the pipe to communicate using it. Process A writes to the pipe as if it were an output file when it needs to deliver data to Process B. In reality, a pipe's implementation resembles a file in many ways. By reading from the pipe as though it were an input file, Process B can read the data. As a result, file reads and writes between processes under UNIX are remarkably similar. And to make matters worse, a process can only learn that the output file it is writing to is a pipe using a specific system function.

1.3.4. Input/Output

Physical I/O devices are present on every computer (Giraldeau et al., 2014). After all, what use would a computer be if its users couldn't instruct it what to perform or could not access the findings once it completed the task? Keyboards, displays, printers, and other I/O devices come in various shapes and sizes. The OS is in charge of controlling these devices. To manage its I/O devices, every OS has an I/O subsystem. Some I/O software can be applied to many or all I/O devices equally since it is device neutral. Other components, including device drivers, are exclusive to certain I/O devices (Fortier, 1986).

1.3.5. Protection

Users frequently desire to safeguard and maintain the confidentiality of vast computer information. Emails, company ideas, tax returns, and a lot more could be included in this data (Tracz, 1974). The OS controls system security so that, for example, only authorized users can access certain files.

Consider UNIX as a straightforward illustration to understand how security can operate. UNIX protects files by giving each one a unique 9-bit binary protection code (Silberschatz et al., 2006). Three 3-bit fields comprise the protection code: one for the owner, one for other users in the owner's group (the system administrator divides users into groups), and one for everyone else. For read, write, and execute access, there are separate bits for each field. The rwx bits are these three bits. For instance, the protection code rwxr-x-x indicates that the owner, other group members, and everyone else can access the file only for execution (not reading or writing). X denotes a directory's search authorization. The absence of the appropriate permission is indicated by a dash (Anderssen & Myburgh, 1992).

Along with fire protection, there are other security concerns. One of them is defending the system against unauthorized visitors, both human and non-human.

1.3.6. The Shell

The program that executes system calls is known as the OS. Even though they are crucial and helpful, editors, compilers, assemblers, linkers, utility programs, and command interpreters are not a part of the OS. At the risk of slightly confounding matters, they will take a quick look at the shell, the UNIX command interpreter. It heavily utilizes numerous OS features while not being an OS component, making it a useful illustration of how system calls are employed (Sinha, 1998). In addition, unless the user utilizes a graphical user interface (GUI), it serves as the primary interface between the user at his terminal and the OS. Numerous shells exist, such as sh, csh, ksh, and bash (Hill et al., 2003). The functionality shown below, which comes from the original shell (sh), is supported by all of them.

Every time a user logs in, a shell is launched. The terminal serves as both the standard input and standard output for the shell. It begins by entering the prompt, which shows the user that the shell is waiting to take command and looks like a dollar symbol (Silberschatz et al., 1999). The shell generates a child process and launches the date program as the child if the user types of date, for instance. The shell waits for the child process to finish operating while still active. The shell retypes the prompt after the child is finished and tries to read the following input line.

The user can specify that standard output be redirected to a file; for example:

```
date >filename
```

Similarly, standard input can also be redirected; for example:

```
sort <fileA >fileB
```

which triggers the sorting program with input content from fileA and output content sent to fileB (Eckert et al., 2016).

The output of a program can also be used as the input for another by connecting both files with a pipe sign; For example:

```
cat fileA fileB fileC fileD | sort >/dev/lp
```

This triggers the cat command to concatenate four files and saves the output to sort the lines of all four files alphabetically. The output is then redirected to a file in a specific path, in this case, a printer.

If the user puts an ampersand after any command, the terminal does not wait for it to complete and instead, outputs the prompt immediately. Consequently,

```
cat fileA fileB fileC | sort >/dev/lp
```

start a background job to begin the sort, enabling the user to continue their work while the sort is in progress. They do not have enough room to explain all of the intriguing aspects of the shell here. Most UNIX literature goes into some detail on the shell.

The majority of modern personal computers employ a GUI. The GUI program runs over the OS, much like a shell (Silberschatz et al., 2009). This reality is made clear in Linux systems since users have the option of (at least) two GUIs, including Gnome and KDE, or none. By altering specific registry variables in Windows, it is also feasible to substitute a different software for the OS's default GUI desktop (Windows Explorer), albeit few users do this.

1.3.7. Ontogeny Recapitulates Phylogeny

The German naturalist Ernst Haeckel declared that "ontogeny recapitulates phylogeny" after the publication of Charles Darwin's book On the Origin of Species (Fink, 1987). He meant by saying that the phylogeny (species evolution) of a species is repeated (i.e., recapitulated) in the development of an embryo (ontogeny). In other words, a human egg goes through stages of becoming a fish, a pig, and so on after fertilization before developing into a human kid. Although this is considered a crude simplification by contemporary biologists, there is some truth to it.

The computing sector has experienced something vaguely similar (Heldstab et al., 2020). Every new species undergoes the same hardware and software development as its relatives. They frequently overlook how much the computer industry, and many other professions rely on technology. It's not because they like to walk so much that the ancient Romans didn't have cars. It's because they had no idea how to construct automobiles. Personal computers exist because it is feasible to build them affordably rather than because millions of people have a long-standing desire to own one (Behrmann & Avidan, 2022). It is important to remember how much technology influences how they see systems occasionally.

For instance, it commonly occurs that an idea becomes outmoded due to a shift in technology and disappears overnight. Yet another technological advancement might bring it back to life. This is especially true when the change concerns how well various system components perform concerning one another. Caches, for example, became crucial to speed up the "slow" memory when CPUs became considerably quicker than memories. Caches will disappear if new memory technology ever makes memories quicker than CPUs. Caches will reemerge if new CPU technology makes them faster than memories. Extinction in biology lasts forever, whereas it occasionally only lasts a few years in computer science.

Due to its impermanence, this book may occasionally examine "obsolete" concepts or those incompatible with modern technology. However, technological advancements may revive some supposedly "obsolete concepts." Because of this, it's critical to comprehend why a notion has been outmoded and what alterations to the external environment can make it relevant again (Clune et al., 2012). Let's look at a straightforward example to illustrate this notion better. Early computers featured instruction sets that were hardwired. The instructions could not be modified because they were immediately carried out by the hardware. Then came microprogramming, where software's "hardware instructions" were executed by an underlying interpreter (first widely used with the IBM 360). Hardwired execution was no longer necessary. It lacked sufficient flexibility. Microprogramming (i.e., interpreted execution) was rendered obsolete by the development of RISC computers since direct execution was faster (Ohno, 1995). Interpretation is now making a comeback in the shape of Java applets delivered over the Internet and interpreted when they arrive. Execution speed may not always be important because network delays frequently take precedence. As a result, the pendulum between direct execution and interpretation has already swung multiple times and may do so again in the future.

1.3.7.1. Large Memories

Now let's look at some historical hardware improvements and how they have impacted software. Initial mainframes had a meager amount of memory. Just over 128 KB of memory was available in a fully loaded IBM 7090 or 7094, which served as the king of the mountain from late 1959 until 1964 (Verma et al., 2019). To conserve memory, it was primarily programmed in assembly language, as was its OS.

Assembly language was declared extinct as compilers for languages like FORTRAN and COBOL improved over time. However, the PDP-1, the first commercial minicomputer, only had 4096 18-bit words of memory when it was originally produced, and assembly language made an unexpected comeback. Minicomputers eventually gained more memory, and high-level languages started to be used often on them (Shan et al., 2022).

The earliest microcomputers had 4-KB memories when they were introduced in the early 1980s, and assembly-language programming came back to life. Embedded computers first had assembler programming and frequently used the same CPU chips as microcomputers (Li et al., 2015). Nowadays, its offspring, personal computers, contain a ton of memory and are programmed in high-level languages like C, C++, and Java. Though beyond a certain size, smart cards frequently feature a Java interpreter and run Java programs interpretively rather than having Java compiled to the smart card's machine language. Smart cards are now experiencing comparable development.

1.3.7.2. Protection Hardware

The IBM 7090/7094 and other early mainframes did not have protection hardware; therefore, they could only run one application at a time. An unreliable program could destroy the computer's OS and cause a simple crash. With the release of the IBM 360, a basic type of hardware security was made accessible (Latif et al., 2014). Multiprogramming was possible on these machines by allowing multiple programs to run concurrently in memory. Programming in isolation was deemed unnecessary.

Multiprogramming was not possible, at least not until the first minicomputer appeared, which lacked security hardware (Molho, 1970). Although the PDP-

1 and PDP-8 lacked hardware for protection, the PDP-11 soon did, and this capability paved the way for multiprogramming and, ultimately, UNIX.

Since the Intel 8080 CPU chip, used in the earliest microcomputers, lacked hardware security, mono-programming—running one program at a time in memory—was once again the norm. Protection hardware wasn't installed, and multiprogramming wasn't made possible until the Intel 80286 CPU. Many embedded devices still today only run a single software and lack any hardware for safety.

Let's now examine OSs. Due to the lack of protection hardware and multiprogramming capability in the early mainframes, they could only run rudimentary OSs that could manage one manually loaded program at a time. Later, they managed numerous programs at once thanks to hardware and OS support, followed by complete timesharing features.

Did you Know?

The concept of virtual memory was first introduced in 1950s by IBM engineer John Backus.

They gradually acquired hardware for protection and the capacity to run two or more programs simultaneously. The original microcomputers could only run one program simultaneously, but they subsequently developed a multitasking capacity (Szefer & Lee, 2011). Smart cards and handheld computers both followed the same path.

Technology has always ruled the software development process (Demigha & Larguet, 2021). For instance, the original microcomputers had no security hardware and about 4 KB of memory. Multiprogramming and high-level languages were too much for such a little system. The hardware and software needed to handle increasingly complex functions were obtained as microcomputers developed into contemporary personal computers. This trend is probably going to last for years to come. This wheel of reincarnation may exist in other fields, but it tends to spin more quickly in the computer business.

1.3.7.3. Disks

Most early mainframes relied heavily on magnetic tape. A program would be read from tape, compiled, run, and the output would be written back to another cassette (Ananthanarayanan et al., 2011). Disks and the idea of a file system didn't exist. When IBM unveiled the RAMAC (RandoM ACcess), the first hard disk, in 1956, this started to alter. Its storage capacity of 5 million 7-bit characters, or enough for one medium-resolution digital photo, took up around 4 square meters of floor area. But putting together enough of them to store the equivalent of a roll of the film quickly became expensive due to the $35,000 annual rental rate. However, costs subsequently decreased, and simple file systems were created.

The CDC 6600, which debuted in 1964 and for many years the world's fastest computer, is an example of these revolutionary advancements. By assigning file names and hoping that no other users had already chosen names like, say, "data," users may create so-called "permanent files." This residence only had one story. A complicated hierarchical file system for mainframes eventually emerged, perhaps culminating in the MULTICS file system (Hwang et al., 2000).

Minicomputers ultimately acquired hard disks as they became more prevalent. When the PDP-11 was first released in 1970, the RK05 disk, which had a 2.5 MB capacity and was just 40 cm in diameter and 5 cm in height, was the standard disk. But at first, it also had a single-level directory. When microcomputers first became available, CP/M was the most popular OS at first, and it too only supported one directory on the (floppy) drive (Almohamad & Selim, 2003).

ACTIVITY 1.1:

Research and compare various operating systems such as Windows, Linux, and macOS and also investigate their history, features, pros, and cons.

1.3.7.4. Virtual Memory

Virtual memory allows for faster switching of data between RAM and disk, allowing for the execution of programs with a greater memory footprint than the machine's physical memory (Li, 1988). It developed similarly, first showing up on mainframes before going on to minis and micros. A program could dynamically link in a library at runtime rather than having to compile it, thanks to virtual memory. The first system to support this was MULTICS. The concept eventually spread throughout the system and is now utilized by most Windows and UNIX systems (Carr & Hennessy, 1981).

In all of these advances, concepts like assembly-language programming, monoprogramming, single-level directories, etc., that were first developed in one context and afterward abandoned when the context changed have since reemerged, frequently a decade later. Due to this, there may be concepts and techniques in this book that seem archaic on gigabyte PCs today but may be revived in the future on embedded systems and smart cards.

1.4. SUMMARY

Resource managers and extended machines are two perspectives on OSs. According to the resource-manager viewpoint, the task of the OS is to manage the many components of the machine effectively. According to the extended-machine approach, the system's responsibility is to give users abstractions that are easier to use than the actual machine. These consist of files, processes, and address spaces. OSs have a lengthy past, going back to when the operator was moved through the present day of multiprogramming systems. Early multiprogramming systems, batch systems, and personal computer systems are among the highlights (Li & Hudak, 1989).

Understanding OSs requires some familiarity with computer hardware because of their tight relationship. Processors, memory, and I/O devices make up computers. Buses connect these components. Processes, memory management, I/O management, the file system, and security are the fundamental ideas on which all OSs are based (Fenichel & Yochelson, 1969). There are numerous ways that OSs might be organized. Typical ones include monolithic systems, layer hierarchies, microkernels, client-server, virtual machines (VMs), or exokernel architectures.

REVIEW QUESTIONS

1. What is an operating system and what are its primary functions?
2. What is process management and how an operating system handle it?
3. What is memory management and how an operating system handle it?
4. Define different types of operating systems?
5. What are some of the challenges in developing and maintaining an operating system?

MULTIPLE CHOICE QUESTIONS

1. Which of the following is not one of the primary functions of an operating system?

a. Process management
b. Memory management
c. File management
d. Program creation

2. What is the purpose of file management in an operating system?

a. To manage input/output devices
b. To manage problems running on the computer
c. To manage files on the computer

d. To allocate resources to processes running on the computer

3. What are some examples of different operating systems?

a. Windows, Mac OS, Linux

b. Facebook, Twitter, Instagram

c. Python, Java, C++

d. None of the above

4. What security mechanisms does on operating system provide?

a. Protection against malicious software and unauthorized access

b. Protection against hardware failures

c. Protection against network failures

d. None of the above

Answers to Multiple Choice Questions

1. (d); 2. (c); 3. (a); 4. (a)

REFERENCES

1. Agne, A., Happe, M., Keller, A., Lübbers, E., Plattner, B., Platzner, M., & Plessl, C., (2013). ReconOS: An operating system approach for reconfigurable computing. *IEEE Micro, 34*(1), 60–71.
2. Almohamad, H. A., & Selim, S. Z., (2003). An algorithm for computing the distance between two circular disks. *Applied Mathematical Modeling, 27*(2), 115–124.
3. Amoroso, E. G., (1994). *Fundamentals of Computer Security Technology* (Vol. 1, pp. 4–8). Prentice-Hall, Inc.
4. Ananthanarayanan, G., Ghodsi, A., Shenker, S., & Stoica, I., (2011). Disk-locality in datacenter computing considered irrelevant. In: *HotOS* (Vol. 13, pp. 1–12).
5. Anderson, T. E., Levy, H. M., Bershad, B. N., & Lazowska, E. D., (1991). The interaction of architecture and operating system design. *ACM SIGPLAN Notices, 26*(4), 108–120.
6. Anderssen, E. C., & Myburgh, C. P. H., (1992). The acquisition of operating systems concepts by computer science students. *Computers & Education, 19*(3), 309–320.
7. Barak, A., & La'adan, O., (1998). The MOSIX multicomputer operating system for high performance cluster computing. *Future Generation Computer Systems, 13*(4, 5), 361–372.
8. Bardram, J., Bunde-Pedersen, J., & Soegaard, M., (2006). Support for activity-based computing in a personal computing operating system. In: *Proceedings of the SIGCHI Conference on Human Factors in Computing Systems* (Vol. 1, pp. 211–220).

9. Behrmann, M., & Avidan, G., (2022). Face perception: Computational insights from phylogeny. *Trends in Cognitive Sciences, 1*, 2–6.
10. Bigum, C., (2005). Design sensibilities, schools and the new computing and communication technologies. In: *Silicon Literacies* (Vol. 1, pp. 130–140). Routledge.
11. Boeckmann, L., Kietzmann, P., Lanzieri, L., Schmidt, T., & Wählisch, M., (2022). *Usable Security for an IoT OS: Integrating the Zoo of Embedded Crypto Components Below a Common API, 1,* 2–5.
12. BORGMAN, C., & DALTON, L., (1987). An embedded multiprocessor computer for proof-of-principle testing of exploratory systems concepts. In: *6th Computers in Aerospace VI Conference* (Vol. 1, pp. 2813).
13. Brown, A. B., & Seltzer, M. I., (1997). Operating system benchmarking in the wake of lmbench: A case study of the performance of NetBSD on the intel x86 architecture. In: *Proceedings of the 1997 ACM SIGMETRICS International Conference on Measurement and Modeling of Computer Systems* (Vol. 1, pp. 214–224).
14. Çakiroğlu, Ü., & Öngöz, S., (2017). The effectiveness of peer tutoring in remedying misconceptions of operating system concepts: A design-based approach. *Education and Information Technologies, 22*(1), 1249–1269.
15. Carr, R. W., & Hennessy, J. L., (1981). WSCLOCK—a simple and effective algorithm for virtual memory management. In: *Proceedings of the Eighth ACM Symposium on Operating Systems Principles* (Vol. 1, pp. 87–95).
16. Chen, S., & Zhou, M., (2021). Evolving container to unikernel for edge computing and applications in process industry. *Processes, 9*(2), 351.
17. Cheong, W. S., Kamarulzaman, S. F., & Rahman, M. A., (2020). Implementation of robot operating system in smart garbage bin robot with obstacle avoidance system. In: *2020 Emerging Technology in Computing, Communication and Electronics (ETCCE)* (Vol. 1, pp. 1–6). IEEE.
18. Christopher, W. A., Procter, S. J., & Anderson, T. E., (1993). The nachos instructional operating system. In: *USENIX Winter* (Vol. 1, pp. 481–488).
19. Clune, J., Pennock, R. T., Ofria, C., & Lenski, R. E., (2012). Ontogeny tends to recapitulate phylogeny in digital organisms. *The American Naturalist, 180*(3), E54–E63.
20. Cohen, F. B., (1993). Operating system protection through program evolution. *Comput. Secur., 12*(6), 565–584.
21. Cole, J. B., (2007). PyPedal: A computer program for pedigree analysis. *Computers and Electronics in Agriculture, 57*(1), 107–113.
22. Curry, B. J., (1984). OCCAM solves classical operating system problems. *Microprocessors and Microsystems, 8*(6), 280–283.
23. Dannenberg, R. B., & Bencina, R., (2005). Design patterns for real-time computer music systems. In: *ICMC 2005 Workshop on Real Time Systems Concepts for Computer Music* (Vol. 1, p. 129).

24. Dasgupta, P., LeBlanc, R. J., Ahamad, M., & Ramachandran, U., (1991). The clouds distributed operating system. *Computer, 24*(11), 34–44.
25. Davey, A., & Ince, C. S., (1999). *Fundamentals of Operating Department Practice* (Vol. 1, pp. 3–5). Cambridge University Press.
26. Demigha, O., & Larguet, R., (2021). Hardware-based solutions for trusted cloud computing. *Computers & Security, 103*(1), 102–117.
27. Denning, P. J., & Stone, H. S., (1980). An exchange of views on operating systems courses. *ACM SIGOPS Operating Systems Review, 14*(4), 71–82.
28. Doane, S. M., Pellegrino, J. W., & Klatzky, R. L., (1990). Expertise in a computer operating system: Conceptualization and performance. *Human–Computer Interaction, 5*(2, 3), 267–304.
29. Dongarra, J., Geist, G. A., Manchek, R., & Sunderam, V. S., (1993). Integrated PVM framework supports heterogeneous network computing. *Computers in Physics, 7*(2), 166–175.
30. Dulman, S., & Havinga, P., (2002). *Operating System Fundamentals for the Eyes Distributed Sensor Network* (Vol. 1, pp. 4–6). Progress Report.
31. Eckert, M., Meyer, D., Haase, J., & Klauer, B., (2016). Operating system concepts for reconfigurable computing: Review and survey. *International Journal of Reconfigurable Computing, 1*, 6–9.
32. Fedorova, A., Seltzer, M. I., Small, C., & Nussbaum, D., (2005). Performance of multithreaded chip multiprocessors and implications for operating system design. In: *USENIX Annual Technical Conference, General Track* (Vol. 1, pp. 395–398).
33. Fenichel, R. R., & Yochelson, J. C., (1969). A LISP garbage-collector for virtual-memory computer systems. *Communications of the ACM, 12*(11), 611–612.
34. Fink, K. J., (1987). Ontogeny recapitulates phylogeny: A classic formula of organicism. *Approaches to Organic Form: Permutations in Science and Culture, 1,* 87–112.
35. Fortier, P. J., (1986). *Design of Distributed Operating Systems: Concepts and Technology* (Vol. 1, pp. 3–6). McGraw-Hill, Inc.
36. Francis-Mezger, P., & Weaver, V. M., (2018). A raspberry pi operating system for exploring advanced memory system concepts. In: *Proceedings of the International Symposium on Memory Systems* (Vol. 1, pp. 354–364).
37. Giraldeau, F., Dagenais, M. R., & Boucheneb, H., (2014). Teaching operating systems concepts with execution visualization. In: *2014 ASEE Annual Conference & Exposition* (Vol. 1, pp. 24–1168).
38. Goullon, H., Isle, R., & Lohr, K. P., (1978). Dynamic restructuring in an experimental operating system. *IEEE Transactions on Software Engineering, 3*(4), 298–307.
39. Gu, L., Vaynberg, A., Ford, B., Shao, Z., & Costanzo, D., (2011). CertiKOS: A certified kernel for secure cloud computing. In: *Proceedings of the Second Asia-Pacific Workshop on Systems* (Vol. 1, pp. 1–5).
40. Halvorsen, O. H., Clarke, D., Halvorsen, O. H., & Clarke, D., (2011). Operating

system fundamentals. *OS X and iOS Kernel Programming, 1*, 1–13.

41. Heldstab, S. A., Isler, K., Schuppli, C., & Van, S. C. P., (2020). When ontogeny recapitulates phylogeny: Fixed neurodevelopmental sequence of manipulative skills among primates. *Science Advances, 6*(30), 2–7.
42. Hermocilla, J. A. C., (2009). ICS-OS: A kernel programming approach to teaching operating system concepts. *Philippine Information Technology Journal, 2*(2), 25–30.
43. Hill, J. H., & Gokhale, A. S., (2005). Visual OS: Design and implementation of a visual framework for learning operating system concepts. In: *Proceedings of the 43rd Annual Southeast Regional Conference* (Vol. 1, pp. 355–358).
44. Hill, J. M., Ray, C. K., Blair, J. R., & Carver, Jr. C. A., (2003). Puzzles and games: Addressing different learning styles in teaching operating systems concepts. In: *Proceedings of the 34th SIGCSE Technical Symposium on Computer Science Education* (Vol. 1, pp. 182–186).
45. Hughes, L., (2000). An applied approach to teaching the fundamentals of operating systems. *Computer Science Education, 10*(1), 1–23.
46. Hwang, K., Jin, H., & Ho, R., (2000). RAID-x: A new distributed disk array for I/O-centric cluster computing. In: *Proceedings the Ninth International Symposium on High-Performance Distributed Computing* (Vol. 1, pp. 279–286). IEEE.
47. Jackson, K. R., (2011). Introduction to cloud computing. In: *Cloud Computing Workshop* (Vol. 1, pp. 5–8).
48. Jeffrey, J. M., (1991). Using petri nets to introduce operating system concepts. *ACM SIGCSE Bulletin, 23*(1), 324–329.
49. Karne, R. K., Jaganathan, K. V., Rosa, Jr. N., & Ahmed, T., (2005). DOSC: Dispersed operating system computing. In: *Companion to the 20th Annual ACM SIGPLAN Conference on Object-Oriented Programming, Systems, Languages, and Applications* (Vol. 1, pp. 55–62).
50. Krzyzanowski, P., (2014). *Operating System Concepts What is an Operating System, What Does it do, and How do You Talk to it?* (Vol. 1, pp. 6–10). Rutgers Univ.
51. Laadan, O., Nieh, J., & Viennot, N., (2011). Structured Linux kernel projects for teaching operating systems concepts. In: *Proceedings of the 42nd ACM Technical Symposium on Computer Science Education* (Vol. 1, pp. 287–292).
52. Lamie, E. L., (1976). Using GPSS to teach operating systems concepts. In: *Proceedings of the ACM SIGCSE-SIGCUE Technical Symposium on Computer Science and Education* (Vol. 1, pp. 174–178).
53. Laprie, J. C., (1995). Dependability of computer systems: Concepts, limits, improvements. In: *Proceedings of Sixth International Symposium on Software Reliability Engineering. ISSRE'95* (Vol. 1, pp. 2–11). IEEE.
54. Latif, R., Abbas, H., Assar, S., & Ali, Q., (2014). Cloud computing risk assessment: A systematic literature review. *Future Information Technology: FutureTech 2013, 1*, 285–295.

55. Letia, M., Preguiça, N., & Shapiro, M., (2010). Consistency without concurrency control in large, dynamic systems. *ACM SIGOPS Operating Systems Review, 44*(2), 29–34.

56. Levy, E., & Silberschatz, A., (1990). Distributed file systems: Concepts and examples. *ACM Computing Surveys (CSUR), 22*(4), 321–374.

57. Li, H., Gao, B., Chen, Z., Zhao, Y., Huang, P., Ye, H., & Kang, J., (2015). A learnable parallel processing architecture towards unity of memory and computing. *Scientific Reports, 5*(1), 1–8.

58. Li, K., & Hudak, P., (1989). Memory coherence in shared virtual memory systems. *ACM Transactions on Computer Systems (TOCS), 7*(4), 321–359.

59. Li, K., (1988). IVY: A shared virtual memory system for parallel computing. *ICPP (2), 88*(1), 94.

60. Linden, T. A., (1976). Operating system structures to support security and reliable software. *ACM Computing Surveys (CSUR), 8*(4), 409–445.

61. Lister, A. M., Eager, R. D., Lister, A. M., & Eager, R. D., (1993). Functions and characteristics of an operating system. *Fundamentals of Operating Systems, 1*, 9–16.

62. Lumia, R., Shapiro, L., & Zuniga, O., (1983). A new connected components algorithm for virtual memory computers. *Computer Vision, Graphics, and Image Processing, 22*(2), 287–300.

63. Molho, L. M., (1970). Hardware aspects of secure computing. In: *Proceedings of the May 5–7, 1970, Spring Joint Computer Conference* (Vol. 1, pp. 135–141).

64. Mondal, R. K., & Sarddar, D., (2016). Web OS in cloud computing: A case study. *International Journal of Advanced Networking and Applications, 7*(5), 28–68.

65. Morris, J. H., Satyanarayanan, M., Conner, M. H., Howard, J. H., Rosenthal, D. S., & Smith, F. D., (1986). Andrew: A distributed personal computing environment. *Communications of the ACM, 29*(3), 184–201.

66. Mugendi, D., Mwangi, W., & Kimwele, M., (2016). Operating system integrity check framework algorithm for threat posed by rootkits. *Journal of Theoretical & Applied Information Technology, 83*(2), 6, 7.

67. Mustafa, B., (2013). YASS: A system simulator for operating system and computer architecture teaching and learning. *European Journal of Science and Mathematics Education, 1*(1), 34–42.

68. O'Brien, D., (2017). Teaching operating systems concepts with SystemTap. In: *Proceedings of the 2017 ACM Conference on Innovation and Technology in Computer Science Education* (Vol. 1, pp. 335–340).

69. Ohno, S., (1995). Why ontogeny recapitulates phylogeny. *Electrophoresis, 16*(1), 1782–1786.

70. Pfiffer, A. K., (1998). Moving paragon™ operating system to a new hardware platform. *Computers & Mathematics with Applications, 35*(7), 33–43.

71. Pinkert, J. R., & Wear, L. L., (1988). *Operating Systems: Concepts, Policies, and Mechanisms* (Vol. 1, pp. 1–6). Prentice-Hall, Inc.

72. Power, R., & Ford, R., (2009). *Operating System Fundamentals* (Vol. 1, pp. 1–10). Power, R. Ford/Boston, MA, USA: Thomson Course Technology.
73. Quigley, M., Gerkey, B., & Smart, W. D., (2015). *Programming Robots with ROS: A Practical Introduction to the Robot Operating System* (Vol. 1, pp. 7–9). "O'Reilly Media, Inc."
74. Redell, D. D., Dalal, Y. K., Horsley, T. R., Lauer, H. C., Lynch, W. C., McJones, P. R., & Purcell, S. C., (1980). Pilot: An operating system for a personal computer. *Communications of the ACM, 23*(2), 81–92.
75. Royce, W. W., (1987). Managing the development of large software systems: Concepts and techniques. In: *Proceedings of the 9th International Conference on Software Engineering* (Vol. 1, pp. 328–338).
76. Salvucci, D. D., & Anderson, J. R., (2000). Intelligent gaze-added interfaces. In: *Proceedings of the SIGCHI Conference on Human Factors in Computing Systems* (Vol. 1, pp. 273–280).
77. Shan, G., Zheng, Y., Xing, C., Chen, D., Li, G., & Yang, Y., (2022). Architecture of computing system based on chiplet. *Micromachines, 13*(2), 205.
78. Silberschatz, A., Galvin, P. B., & Gagne, G., (1999). *Applied Operating System Concepts* (Vol. 1, pp. 6–8). John Wiley & Sons, Inc.
79. Silberschatz, A., Galvin, P. B., & Gagne, G., (2006). *Operating System Concepts, Windows XP Update* (Vol. 2, No. 1, pp. 6, 7). John Wiley & Sons.
80. Silberschatz, A., Galvin, P. B., & Gagne, G., (2009). *Operating System Concepts with Java* (Vol. 2, No. 1, pp. 7–10). Wiley Publishing.
81. Silberschatz, A., Peterson, J. L., & Galvin, P. B., (1991). *Operating System Concepts* (Vol. 1, pp. 6–18). Addison-Wesley Longman Publishing Co., Inc.
82. Sinha, P. K., (1998). *Distributed Operating Systems: Concepts and Design* (Vol. 1, pp. 4–8). PHI Learning Pvt. Ltd.
83. Skipper, J., (1998). The computer zoo-evolution in a box. *Computational Intelligence in Software Engineering, 151*(1), 7–9.
84. Skousen, A., & Miller, D., (2000). The sombrero single address space operating system prototypes a testbed for evaluating distributed persistent system concepts and implementation. In: *PDPTA* (Vol. 1, pp. 6–8).
85. Studiawan, H., Sohel, F., & Payne, C., (2020). Anomaly detection in operating system logs with deep learning-based sentiment analysis. *IEEE Transactions on Dependable and Secure Computing, 18*(5), 2136–2148.
86. Szefer, J., & Lee, R. B., (2011). A case for hardware protection of guest VMS from compromised hypervisors in cloud computing. In: *2011 31st International Conference on Distributed Computing Systems Workshops* (Vol. 1, pp. 248–252). IEEE.
87. Tanenbaum, A. S., & Woodhull, A. S., (1997). *Operating Systems: Design and Implementation* (Vol. 2, pp. 4–7). Englewood Cliffs: Prentice Hall.
88. Theimer, M., Demers, A., & Welch, B., (1993). Operating system issues for PDAs.

In: *Proceedings of IEEE 4th Workshop on Workstation Operating Systems; WWOS-III* (Vol. 1, pp. 2–8). IEEE.

89. Tracz, W., (1974). The use of ATOPSS for presenting elementary operating system concepts. In: *Proceedings of the Fourth SIGCSE Technical Symposium on Computer Science Education* (Vol. 1, pp. 74–78).
90. Verma, N., Jia, H., Valavi, H., Tang, Y., Ozatay, M., Chen, L. Y., & Deaville, P., (2019). In-memory computing: Advances and prospects. *IEEE Solid-State Circuits Magazine, 11*(3), 43–55.
91. Wang, F. Y., (2010). Parallel control and management for intelligent transportation systems: Concepts, architectures, and applications. *IEEE Transactions on Intelligent Transportation Systems, 11*(3), 630–638.
92. Weber, S., (2008). Using virtualization technology to teach operating system concepts: Tutorial presentation. *Journal of Computing Sciences in Colleges, 23*(6), 72.
93. Wulf, C., Willig, M., Akgün, G., & Göhringer, D., (2021). Operating systems for reconfigurable computing: Concepts and survey. *Towards Ubiquitous Low-power Image Processing Platforms, 1,* 61–78.
94. Zareie, F., & Najaf-Zadeh, M., (2013). *OSLab: A Hand-on Educational Software for Operating Systems Concepts Teaching and Learning* (Vol. 1, No. 2, pp. 31–37). WebPub.
95. Zeng, L., Xiao, Y., Chen, H., Sun, B., & Han, W., (2016). Computer operating system logging and security issues: A survey. *Security and Communication Networks, 9*(17), 4804–4821.

CHAPTER 2

HISTORY OF OPERATING SYSTEMS

UNIT INTRODUCTION

Operating systems (OSs) have seen significant changes during their history. In the following parts, they will glance at a few of the most important aspects. Because OSs have always been very closely related to the structure of the pcs on which they operate, they will examine the OSs that came pre-installed on various generations of computers to get an idea of how OSs have evolved. This crude mapping of computer generations to OS generations provides some structure where there might have been none, notwithstanding its flaws (Hansen, 2001).

The progression described below is chronological, although getting here has not been smooth. Each new advancement did not wait until the one that came before it was completed before beginning work on itself. There was a great deal of redundancy, not to mention many unproductive beginnings and fruitless efforts (Choi et al., 2017). Use what is shown here as a guide, but do not consider it definitive.

Charles Babbage, a British mathematician from 1792 to 1871, is accredit for designing the very first "true" digital computer. Even though Babbagea spent most of his life and fortune attempting to construct the analytical engine, he was never successful. This was because the machine was entirely mechanical, and the technology of the time was unable to make the necessary wheels, gears, and cogs with the level of precision that was required by Babbage (Stevens, 1968). If they were wondering, the analytical engine was not equipped with any OS. Ada Lovelace, the daughter of renowned British poet Lord Byron, was hired by Babbage as the first programmer in history after he comprehended that his analytical engine would need software. This historical side trip is fascinating. Babbage was predictable that his analytical engine would want software. The electronic system known as Ada® honors her name (Stuart, 2009).

Learning Objectives

After the chapter, students will be able to understand the following:

- Basic concept of operating systems;
- Learn about the first generation of operating systems;
- Understanding the second generation of operating systems;
- Knowledge about the third, fourth, and fifth generations of operating systems.

Key Terms

- Evolution
- Features
- Generation
- IBM
- MacOS
- Mainframe computers
- Mobile operating systems
- MS-DOS
- Programming
- Punch cards

2.1. THE FIRST GENERATION: VACUUM TUBES (1945–1955)

Following Babbage's failed attempts, and very little progress had been achieved in developing digital computers until the start of World War II, which triggered an outburst of activity. The first functional digital computer was built by Iowa State University instructor John Atanasoff and his graduate pupil Clifford Berry (Ceruzzi, 1997). There were 300 vacuum tubes in use. In the same period, Berlin's Konrad Zuse constructed the Z3 computer utilizing the electro-mechanical relays. Howard Aiken developed the Mark I at Harvard, a group of researchers at Bletchley Park in England developed the Colossus, and William Mauchley and his PhD student J. Presper Eckert developed the ENIAC at the University of Pennsylvania in 1944. Even though some were programmed, others used vacuum tubes, some used binary, and all were very rudimentary, the simplest computation took several seconds to complete on all of them (Bergles, 2003).

Did you Know?

The first operating system, GM-NAA I/O was developed in the 1950s for the IBM 704 computer.

In those early times, each machine was conceived, constructed, programmed, operated, and maintained by a single team of individuals. To manage the system's fundamental operations, The only programming language (PL) used was rigid machine-oriented language, or even worse, by constructing electrical circuits by attaching many wires to plugboards (Franke, 1987). Even assembly language was unknown, let alone PLs. Operating systems (OSs) didn't exist. The typical procedure for the programmer was to reserve a "block" of time by using the sign-up sheets on the wall, and then descend to the "machine room," plug their plugboard in the computer, and wait for a few hours, believing, not one of the over 17,000 or therefore vacuum tubes might blow during execution (Guarnieri, 2012). Most issues included fundamental mathematical and numerical computations, such as determining artillery trajectories or calculating sine, cosine, and logarithm tables.

2.2. THE SECOND GENERATION: TRANSISTORS AND BATCH SYSTEMS (1955–1965)

The picture was drastically altered by the transistor's invention in 1947. As time went on, computers' dependability increased to the point to be produced and sold to clients with the knowledge that they could work for at least long enough to complete a certain valuable task. The distinction between developers, constructors, operators, coders, and maintenance staff was distinct for the first time. The operator walks to the printer, takes out the output, and transports it to output room whenever computer completed whatever task it was working on so that the programmer could later retrieve it. He would then read from a deck of cards from the input room. The operator would have to read in the FOR-TRAN compiler from a file cabinet if required (Gray & Smith, 1998). Operators were wasting much computer time by moving around the engine room.

Given the high cost of the technology, it's not surprising that the people were looking for ways to reduce the significant amount of time which was lost. The fixture that saw the greatest amount of adoption was the batch processing method. The plan was to use a minicomputer, which was fairly adequate at copying tapes, reading the cards, and printing the output but not at all outstanding at quantitative computations, creating a tray which is full of jobs in the input room and write it on magnetic tape. IBM 1401 was great at copying tapes, reading the cards, and printing the output. However, it was lackluster in numeric calculations. Some other, more luxurious devices, like the IBM 7094, were used to perform computational tasks. This scenario is depicted in Figure 2.1 (Nisenoff, 1966).

After gathering a batch of jobs for about an hour, the cards were read and then written onto magnetic tapes. This tape then taken to a "machine room" and installed on a tape drive. The first job was run by the operator after loading a specific program. Instead of printing, the output was recorded onto a second cassette. After each job finished, the operating system automatically read the next job from the tape and began running (Bell, 2016).

Figure 2.1. Representation of an early batch system.

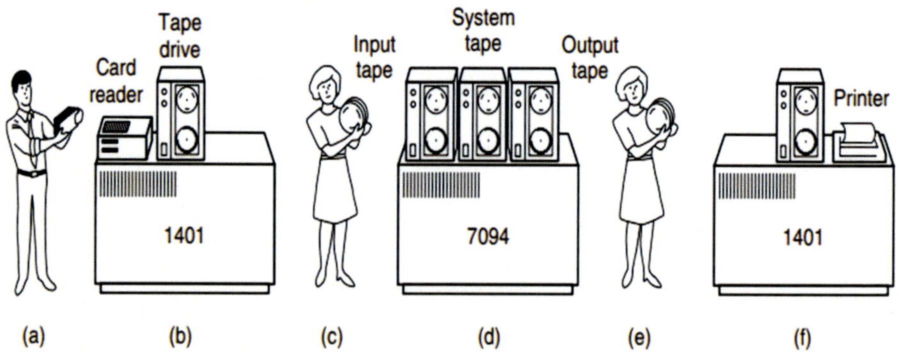

Source: Carole Snyder, Creative Commons License.

After finishing the full batch, the technician takes out the I/O tapes, changes the input tape with the next bunch, and after that, takes the end result tape to the 1401 for printing it offline. Figure 2.2 depicts the framework of a typical input job (Gray & Smith, 2004). It began with a $JOB card with the programmer's name, the number of the account that will be charged, and the maximum run duration in minutes. The OS was then instructed to load the Formula Translation compiler or simply, FORTRAN compiler from the system tape with a $FORTRAN card. The program to be synthesized and a card of $LOAD that instructed the OS to load the recently compiled object program was placed immediately after it. The $RUN card followed next, instructing the OS to execute program with data after it (Grudin, 2017). $END card signaled the completion of the task in the end. The ancestors of contemporary shells and command-line interpreters were these archaic control cards.

Most calculations performed on large second-generation computers were in the engineering and sciences, e.g., the solution of partial differential equations frequently appearing in these fields. They were mostly written in assembly language and FORTRAN. FMS (the Fortran monitor system) and IBSYS, IBM's OS for the 7094, were typical OSs (Aspray & Beaver, 1986).

2.3. THE THIRD GENERATION: ICS AND MULTIPROGRAMMING (1965–1980)

Most manufacturers of computers had two independent, incompatible product lines by the early 1960s. On the other hand, word-oriented, massively parallel scientific computers, like the 7094, were employed in science and engineering for industrial-strength numerical calculations (Rosen, 1972). However, there were also character-oriented, commercial computers, such as the 1401, which were widely used for tape sorting and printing by banks and insurance companies.

It costs the manufacturers a lot of money to create and maintain two different product lines. Moreover, many new pc users found they needed a modest system but ultimately outgrew it. They desired a larger computer that could run their previous applications faster (Hennessy & Jouppi, 1991).

IBM introduced the System/360 to address both of these issues simultaneously. The IBM's 360 is a line of software compatible devices that included "1401" sized units and far larger, more potent devices than the formidable 7094. Only the pricing and capabilities (i.e., allowed I/O devices, maximum RAM, processor speed) varied amongst the computers. Theoretically, programs created for one computer could run on all the others as they shared the same architecture and instruction set. (However, Yogi Berra says that while theory and practice are equivalent in principle, they are not in reality.) A single-family of computers could meet the needs of all clients because the 360 was created to handle both scientific and commercial computing (Tanenbaum, 1992). The 370, 4300, 3080, and 3090 are backward-compatible upgrades to the 360 range that IBM will release in the next years with more advanced technology. The most recent member of this line is the zSeries, even though it has significantly changed since the beginning.

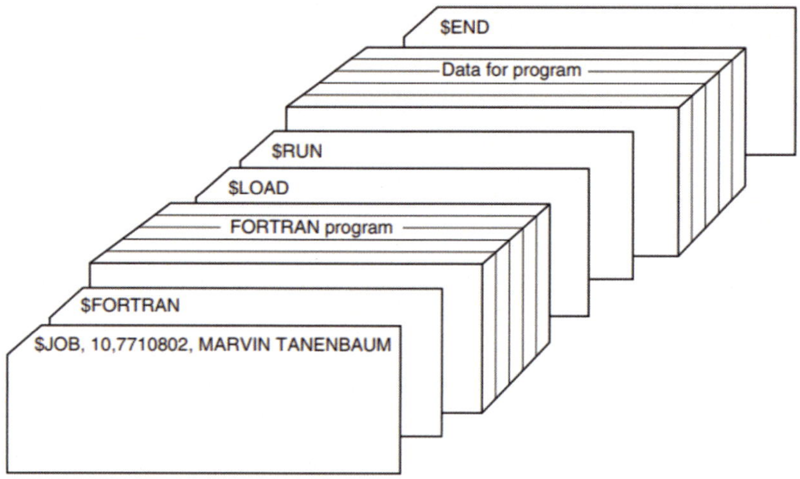

Figure 2.2. Structure of a typical FMS job.

Source: Herbert Bos, Creative Commons License.

When contrasted with computers of the second generation that were built from individual transistors, the IBM 360 was the first significant computer line to use Integrated Circuits (ICs) on a modest scale. This was done with the IBM 360 (Bell, 1985). As a consequence of this, it provided a considerable advantage in terms of price and performance. It was an immediate success, and almost all of the other major computer manufacturers adopted the idea of a family of interoperable computers almost immediately after its introduction. The descendants of these machines can be found working in data centers even to this day. They are commonly used as servers for websites on the Worldwide Web that must process thousands of requests per second or for the management of massive databases (such as those used by airline reservation systems).

The idea of a "single-family" had many positive aspects, but it also had a number of drawbacks. In the initial conception, each and every piece of software, such as the OS/360 OS, was intended to be compatible with each and every model (McKay & Shapiro, 1980). It needed to be able to run on extremely large systems, which commonly replaced 7094s for intensive computing and forecasting the weather, as well as on very tiny systems, which frequently simply substituted 1401s for copying cards to tape. It works well with both systems that require a small number of peripherals and those that require a large number. It was necessary that it work in both an academic and a professional environment. First and foremost, it needed to be useful for all of these different purposes.

It was impossible for IBM or anybody else to develop a piece of software that could meet all of those conflicting requirements at the same time. The final product was two to three orders of magnitude larger than the FMS OS, which was also exceptionally complex. It was built of millions of lines of assembly language that were produced by tens of thousands of programmers, and it was afflicted with a large number of bugs that required a consistent stream of updates in order to attempt to fix them. It is possible that the total number of bugs has remained the same throughout time due to the fact that each new version has both added and removed bugs (Denning, 1971).

Fred Brooks, one of the OS/360 designers, later penned a sharp and funny book (Brooks, 1996) detailing his interactions with the OS. It is impossible to characterize the book in this space but suffice it to say that the cover features a herd of extinct animals trapped in a tar pit. OSs are described as "dinosaurs" on the cover of Rosen (1969).

Did you Know?

The first popular personal computer operating system was MS-DOS, which was developed by Microsoft and released in 1981.

Despite their large size and flaws, third-generation OSs like OS/360 and those made by other computer manufacturers were able to serve the majority of their consumers satisfactorily. They also helped to popularize several crucial methods that were not present in second-generation OSs. One of these, multiprogramming, was probably the most significant. On the 7094, the CPU just sat idle while the present job was put on hold while it waited for a tape or other I/O operation to finish. I/O is infrequent in highly CPU-bound scientific calculations; therefore, this lost time is unimportant (Popek & Goldberg, 1974). Something had to be done to stop the (expensive) CPU from being idle for such a long time since, with commercial data processing, the I/O wait time can frequently be 80 or 90% of the entire time.

The solution that emerged involved breaking up the memory into numerous sections and assigning a separate task to each section, as shown in Figure 2.3 (Barroso et al., 2000). A job could be using the CPU while another was waiting for I/O to finish. The CPU could be kept active almost constantly if enough tasks could be held in the main memory simultaneously. The 360 and other third-generation systems were equipped with this technology, making it possible to run multiple programs safely in memory at once. This required specialized hardware to guard against spying and other mischief by the other jobs (Arora et al., 1998).

Figure 2.3. Illustration of a multi-programming system with three jobs in memory.

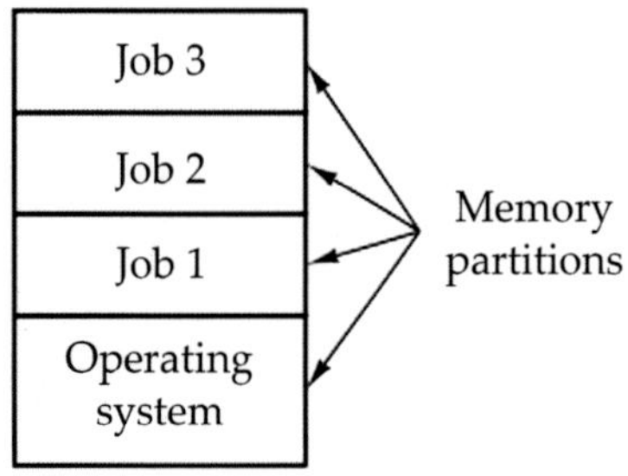

Source: Dianne, Creative Commons License.

An important function of OSs of the third generation was that they could read jobs from cards directly onto disks as soon as the cards were brought into the computer room. This was an extremely useful function. When a work that was now running ended, the OS may then load a new job from the disk into the partition that was previously empty and begin executing it. A technique known as "spooling," which is an acronym for "simultaneous peripheral operation on-line," was also used for the output of data (Fineberg & Serlin, 1967). Since spooling was no longer necessary, 1401s were no longer needed, and the amount of carrying tapes significantly decreased.

Third-generation OS remained mostly batch systems, despite being well suited for large-scale commercial data processing runs and complex scientific calculations. Many programmers yearned for the first-generation era when they could swiftly debug their programs since they had the machine to themselves for a few hours (Park et al., 2015). With third-generation systems, it could take several hours between submitting a job and receiving the results, so one incorrectly placed comma could ruin a compilation and cost the programmer a whole day's work. That did not sit well with programmers.

Due to this need for speedy responses, timesharing—a type of multiprogramming in which each user has an online terminal—was made possible. If 20 users are enrolled in a timesharing system, and 17 are talking, thinking, or drinking coffee, the CPU can be distributed to the three active tasks. Since short commands like "compile a five-page procedure" are more frequently used when debugging programs than longer ones like "sort a million-record file," the computer can offer quick, interactive service to many users while also possibly working on large batch tasks in the background when the CPU is otherwise idle. At M.I.T., using a specially modified 7094 (DeHon, 1994).

Following the CTSS system's success, M.I.T., Bell Labs, and General Electric started developing a "computer utility," or a device that would handle many concurrent timesharing users (Chilipi et al., 2016). They used the electricity system as their example; if they need electricity, all they have to do is plug a plug into the wall, and, within reason, they will have all the power they require. The MULTICS (MULTiplexed Information and Computing Service) system's creators had an enormous machine in mind to provide computing capacity for everyone in the Boston area (Wang et al., 2021). It was pure science fantasy to think that only 40 years later, machines 10,000 times faster than their GE-645 mainframe would be marketed in the millions (for far under $1,000). Similar to the concept of the current supersonic submarine trains crossing the Atlantic.

Success for MULTICS was uneven. Although it had substantially higher I/O capacity, it was built to accommodate hundreds of users on a system that was only marginally more powerful than an Intel 386-based PC (Chen & Yan, 2016). Since individuals back then knew how to create compact, effective programs—a talent that has since been entirely lost—this is not quite as absurd as it may seem. There are several reasons why MULTICS did not conquer the globe, not the least of which is that it was created using the PL/I programming language and that, when it eventually did, the PL/I compiler was years late and hardly functional (Gupta et al., 2022).

To cut a long tale short, MULTICS offered several groundbreaking concepts in computer literature, but it was far more difficult than anyone had anticipated to transform it into a significant product and commercial success. Bell Labs pulled out of the project, and General Electric completely gave up on the computer industry (Srivastava et al., 2016). However, M.I.T. persevered, and MULTICS eventually began to function. Eventually, the business that acquired GE's computer division (Honeywell) offered it as a commercial product, and roughly 80 large corporations and institutions installed it across the globe. Users of MULTICS were fervently devoted despite their very tiny numbers. After years of attempting to convince Honeywell to upgrade the hardware, companies including General Motors, Ford, and the U.S. National Security Agency, for instance, finally shut down their MULTICS systems in the late 1990s, 30 years after MULTICS was first introduced.

By the end of the 20th century, the concept of a computer utility had become extinct. Yet, it may come back in the type of cloud computing, in which relatively small computers are linked to servers located in enormous and remote data centers. These servers perform all of the processing, while the local computer only manages the user interface (UI). The rationale behind this assertion is that the vast majority of people believe it to be more convenient for an experienced group of individuals, such as the employees of the corporation that is in charge of maintaining the data center, to be in charge of the administration of an increasingly intricate and finicky computer system. Numerous companies are already pushing their e-commerce operations in this direction by carrying out email processing on multiprocessor servers to which straightforward customer personal computers connect. This fits in perfectly with the MULTICS philosophy and makes a lot of sense (Bian & Xie, 2018).

MULTICS had a significant impact on later OSs, particularly UNIX and its descendants, FreeBSD, Linux, iOS, and Android, despite its lack of economic success. Corbato et al. (1972); Corbato & Vyssotsky (1965); Daley & Dennis (1968); Organick (1972); and Saltzer (1974) are a few of the papers and books that discuss it. The website, accessed at www.multicians.org, is active and contains a wealth of knowledge on the system, its creators, and its users.

The explosive expansion of minicomputers during the third generation, which began with the DEC PDP-1 in 1961, was another significant breakthrough. Even though the PDP-1 only had 4K of 18-bit words and cost $1,20,000 per machine (less than 5% of a 7094's price), it was a huge success. It created an entirely new industry and was nearly as quick as the 7094 for some non-numerical tasks. It was swiftly followed by several other PDPs, the last of which was the PDP-11. These PDPs were all incompatible, unlike IBM's family (Kamble et al., 2014).

Later, Ken Thompson, a computer scientist at Bell Labs who had worked on the MULTICS project, discovered a small PDP-7 minicomputer that was not in use and began to develop a simplified, single-user version of MULTICS. This work later evolved into the UNIX OS, which gained popularity among academic institutions, governmental organizations, and several businesses (Cebollero-Salinas et al., 2022).

Other sources (such as McCrickard et al., 2003) have detailed the story of UNIX. It will have to do for now to mention that because the source code was widely available, other businesses created their own (incompatible) versions, which resulted in mayhem. System V from AT&T and BSD (Berkeley software distribution) from the University of California, Berkeley, were the two main versions that were created. These also have small variations. The IEEE created the POSIX UNIX standard, now supported by most UNIX versions, to enable programmers to create applications that could operate on any UNIX system. A minimum system-call interface is specified by POSIX and must be supported by conformant UNIX systems. The POSIX interface is now supported by a few other OSs (Abeykoon et al., 2017).

As a side note, it's important to note that the creator published a tiny UNIX clone called MINIX in 1987 for instructional purposes. With POSIX support, MINIX functions fairly similarly to UNIX. Since then, the original version has developed into MINIX 3, a highly modular OS with a strong reliability emphasis (Saraswat et al., 1994). It can instantly identify and swap out damaged or crashed modules (such as I/O device drivers) without rebooting or interrupting running processes. Its main goals are to offer extremely high dependability and availability. It's also possible to buy a book that explains how it works internally and includes the source code as an appendix (Rohlf & Helman, 1994). The MINIX 3 system can be downloaded from the www.minix3.org website, along with the source code.

A student from Finland named Linus Torvalds created Linux out of a need for a freely distributable production (as opposed to instructional) version of MINIX. This system originally supported several MINIX features, such as the MINIX file system, and was directly influenced by and developed on MINIX. Even though it has since undergone numerous extensions, it still shares some fundamental structure with UNIX and MINIX (Zhou et al., 2016). The book by Glyn Moody (2001), which provides a thorough history of Linux and the open-source movement, might interest readers. Thus, most of what is discussed about UNIX in this book also applies to System V, MINIX, Linux, and other UNIX versions and clones.

2.4. THE FOURTH GENERATION: PERSONAL COMPUTERS (1980–PRESENT)

The development of LSI (large scale integration) circuits, which are processors that include thousands of transistors on a square centimeter of silicon, marked the beginning of the era of the personal computer (Landsbergen & Wolken, 2001). Although personal computers, which were first referred to as microcomputers, did not fundamentally differ in architecture from miniature computers of the PDP-11 class, there was a large price difference between the two types of machines. A microprocessor chip has made it possible for a single person to have their own personal computer, while the minicomputer has made it possible for an entire department in a company or university to have its own computer.

When Intel released the 8080 in 1974, the first all-purpose 8-bit CPU, it sought an OS for it so that it could test it. Gary Kildall, one of Intel's consultants, was tasked with creating one. Kildall and a friend created the first microcomputer with a disk when they constructed a controller for the recently announced Shugart Associates 8-inch floppy disk and connected it to the 8080. Then Kildall created CP/M (control program for microcomputers), a disk-based OS, for it. Kildall's request for the rights to CP/M was granted by Intel since the company did not see much of a future for disk-based microcomputers. Kildall then established a business called Digital Research to continue working on and marketing CP/M (Rajan & Jairath, 2011).

To make CP/M compatible with running on the numerous microcomputers using the Zilog Z80, 8080, and other CPU processors, Digital Research redesigned it in 1977 (Miller, 1984). For around five years, CP/M dominated the microcomputer industry thanks to the abundance of application programs created to run on it.

The IBM PC was created by IBM in the early 1980s, and IBM scoured the market for software to run on it. Bill Gates was contacted by IBM representatives about licensing his BASIC interpreter. They also questioned whether he was familiar with any PC OSs. Gates advised IBM to contact Digital Research, the leading OS provider (van Hintum, 1987). Kildall sent a subordinate in place of himself when he declined to meet with IBM, making what is unquestionably the worst business decision ever made in history. Even worse, his attorney refused to sign the nondisclosure agreement that IBM had prepared for the upcoming PC. As a result, IBM contacted Gates once more to ask whether he could give them an OS.

Did you Know?

The first graphical user interface (GUI) for a personal computer was developed by Xerox in the 1970s.

When IBM returned, Gates discovered that Seattle Computer Products, a local computer maker, had an appropriate OS, DOS. They quickly agreed when he contacted them and offered to buy it (supposedly for $75,000). Gates then made an offer to IBM, which IBM accepted: a DOS/BASIC bundle (Crecine, 1986). Gates employed Tim Paterson, the author of DOS, as an employee of his startup business, Microsoft, to perform some of the modifications IBM requested. The updated system was given the new name MS-DOS (Microsoft disk operating system), and it immediately dominated the market for IBM PCs. As opposed to Kildall's (at least originally) attempt to sell CP/M to end customers one at a time, Gates made the (in retrospect, quite prudent) decision to sell MS-DOS to computer firms for bundling with their hardware (Rowe & Shiavi, 2004). After all this, Kildall passed away unexpectedly and suddenly from circumstances that have not yet been fully explained.

When the IBM PC/AT, which replaced the IBM PC and had an Intel 80286 CPU, was released in 1983, MS-DOS had gained widespread adoption, and CP/M was nearing the end of its useful life. Later, the 80386 and 80486 were frequently utilized with MS-DOS. Although MS-DOS's first iteration was very archaic, later iterations included more sophisticated features, many of which were derived from UNIX. (During the early years of the corporation, Microsoft even offered a microcomputer version of UNIX called XENIX) (Necco & Tsai, 1988).

Early microcomputer OSs like CP/M and MS-DOS relied on user keyboard input to execute commands. That later altered due to Doug Engelbart's 1960s study at Stanford Study Institute. The graphical user interface (GUI), which includes windows, icons, menus, and a mouse, was created by Engelbart. Researchers at Xerox PARC accepted these concepts and used them to create their machinery (Thompson et al., 1991).

When Steve Jobs, who co-invented the Apple computer in his garage, visited PARC one day, he noticed a GUI and immediately understood its potential worth, unlike Xerox management, which is infamous for failing to do so. This massive strategic error inspired the book Fumbling the Future (Rugaber & Doddapaneni, 1993). Jobs started work on an Apple with a GUI after that. The Lisa, a project that resulted from this one, was overpriced and a commercial failure. The Apple Macintosh, Jobs' second attempt, was a huge success not only because it was much less expensive than the Lisa but also because it was designed for users who knew nothing about computers and had no intention of ever learning. Professional digital video production, professional digital photography, and graphic design are all creative industries (Igbaria et al., 1997). The use of Macs is extremely widespread, and its users love them. Created to replace the BSD UNIX kernel, the Mach microkernel from Carnegie Mellon University was adopted by Apple in 1999. Thus, although having a very different UI, Mac OS X is a UNIX-based OS.

The popularity of the Macintosh had a big impact on Microsoft's decision to create a replacement for MS-DOS. It created Windows, a GUI-based OS initially built on MS-DOS (more of a shell than an actual OS). From 1985 to 1995, Windows was merely a graphical interface on top of MS-DOS for nearly 10 years. But starting in 1995, a standalone version called Windows 95 was made available. This version included numerous OS features and only used the underlying MS-DOS system to boot and run legacy programs. A slightly altered version of the OS known as Windows 98 was launched in 1998 (Tesone, 2004). However, there was still a significant amount of 16-bit Intel assembly code in Windows 95 and 98.

Windows NT, another Microsoft OS, was internally completely rewritten from scratch but was internally compatible with Windows 95 to a certain extent (the NT stands for New Technology) (Verner & Tate, 1988). A complete 32-bit system was used. Since David Cutler served as the principal developer of Windows NT and was also one of the designers of the VAX VMS OS, NT incorporates several concepts from VMS. It contained so many ideas from VMS that DEC, the owner of VMS, sued Microsoft. A settlement was reached outside of court for a sum requiring numerous digits to represent. Since the original edition of NT was a considerably improved system, Microsoft anticipated that it would eradicate MS-DOS and all earlier iterations of Windows, but it fizzled. It didn't take off until Windows NT 4.0, especially on business networks. Early in 1999,

Windows NT version 5 underwent a name change to Windows 2000. It was created to replace both Windows 98 and Windows NT 4.0 (Press, 1999).

Microsoft released Windows Me (Millennium Edition), a new version of Windows 98; after that also did not exactly work out. Windows XP, a somewhat improved version of Windows 2000, was introduced in 2001. It lasted for six years, effectively superseding all earlier iterations of Windows.

The creation of new variants carried on unabatedly. Microsoft divided the Windows family into a client and a server line following the release of Windows 2000. While Windows Server 2003 and Windows 2008 were part of the server line, XP and its successors served as the foundation for the client line (Mollah et al., 2012). Later, a third line for the embedded world was added. Service packs were the vehicle via which these Windows iterations split off their variations. Some administrators (and authors of OSs textbooks) were sufficiently enraged by it.

Did you Know?

The Linux operating system was created by Linux programmer Linus Torvalds in 1991.

Then, in January 2007, Microsoft officially unveiled Windows Vista, the replacement for XP. It came with several new or upgraded user programs, an updated GUI, and enhanced security. Microsoft had hoped to replace Microsoft Win-XP, but it never did. Instead, because of the stringent license terms, high system requirements, and the support for the DDM or digital rights management procedure that made it significantly more difficult for consumers to duplicate protected content—it garnered a lot of criticism and negative attention (Ray & Misra, 2006).

Many others chose not to use Vista at all after the release of Win-7s, a new and much optimized not to mention less resource-hungry version of the OS. Although Windows 7 didn't include a ton of new features and changes, it was a comparatively much lightweight and a much stable OS. Windows 7 gained greater market share in less than three weeks than Vista in seven. Microsoft released Win-8, a new OS build specifically for touch displays, as its replacement in 2012. The business anticipates that a considerably wider range of devices, including phones, tablets, laptops, desktops computers, notebooks, and home theater computers, would adopt the new design as the standard OS. However, compared to Windows 7, the market penetration is now modest.

UNIX (and its several variations) is the other top competitor in personal computers. Even though network and enterprise servers are where UNIX performs best, it is frequently found on desktops, laptops, tablets, and smartphones. Students and an increasing number of business users are switching from Windows to Linux on x86-based systems (Chute & Westall, 1996).

As a side note, they will mention all contemporary processors built on the hierarchy of instructions-set architecture that began with the assembly 8086 in the early 70s as "x86" throughout this book. There are many of these processors available, made by firms like AMD and Intel, and they frequently differ greatly from one another on the inside. For example, processors may be 32 bits or 64 bits, have a few or many cores, have deep or shallow pipelines, or any combination of these. Nevertheless, they all appear quite similar to a coder and can still execute 8086 codes created 35 years ago. Where the difference is significant, they shall refer to explicit models instead, designating the 32-bit and 64-bit versions with the abbreviations x86–32 and x86–64 (Stein, 1995).

FreeBSD was another well-known UNIX variant that emerged from the Berkeley BSD project. A modified variant of Free-BSD (OS X) is used by all current Macintosh systems (Evans, 1989). Workstations powered by high-performance RISC CPUs also come standard with UNIX. On mobile phones, such as those running iOS-7 or Google's Android, its variations are frequently utilized.

Since the majority of UNIX users, especially seasoned programmers, favors a command-line interface to a GUI, practically all UNIX systems support the X Window System (commonly known as X11), a windowing system developed at M.I.T. Users can create, delete, move, and resize windows with a mouse thanks to this system, which also handles basic window management. For UNIX users who desire it, a full GUI, like Gnome or KDE, is frequently offered to run on top of X11 and provide UNIX a look and feel similar to the Macintosh or Microsoft Windows (Elder, 1984).

The expansion of networks of personal computers running a network OS and distributed OSs is an intriguing phenomenon that started in the middle of the 1980s (Zhao & Qing, 2023). In a network OS, consumers are aware that there are numerous computers present and have the ability to log in to distant machines and transfer files from one machine to another. Each computer has its local user (or users) and local OS.

OSs for single processors and networks are not fundamentally dissimilar. While it is evident that they require a network interface controller, some low-level software to operate it, and applications to enable remote login and remote file access, these additions do not alter the OS's fundamental design.

While consisting of numerous processors, a distributed OS presents itself to its users as a conventional uniprocessor system. Users shouldn't know where their applications are being executed, or their files are stored; the OS should handle everything automatically and effectively. Because distributed and centralized systems differ in a few crucial areas, true distributed OSs involve more than simply adding a little code to a uniprocessor OS (Berry, 1987). For instance, distributed systems frequently permit programs to execute concurrently on several processors, necessitating more sophisticated processor scheduling techniques.

These (and other) algorithms frequently have to operate with partial, out-of-date, or even inaccurate data due to network communication delays. This drastically differs from a single-processor system, where the OS has full knowledge of the system status.

2.5. THE FIFTH GENERATION: MOBILE COMPUTERS (1990–PRESENT)

Did you Know?

The first mobile operating system, Symbian, was developed in 1990s and was used in Nokia phones.

People all over the world have desired for a pocketable, communication device ever since detective Dick Tracy in the 1940s comic strip began conversing with his "two-way radio wristwatch." In 1946, a real mobile phone made its debut, and it weighed about 40 kilograms (Rajan & Jairath, 2011). As long as they had a car to transport it in, they could take it anywhere.

The first portable phone debuted in the 1970s and was positively featherweight at about one kilogram. It was jokingly referred to as "the brick." Soon, everyone was clamoring for one. Nearly 90% of people on the planet have cell phones today. Shortly, eyeglasses and other wearable devices will be able to make calls in addition to our portable phones and wristwatches. Additionally, the phone component is no longer all that fascinating. They do not give it a second thought while they receive emails, browse the web, text pals, play games, and maneuver through congested traffic (Vij & Jain, 2016).

The idea of combining computing and telephony in a phone-like device has been around since the 1970s, but the first genuine smartphone wasn't produced until Nokia's N9000 in the middle of the 1990s. This device combined a phone and a PDA (personal digital assistant), two functions that were previously mostly separate. For its GS88 "Penelope," Ericsson first used the word smartphone in 1997 (Yang, 2021).

The battle between the various OSs is severe now that cell phones are commonplace, and the outcome is even-less certain than in the Personal Computer's industry. Currently, iOS by Apple and Android by Google, are the two most widely used and popular OS, but this was not always the case. In a few years, things could change drastically (Forman & Zahorjan, 1994). In smartphones, it is evident that it is difficult to hold the top spot for very long.

ACTIVITY 2.1:

Create a timeline of the major milestones in the development of operating systems, including the introduction of key features and the release of significant operating system versions.

After all, Symbian OS powered most smartphones over the first 10 years after their introduction. Popular companies like Sony, Samsung, Nokia, and Motorola used it as their preferred OS. However, Symbian's market share began to decline as other OSs, such as Apple's iOS and RIM's Blackberry OS, both of which debuted in 2002 for smartphones. Many predicted that RIM would rule the complete business while the iOS rule's the consumer electronics market. The market share of Symbian decreased. Nokia said in 2011 that it would stop supporting Symbian and instead concentrate on the Windows Phone OS. Although not nearly as popular as Symbian (Nokia) had been, Apple and RIM were once the talks of the town (Mukherjee & De, 2016). However, Android (currently the used in smartphones), the OS based on Linux was introduced by Google in the year 2008, quickly surpassed all the competitors in the market.

The fact that Android was open source and offered under a permissive license was advantageous for phone manufacturers. They could, therefore, easily modify it and fit it into their hardware. Additionally, it has a sizable developer community that produces programs, most frequently in the well-known Java PL. The supremacy may not endure, though, as evidenced by recent years, and Android's rivals are anxious to reclaim some of its market shares (Huang et al., 2019).

2.6. SUMMARY

OSs have a long and complex history dating back to the early days of computing. In 1950s early computers were programmed using machine language, which was a laborious and time-consuming process. The first OSs were developed to make programming more efficient. The rise of mainframe OSs became more prevalent and systems like IBM's OS/360 were developed. In 1980s personal computers became more popular and OSs like MS-DOS and Apple's Macintosh system were developed. In 1990s OSs like Windows 95 and MacOS 7 introduced GUI making computers more user-friendly. In 2000s OSs like Symbian, iOS ad Android were developed to run on mobile devices like smartphones and tablets. The history of OSs is a story of constant innovation and evolution as developers have sought to meet the changing needs of users and businesses.

REVIEW QUESTIONS

1. What was the first operating system and why was it developed?
2. How did the rise of mainframe computers in the 1960s and 1970s impact the development of operating systems?
3. What were some of the challenges involved in developing operating systems for mobile devices?
4. How has the evolution of operating systems impacted the way we use computers and other devices in our daily life?
5. What are some of the current trends and developments in the field of operating systems?

MULTIPLE CHOICE QUESTIONS

1. What was the first operating system?

a. MS-DOS
b. GM-NAA I/O
c. MacOS
d. Symbian

2. Which operating system introduced graphical user interface in the 1990s?

a. Windows 31
b. Windows 95
c. MacOS 7
d. Linux

3. Which operating system is commonly used for cloud computing?

a. MacOS

b. Windows 10
c. Linux
d. iOS

4. What were some of the challenges involved in developing operating systems for mobile devices?

a. Limited processing power and memory
b. Limited battery life
c. Small screen size
d. All of the above

Answers to Multiple Choice Questions

1. (b); 2. (b); 3. (c); 4. (d)

REFERENCES

1. Abeykoon, S. K., Lin, M., & Van, D. K. K., (2017). Parallelizing x-ray photon correlation spectroscopy software tools using python multiprocessing. In: *2017 New York Scientific Data Summit (NYSDS)* (Vol. 1, pp. 1–10). IEEE.
2. Arora, N. S., Blumofe, R. D., & Plaxton, C. G., (1998). Thread scheduling for multiprogrammed multiprocessors. In: *Proceedings of the Tenth Annual ACM Symposium on PARALLEL Algorithms and Architectures* (Vol. 1, pp. 119–129).
3. Aspray, W., & Beaver, D. D., (1986). Marketing the monster: Advertising computer technology. *Annals of the History of Computing, 8*(2), 127–143.
4. Barroso, L. A., Gharachorloo, K., McNamara, R., Nowatzyk, A., Qadeer, S., Sano, B., & Verghese, B., (2000). Piranha: A scalable architecture based on single-chip multiprocessing. *ACM SIGARCH Computer Architecture News, 28*(2), 282–293.
5. Bell, C. G., (1985). Multis: A new class of multiprocessor computers. *Science, 228*(4698), 462–467.
6. Bell, G., (2016). *Bell's Law for the Birth and Death of Computer Classes: A Theory of the Computer's Evolution Gordon Bell, 1*, 2–6.
7. Bergles, A. E., (2003). Evolution of cooling technology for electrical, electronic, and microelectronic equipment. *IEEE Transactions on Components and Packaging Technologies, 26*(1), 6–15.
8. Berry, J. K., (1987). Fundamental operations in computer-assisted map analysis. *International Journal of Geographical Information System, 1*(2), 119–136.
9. Bian, Y., & Xie, X. Q., (2018). Computational fragment-based drug design: Current trends, strategies, and applications. *The AAPS Journal, 20*(1), 1–11.

10. Brooks, F. P., (1996). Keynote address: Language design as design. In: *History of Programming Languages—II* (Vol. 1, pp. 4–16).
11. Cebollero-Salinas, A., Cano-Escoriaza, J., & Orejudo, S., (2022). Are emotional e-competencies a protective factor against habitual digital behaviors (media multitasking, cybergossip, phubbing) in Spanish students of secondary education? *Computers & Education, 181*(1), 104464.
12. Ceruzzi, P., (1997). Crossing the divide: Architectural issues and the emergence of the stored program computer, 1935–1955. *IEEE Annals of the History of Computing, 19*(1), 5–12.
13. Chen, Q., & Yan, Z., (2016). Does multitasking with mobile phones affect learning? A review. *Computers in Human Behavior, 54*(1), 34–42.
14. Chilipi, R. R., Al Sayari, N., Beig, A. R., & AlHosani, K., (2016). A multitasking control algorithm for grid-connected inverters in distributed generation applications using adaptive noise cancellation filters. *IEEE Transactions on Energy Conversion, 31*(2), 714–727.
15. Choi, N., Kim, D., Lee, S. J., & Yi, Y., (2017). A fog operating system for user oriented IoT services: Challenges and research directions. *IEEE Communications Magazine, 55*(8), 44–51.
16. Chute, D. L., & Westall, R. F., (1996). Fifth-generation research tools: Collaborative development with power laboratory. *Behavior Research Methods, Instruments, & Computers, 28*(2), 311–314.
17. Crecine, J. D., (1986). The next generation of personal computers. *Science, 231*(4741), 935–943.
18. DeHon, A., (1994). DPGA-coupled microprocessors: Commodity ICs for the early 21st century. In: *Proceedings of IEEE Workshop on FPGAs for Custom Computing Machines* (Vol. 1, pp. 31–39). IEEE.
19. Denning, P. J., (1971). Third generation computer systems. *ACM Computing Surveys (CSUR), 3*(4), 175–216.
20. Elder, M., (1984). SALVO: A fourth-generation language for personal computers. In: *Proceedings of the July 9–12, 1984, National Computer Conference and Exposition* (Vol. 1, pp. 561–566).
21. Evans, M. W., (1989). *The Software Factory: A Fourth Generation Software Engineering Environment* (Vol. 1, pp. 2–5). John Wiley & Sons, Inc.
22. Fineberg, M. S., & Serlin, O., (1967). Multiprogramming for hybrid computation. In: *Proceedings of the November 14–16, 1967, Fall Joint Computer Conference* (Vol. 1, pp. 1–13).
23. Forman, G. H., & Zahorjan, J., (1994). The challenges of mobile computing. *Computer, 27*(4), 38–47.
24. Franke, R. H., (1987). Technological revolution and productivity decline: Computer introduction in the financial industry. *Technological Forecasting and Social Change, 31*(2), 143–154.

25. Gray, G. T., & Smith, R. Q., (2004). Sperry rand's first-generation computers, 1955–1960: Hardware and software. *IEEE Annals of the History of Computing, 26*(4), 20–34.
26. Gray, G., & Smith, R., (1998). Sperry rand's transistor computers. *IEEE Annals of the History of Computing, 20*(3), 16–26.
27. Grudin, J., (2017). From tool to partner: The evolution of human-computer interaction. *Synthesis Lectures on Human-Centered Interaction, 10*(1), 1–183.
28. Guarnieri, M., (2012). The age of vacuum tubes: Merging with digital computing [historical]. *IEEE Industrial Electronics Magazine, 6*(3), 52–55.
29. Gupta, A., Zhou, L., Ong, Y. S., Chen, Z., & Hou, Y., (2022). Half a dozen real-world applications of evolutionary multitasking, and more. *IEEE Computational Intelligence Magazine, 17*(2), 49–66.
30. Hansen, P. B., (2001). The evolution of operating systems. *Classic Operating Systems: From Batch Processing to Distributed Systems, 1*, 1–34.
31. Hennessy, J. L., & Jouppi, N. P., (1991). Computer technology and architecture: An evolving interaction. *Computer, 24*(9), 18–29.
32. Huang, D., Du, Z., & Wang, Y., (2019). Slot antenna array for fifth generation metal frame mobile phone applications. *International Journal of RF and Microwave Computer-Aided Engineering, 29*(9), e21841.
33. Igbaria, M., Zinatelli, N., Cragg, P., & Cavaye, A. L., (1997). Personal computing acceptance factors in small firms: A structural equation model. *MIS Quarterly, 2*(1), 279–305.
34. Kamble, S., Meshram, S., Thokal, R., & Gakre, R., (2014). Developing a multitasking shopping trolley based on RFID technology. *International Journal of Soft Computing and Engineering (IJSCE), 3*(6), 4–8.
35. Landsbergen, Jr. D., & WolkenJr, G., (2001). Realizing the promise: Government information systems and the fourth generation of information technology. *Public Administration Review, 61*(2), 206–220.
36. McCrickard, D. S., Chewar, C. M., Somervell, J. P., & Ndiwalana, A., (2003). A model for notification systems evaluation—Assessing user goals for multitasking activity. *ACM Transactions on Computer-Human Interaction (TOCHI), 10*(4), 312–338.
37. McKay, D. P., & Shapiro, S. C., (1980). MULTI-a LISP based multiprocessing system. In: *Proceedings of the 1980 ACM Conference on LISP and Functional Programming* (Vol. 1, pp. 29–37).
38. Miller, B. B., (1984). Fourth-generation languages (4GLs) and personal computers. In: *Proceedings of the July 9–12, 1984, National Computer Conference and Exposition* (Vol. 1, pp. 555–559).
39. Mollah, M. B., Islam, K. R., & Islam, S. S., (2012). Next generation of computing through cloud computing technology. In: *2012 25th IEEE Canadian Conference on Electrical and Computer Engineering (CCECE)* (Vol. 1, pp. 1–6). IEEE.
40. Mukherjee, A., & De, D., (2016). Femtolet: A novel fifth generation network device

for green mobile cloud computing. *Simulation Modeling Practice and Theory, 62*(1), 68–87.

41. Necco, C. R., & Tsai, N. W., (1988). Use of fourth generation languages: Application development. *Journal of Systems Management, 39*(8), 26.
42. Nisenoff, N., (1966). Hardware for information processing systems: Today and in the future. *Proceedings of the IEEE, 54*(12), 1820–1835.
43. Park, J. J. K., Park, Y., & Mahlke, S., (2015). Chimera: Collaborative preemption for multitasking on a shared GPU. *ACM SIGARCH Computer Architecture News, 43*(1), 593–606.
44. Popek, G. J., & Goldberg, R. P., (1974). Formal requirements for virtualizable third generation architectures. *Communications of the ACM, 17*(7), 412–421.
45. Press, L., (1999). Personal computing: The next generation of business data processing. *Communications of the ACM, 42*(2), 13–16.
46. Rajan, S., & Jairath, A., (2011). Cloud computing: The fifth generation of computing. In: *2011 International Conference on Communication Systems and Network Technologies* (Vol. 1, pp. 665–667). IEEE.
47. Ray, S. K., & Misra, I. S., (2006). Fourth generation (4G) networks: Roadmap-migration to the future. *IETE Technical Review, 23*(4), 253–265.
48. Rohlf, J., & Helman, J., (1994). IRIS performer: A high performance multiprocessing toolkit for real-time 3D graphics. In: *Proceedings of the 21st Annual Conference on Computer Graphics and Interactive Techniques* (Vol. 1, pp. 381–394).
49. Rosen, S., (1969). Electronic computers: A historical survey. *ACM Computing Surveys (CSUR), 1*(1), 7–36.
50. Rosen, S., (1972). Programming systems and languages 1965–1975. *Communications of the ACM, 15*(7), 591–600.
51. Rowe, C., & Shiavi, R., (2004). Incorporation of fourth generation computing environment into freshmen engineering program: A historical perspective. In: *2004 Annual Conference* (Vol. 1, pp. 9–719).
52. Rugaber, S., & Doddapaneni, S., (1993). The transition of application programs from COBOL to a fourth-generation language. In: *1993 Conference on Software Maintenance* (Vol. 1, pp. 61–70). IEEE.
53. Saraswat, K. C., Apte, P. P., Booth, L., Chen, Y., Dankoski, P. C. P., Degertekin, F. L., & Wood, S. C., (1994). Rapid thermal multiprocessing for a programmable factory for adaptable manufacturing of ICs. *IEEE Transactions on Semiconductor Manufacturing, 7*(2), 159–175.
54. Srivastava, J., Nakazawa, M., & Chen, Y. W., (2016). Online, mixed, and offline media multitasking: Role of cultural, socio-demographic, and media factors. *Computers in Human Behavior, 62*(1), 720–729.
55. Stein, A., (1995). Re-engineering the executive: The 4th generation of EIS. *Information & Management, 29*(1), 55–62.

56. Stevens, D. F., (1968). Operating systems: On overcoming high-priority paralysis in multiprogramming systems: A case history. *Communications of the ACM, 11*(8), 539–541.
57. Stuart, B. L., (2009). Principles of operating systems: Design & applications. *Course Technology, 1*, 2–6.
58. Tanenbaum, A. S., (1992). Operating systems—The state of the art. *Handbooks in Operations Research and Management Science, 3*(1), 91–131.
59. Tesone, D. V., (2004). Fourth generation online learning for business and hospitality management schools: So far, so fast. *Journal of Applied Management and Entrepreneurship, 9*(2), 57.
60. Thompson, R. L., Higgins, C. A., & Howell, J. M., (1991). Personal computing: Toward a conceptual model of utilization. *MIS Quarterly, 1*, 125–143.
61. Van, H. T. J., (1987). GENIS: A fourth generation information system for the database management of genebanks. *Plant Genet. Resour. Newsl., 75*(76), 13–15.
62. Verner, J., & Tate, G., (1988). Estimating size and effort in fourth-generation development. *IEEE Software, 5*(4), 15–22.
63. Vij, S., & Jain, A., (2016). 5G: Evolution of a secure mobile technology. In: *2016 3rd International Conference on Computing for Sustainable Global Development (INDIACom)* (Vol. 1, pp. 2192–2196). IEEE.
64. Wang, H., Feng, L., Jin, Y., & Doherty, J., (2021). Surrogate-assisted evolutionary multitasking for expensive minimax optimization in multiple scenarios. *IEEE Computational Intelligence Magazine, 16*(1), 34–48.
65. Yang, H., (2021). Research on network security of the fifth-generation mobile communication technology. In: *2021 International Wireless Communications and Mobile Computing (IWCMC)* (Vol. 1, pp. 919–923). IEEE.
66. Zhao, Z., & Qing, R., (2023). The fourth-generation text processing system. *Office Informatization, 9718*(1), 100-7001X.
67. Zhou, L., Feng, L., Zhong, J., Ong, Y. S., Zhu, Z., & Sha, E., (2016). Evolutionary multitasking in combinatorial search spaces: A case study in capacitated vehicle routing problem. In: *2016 IEEE Symposium Series on Computational Intelligence* (SSCI) (Vol. 1, pp. 1–8). IEEE.

CHAPTER 3

STRUCTURE OF OPERATING SYSTEMS

UNIT INTRODUCTION

Over an operating system's (OS) lifespan, it is reasonable to anticipate multiple modifications occurring within computer systems and environments for computing. To accommodate modifications to an OS, it is imperative that implementing said OS on a novel computer system is facile and that adding supplementary functionalities is uncomplicated. The two fundamental requirements that an OS must possess are portability and extensibility (Tanenbaum & Woodhull, 1997).

Historically, OSs were closely intertwined with the design and structure of a particular computer system. The characteristic above had an impact on their level of portability. Contemporary OSs incorporate the fundamental components of an OS through a kernel or microkernel architecture and construct supplementary OS functionalities by leveraging the core's service provisions (Chen & Bershad, 1993). The configuration above limits the interdependence of architectural components to the fundamental framework of the OS, thereby establishing the extent of an OS's transferability based on the characteristics of its kernel or the micro-kernel (Boos et al., 2020). The extensibility of an OS is contingent upon the types of services its core provides.

The configuration of an OS pertains to the fundamental characteristics of the OS kernel and additional components of the OS, as well as their interrelationships (Cook, 1979).

This book outlines various philosophical approaches to the design of OSs and examines their impact on the extensibility and portability of such systems.

Learning Objectives

After the chapter, students will be able to understand the following:

- Basic idea regarding operation of an operating system;
- Understanding structure of an operating system;
- Learn about operating systems with monolithic and layered structure;
- Fundamental concept of kernel-based and microkernel-based operating systems.

Key Terms

- Architecture
- Kernel
- Layered
- Mechanisms
- Microkernel
- Monolithic
- Network management
- Operating system
- Policies
- Security

3.1. OPERATION OF AN OPERATING SYSTEM (OS)

Upon powering on a computer, the boot process analyzes its configuration, encompassing the CPU type, memory capacity, I/O peripherals, and other hardware particulars linked to the system. Subsequently, a segment of the operating system (OS) is loaded into the memory, whereby its data structures are initialized utilizing the data above (Lauer & Needham, 1979). The computer system is then relinquished to the OS.

The schematic diagram of the operation of the OS is presented in Figure 3.1 (Cheriton & Duda, 1995). An interrupt is triggered by an occurrence such as I/O completion or the conclusion of a time slice. If a process initiates a system call, such as to solicit resources or commence an I/O operation, it interrupts software. Interrupting causes the central processing unit (CPU) to transition to a routine that services the interrupt (Christopher et al., 1993).

Did you Know?

In the early days of computing, operating systems were often developed by individual hardware manufacturers for their specific machines.

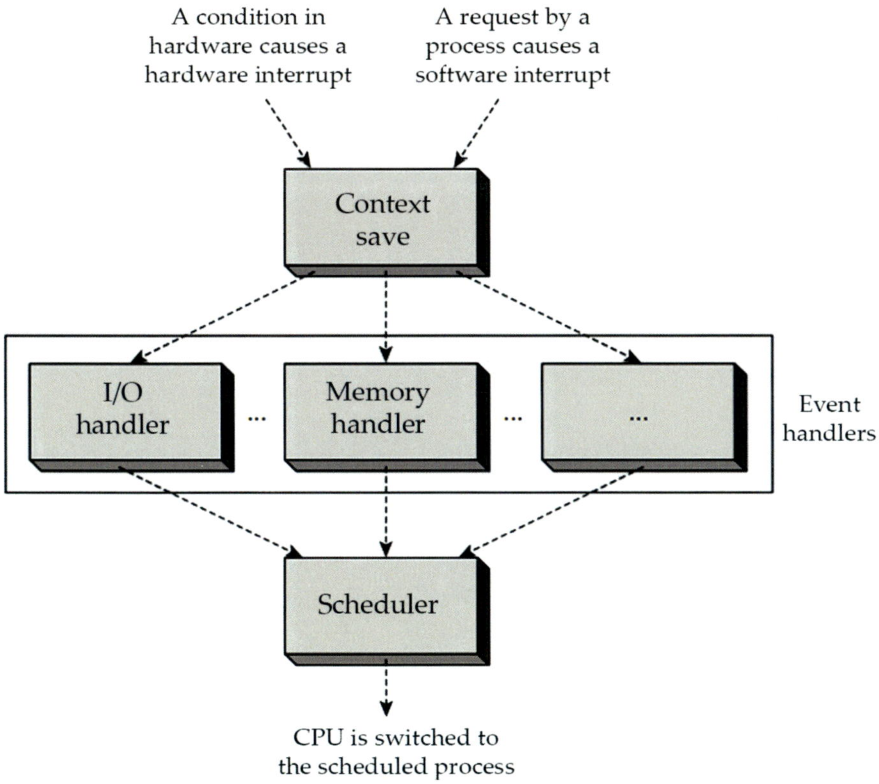

Figure 3.1. Overview of operating system operation.

Source: Dhananjay M. Dhamdhere, Creative Commons License.

The routine is responsible for servicing interrupts and executing a context-save operation to preserve relevant data about the interrupted program. Subsequently, an event handler is triggered to perform the necessary actions to address the event. Subsequently, the scheduler chooses a process and initiates the CPU transition to said process. The process of CPU switching involves two distinct stages in the event processing cycle. Initially, the CPU switches to the kernel to execute event handling, and subsequently, it switches to the process designated by the scheduler (Linden, 1976).

The implementation of the functions of an OS is carried out through the activation of event handlers by interrupting servicing routines. Table 3.1 provides a summary of the functions that are primarily focused on managing processes and resources, as well as preventing any potential interference with them (Auslander et al., 1981).

Table 3.1. The Function of an Operating System

Function	Description
Process management	The commencement and cessation of procedures, as well as the arrangement of their timing.
Memory management	The management of memory allocation and deallocation, swapping, and virtual memory.
I/O management	Servicing of input/output interrupts, the initiation of input/output operations, and the optimization of input/output device performance.
File management	The processes of generating, retaining, and retrieving files.
Security and protection	Mitigating interference with resources and processes.
Network management	The transmission and reception of information across a network.

Source: Dijkstra, Creative Commons License.

3.2. STRUCTURE OF AN OPERATING SYSTEM (OS)

3.2.1. Policies and Mechanisms

When considering the execution of a function within an OS, the designer must contemplate two separate tiers:

1. **Policy:** A policy is a fundamental directive that governs how an OS executes its operations (Gray et al., 1972). In policy implementation, a mechanism refers to a particular course of action required to bring about the intended policy outcome.
2. **Decision-Making:** Policies are responsible for determining the appropriate course of action, whereas mechanisms are tasked with executing and implementing said actions. A policy serves as a module for decision-making, determining the appropriate mechanism modules to invoke based on specific conditions. A mechanism refers to a discrete unit of functionality encapsulated as a module to execute a predetermined task (Ousterhout et al., 1980).

The scheduling policy employed in multiprogramming systems is the priority-based scheduling policy. This policy necessitates implementing a distinct mechanism to keep information about ready processes. However, this mechanism differs from the one utilized in round-robin scheduling as it arranges information based on process priority. The mechanism for dispatching, nonetheless, would be universal among all policies for scheduling.

3.2.2. Portability and Extensibility of Operating Systems (OSs)

The process of designing and implementing OSs entails significant financial investments (Vömel & Freiling, 2011). To safeguard these investments, the OS design must possess a lifespan of at least 10 years. Given the anticipated changes in computer design, I/O device technological advances, and application environments, it is conceivable that an OS could be modified to accommodate these developments. In this context, two crucial aspects are portability and extensibility.

Porting refers to modifying software to make it compatible with a different computer system. The term "portability" pertains to the ease with which an application can be ported and is inversely related to the amount of effort required for porting. The term "extensibility" pertains to the level of the simplicity involved in incorporating additional functionalities into a given software system (Unrau et al., 1995). Porting an OS involves modifying architecture-dependent code components to enable the OS to function with novel hardware. Architecture-dependent information and commands in an OS can include various examples as follows:

1. An interrupt vector is a data structure that holds the necessary information to transfer control of the CPU to an interrupt service routine by loading specific fields of the program status word (PSW) (Stoy & Strachey, 1972). The provided data is specific to the field of architecture.

2. The specifics of memory protection and the necessary information to be supplied to the memory management unit (MMU) depend on the architecture.
3. The effective use of I/O instructions for executing an I/O operation is contingent upon the architecture (Greenwald & Cheriton, 1996).

The portion of an OS's code is specific to a particular architecture and is commonly linked with mechanisms instead of policies. An OS can be considered highly portable if its architecture-dependent code is minimal (Anderson et al., 1991). Its overall code structure allows porting efforts to be mainly decided by the architecture-dependent code size rather than the complete code size. Therefore, the matter of OS portability is resolved through the segregation of architecture-specific and architecture-agnostic components of an OS, along with the provision of clearly defined interfaces between these two components.

The extensibility of an OS is required for two primary objectives: firstly, to facilitate the integration of novel hardware components into a computer system, such as new input/output devices or network adapters; and secondly, to enable the provision of fresh functionalities in response to evolving user demands. In the past, OSs could not offer extensibility of any kind. Therefore, incorporating a novel input/output device necessitated alterations to the OS. Subsequent OSs resolved this issue by incorporating additional features into the boot process. The system would verify the existence of hardware components that were not detected during the previous boot of the OS (Comer, 2011).

Subsequently, it would either request the user to choose a suitable software to manage the new hardware, which commonly comprises a collection of procedures known as a device driver that manages the new device, or autonomously select such software. Subsequently, the novel software was uploaded and incorporated into the kernel to ensure its proper invocation and utilization. Contemporary OSs offer an additional feature of plug-and-play functionality, which enables the addition of new hardware while the OS is in operation. The OS manages the interrupt triggered by introducing new hardware, identifying suitable software, and incorporating it into the kernel (Baumann et al., 2005).

The absence of extensibility can result in challenges when attempting to modify an OS to meet evolving user demands. Numerous instances of such challenges are evident in the chronicles of OSs. During the 1980s and 1990s, there was a demand among personal computer users for a novel functionality that would enable the establishment of multiple sessions with an OS concurrently. During that era, several widely recognized OSs, such as MS-DOS, encountered challenges delivering this capability due to inadequate extensibility (Yokote, 1992). The Unix OS encountered a comparable challenge when facilitating multiprocessor computer systems.

3.3. OPERATING SYSTEMS (OSS) WITH MONOLITHIC STRUCTURE

The OS is a sophisticated software system encompassing many functions and can comprise millions of instructions. The system is structured to comprise a collection of software modules, wherein each module possesses a precisely defined interface that is mandatory for accessing any of its functions or data (Chen & Bershad, 1993). This particular design exhibits the characteristic whereby a module cannot perceive the internal workings of other modules. The property above serves to streamline the OS design, coding, and testing processes.

The initial OSs exhibited a monolithic architecture, wherein the OS constituted a solitary software layer that mediated between the user and the underlying hardware of the computer system, as depicted in Figure 3.2 (Chen et al., 1996). The command interpreter furnished the user interface (UI). The command interpreter is responsible for the organization of user process creation. Using system calls facilitated the invocation of OS functionalities and services by user processes and command interpreters.

Over time, it became apparent that two distinct issues were associated with the monolithic structure. The OS's single layer established a connection with the underlying hardware. Consequently, the presence of architecture-dependent code was pervasive across the OS, leading to suboptimal levels of portability. Furthermore, the issue above resulted in challenges regarding testing and debugging, ultimately resulting in elevated expenses for maintenance and improvement. The above-mentioned issues prompted an exploration of alternative methodologies in organizing an OS. The subsequent sections will expound on three techniques for organizing an OS executed as resolutions to the issues mentioned above:

i. Implementing a layered structure in OSs aims to mitigate the intricacy and expenses associated with their development and upkeep. This is achieved by organizing the system into multiple layers (Kapteijn et al., 2001). The layered OS, exemplified by the multiprogramming system of the 1960s, is a widely recognized paradigm in computer science.

ii. The kernel-based structure is a type of structure that is utilized in certain fields of study. Utilizing a kernel-based structure restricts the reliance on architecture-specific elements to a limited portion of the OS's code, which is the kernel (Biggs et al., 2018). This approach enhances the

Did you Know?

The term "kernel" was first used in the context of operating systems by computer scientist Walter F. Bauer in the late 1960s.

potential for portability. The Unix OS exhibits a structure that is based on a kernel.

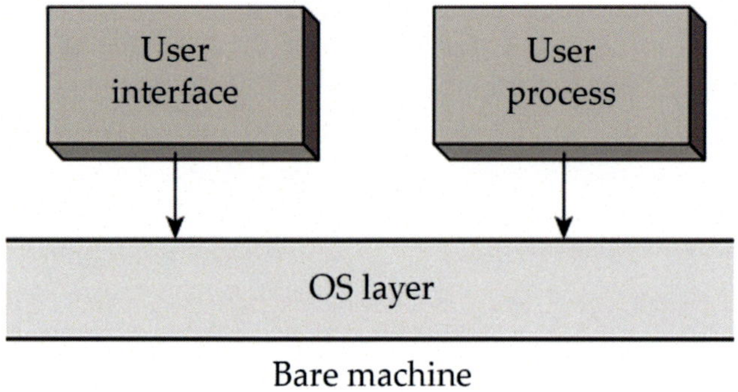

Figure 3.2. Representation of monolithic operating system.

Source: Barham, Creative Commons License.

The OS structure based on a microkernel involves utilizing a fundamental set of functionalities and services to implement an OS. The utilization of it offers mobility. The microkernel architecture offers extensibility as modifications to the OS can be implemented without necessitating alterations in the microkernel (Anderson et al., 1991).

3.4. LAYERED DESIGN OF OPERATING SYSTEMS (OSS)

The issue plagued the monolithic OS architecture in that every constituent of the OS was required to possess the capability to function with the underlying hardware (Feng et al., 2003). This particular feature has resulted in an escalation of expenses and exertion in the OS development process, owing to the significant disparity in meaning between the OS and the fundamental machine.

The concept of the semantic gap may be demonstrated through the following illustration: A machine instruction is responsible for executing a fundamental operation at the machine level, such as arithmetic or logical manipulation of operands. A module within an OS can incorporate an algorithm that utilizes low-level primitive operations of the OS, such as preserving the context of a process and commencing an input/output operation. The operations above exhibit more complexity than the fundamental operations executed at the machine level. This disparity necessitates programming to establish a connection between the two entities. The OS transforms every desired operation into a series of instructions, which may be a routine (*refer* Figure 3.3) (Farooq & Kunz, 2011). The outcome is an increase in programming expenses. One possible approach to narrowing the semantic gap between an OS and its underlying hardware is to employ a more advanced machine that can execute the necessary operations without relying on the OS (Reed, 1976). Alternatively, a software-based solution could emulate a more sophisticated machine to perform the required tasks. The preceding methodology is costly.

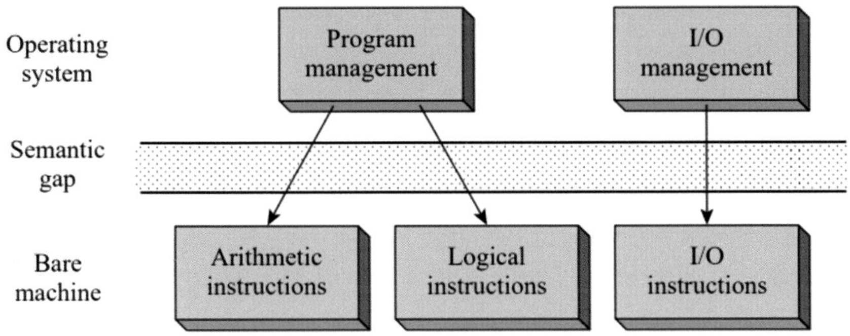

Figure 3.3. Representation of semantic gap.

Source: Solomon, Creative Commons License.

The latter methodology involves using a simulator, a software program that operates on the underlying hardware and emulates a more robust machine that encompasses numerous functionalities sought after by the OS. The novel apparatus is called an extended machine, while its corresponding emulator is denoted as the extended machine software (Coady et al., 2001). The OS establishes communication with the extended machine instead of the bare machine. The extended machine software is an intermediary between the OS and the bare machine.

The fundamental principle underlying the design of a layered OS is that each layer's procedures should solely rely on the resources provided by the layer immediately beneath it. In other words, no layer within the system can be circumvented. Access to lower-layer routines should be limited to the interface between layers (Casado & Tsigas, 2009). Consequently, a procedure located in a given stratum lacks awareness of the addresses of data structures or directives in the underlying stratum; its sole knowledge pertains to invocating a procedure from the lower stratum. The concept of information hiding is employed to avert the potential for misapplication or distortion of data belonging to a particular layer by routines located in other OS layers. In debugging, the localization of errors is facilitated as the root cause of an error within a layer, such as an erroneous value in its data element, is confined solely to that particular layer. The concept of information hiding entails the ability to modify a layer of an OS without causing any impact on the remaining layers. The characteristics above facilitate the process of evaluating and troubleshooting an OS.

The diagram presented in Figure 3.4 depicts a two-tiered OS (Jutla, 2010). The extended machine offers a range of functionalities such as context preservation, dispatching, swapping, and initiating input/output operations. The OS layer is situated above the layer of the extended machine. The separation of a function's algorithm from the implementation of its primitive operations significantly simplifies the coding and testing of OS modules. Testing, debugging, and modifying an OS module is comparatively simpler in a modular OS than in a monolithic OS (Xu & Zhu, 2018). The extended machine is an abstraction provided by the lower layer. The uppermost layer of the OS is commonly referred to as the OS layer.

The evolution of OS layered structures has taken various forms, involving diverse abstractions and layer counts (Dutta & Dunkels, 2012).

Figure 3.4. Depiction of layered OS design.

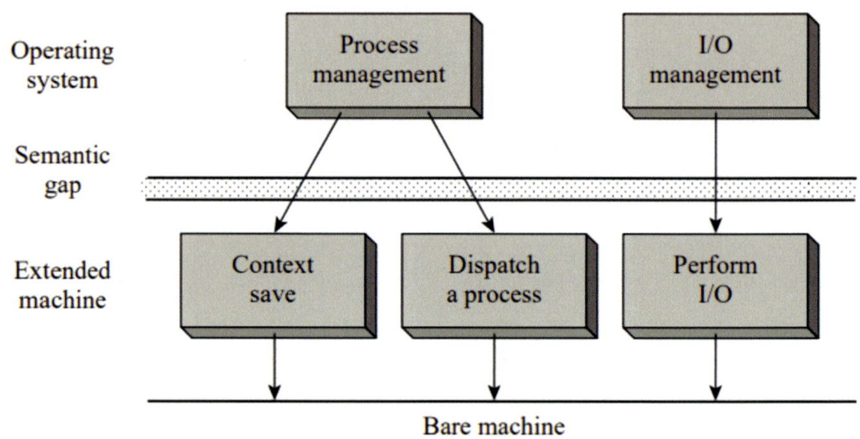

Source: Hartig, Creative Commons License.

The design approach of OSs that involves multiple layers is associated with three issues. The layered structure of a system has the potential to impede its operation. It is important to note that every layer can interact solely with the layers adjacent to it (Watanabe & Sakamura, 1995). The statement suggests that when a user process requests an OS service, the request must traverse from the highest to the lowest numbered layer before the bare machine can execute the necessary action. This characteristic results in a significant increase in operational costs.

The second issue pertains to challenges encountered in developing a stratified architecture. As per the hierarchical structure of networking layers, a layer is restricted to accessing solely the layer directly beneath it. Therefore, any attributes or capabilities required by a given layer must be present in the lower layers. This stipulation presents a predicament in the arrangement of strata that necessitate reciprocal services. The issue above is commonly resolved by dividing a layer into two distinct sections and subsequently interposing additional layers between the halves above. A designer may allocate process handling functions to a specific layer and position memory management in the subsequent higher layer (Lampson & Sturgis, 1976). Memory allocation is a necessary aspect of the process creation procedure. To address this challenge, the management of processes can be bifurcated into two distinct layers. A single layer would undertake process management tasks such as context preservation, switching, scheduling, and synchronization of processes.

The stratum above is expected to remain beneath the layer responsible for managing memory. The additional stratum would undertake the task of generating new processes. It would be situated at a higher level than the memory management layer (Payne et al., 2007).

The third issue pertains to the stratification of OS functionalities. The stratification phenomenon arises due to the need to partition each functionality into layers within a layered OS. The utilization of interfaces is imperative for facilitating communication between the different layers of these components. An illustrative instance involves a specific OS functionality denoted as F, comprising two distinct modules, Fl1 and Fl2, that correspondingly are affiliated with layers l1 and l2.

If access to layer l2 is restricted solely to interrupt-driven mechanisms, Fl1 is required to generate an interrupt to establish communication with Fl2. This phenomenon has the potential to result in an intricate design and reduced operational efficiency (Watson & Fletcher, 1980). The stratification phenomenon can result in limited extensibility as incorporating novel functionalities necessitates the inclusion of fresh code across multiple strata of the OS. This, in turn, may necessitate modifications to the interfaces of the strata.

It is worth mentioning that the multilayered OS design does not prioritize the segregation of architecture-dependent components of the OS code. For example, four of the five layers in the multiprogramming system outlined in Table 3.2 consist of architecture-dependent components. A layered structure does not necessarily ensure a high level of portability.

Table 3.2. Layers in the Multiprogramming System

Layer	Description
Layer 0	Processor allocation and multiprogramming
Layer 1	Memory and drum management
Layer 2	Operator-process communication
Layer 3	I/O management
Layer 4	User processes

Source: M. Cesati, Creative Commons License.

3.5. VIRTUAL MACHINE OPERATING SYSTEMS (VM OSS)

Diverse user groups necessitate distinct types of user services. Consequently, using a solitary OS on a computing system may lead to dissatisfaction among numerous users. Utilizing various OSs at different time intervals to operate the computer is deemed inadequate as it would restrict access to services exclusively available under a single OS at any given time (King et al., 2003). The resolution of this issue is achieved by utilizing a virtual machine operating system (VM OS) to manage the computer system. The VM OS generates multiple VMs. Individual users are assigned to each VM, allowing them to utilize any OS they prefer within the virtual environment and execute their respective programs under the selected OS. By utilizing this approach, the computer system user can concurrently operate multiple OSs. The VM OS is referred to as the host OS, while each other OS is designated as a guest OS. The machine on which the VM OS runs is commonly called the host machine.

A VM can be defined as a simulated computing environment that operates as a virtual resource (Kivity et al., 2014). The discourse concerns a VM with identical architecture to the host machine. Specifically, it is equipped with a virtual CPU that can perform the same set of instructions and analogous memory and input/output devices. The VM's configuration may exhibit discrepancies with the host machine's, particularly about certain aspects such as memory capacity and input/output peripherals. The absence of a semantic gap between the host and VMs results in no performance loss during running a VM.

Additionally, no software intervention is required to execute a guest OS on a VM due to their identical architectures. The VM OS facilitates the concurrent operation of guest OSs through a process that bears a resemblance to that of process scheduling

(King et al., 2005). This involves the selection of a VM and the arrangement of execution of its commands on the CPU by the guest OS. The OS running as a guest has full authority over the host system's surroundings, including the handling of interrupts. The lack of an intermediary software layer across the host machine and guest OS results in optimal utilization of the host machine's resources. The guest OS retains authority over the host machine until the VM OS elects to transition to a different VM, typically prompted by an interrupt. The VM OS can utilize the timer mechanism to implement round-robin scheduling and time-slicing of guest OSs.

An intricate system is required to manage interruptions during the execution of a guest OS (Madnick & Donovan, 1973). Certain interrupts may originate within the VM's domain, such as an I/O interrupt from a device integrated within the VM. Conversely, other interrupts may arise within the domains of other guest OSs. The VM OS can assume control upon the occurrence of an interrupt, identify the corresponding guest OS domain to which the interrupt pertains, and subsequently allocate the responsibility of handling the interrupt to the respective guest OS through a scheduling mechanism. The present configuration results in significant overhead due to two context switch operations. The initial context switch transfers control to the VM OS, while the subsequent switch transfers control to the appropriate guest OS.

Consequently, the VM OS can utilize a configuration whereby the guest OS is directly activated by interrupts originating within its sphere. The implementation is executed in the following manner: During transferring control to a guest OS, the VM's OS substitutes its interrupt vectors with those specified in the guest OS (Dunlap et al., 2002). This measure guarantees that the CPU would transition to an interrupt servicing routine of the guest OS. Suppose the guest OS detects the absence of an interrupt within its designated domain. In that case, it will transfer control to the VM OS by utilizing a distinct system called "invoke VM OS." The VM OS currently implements a mechanism to transfer the interrupt signal to the corresponding guest OS. In situations where a considerable quantity of VMs is present, the processing of interrupts has the potential to result in excessive shuffling between VMs. As a result, the VM's OS may not promptly initiate the guest OS within its domain in response to an interruption. Rather, it may merely take note of the incidence of interrupts that transpired within the domain of a guest OS and furnish this data to the guest OS during its next scheduled activation.

The differentiation between the kernel and user modes of the CPU presents certain challenges in utilizing a VM OS. To ensure self-protection from guest OSs, the VM OS must execute guest OSs utilizing the CPU's user mode (Meyer & Seawright, 1970). Nonetheless, this approach entails that both a guest OS and the user processes running under it operate in the user mode, thereby exposing the guest OS to potential corruption by a user process. The

Intel 80×86 computer family possesses a characteristic that solves this challenge. The CPU of 80×86 computers can operate in four distinct execution modes.

Consequently, the host OS can operate with the CPU in kernel mode. On the other hand, a guest OS can carry out processes that operate under it with the CPU in user mode. However, it can operate with the CPU using one of the intermediary modes.

Remember

Operating systems play a critical role in the modern world, powering everything from personal computers and mobile devices to servers and data centers that support the internet and other critical infrastructure.

Virtualization refers to mapping the resources and interfaces of a VM onto those of the host machine (Martinović et al., 2010). Full virtualization means that the host and VMs possess similar capacities; consequently, an OS may function the same while operating on a bare machine and on a VM that uses a VM OS. Nonetheless, it is worth noting that complete virtualization has the potential to compromise security.

Para-virtualization is a technique utilized in contemporary VM environments to address the challenges of full virtualization (Robin & Irvine, 2000). The technique of para-virtualization involves substituting non-virtualizable instructions, which cannot be implemented within a virtual machine (VM), with readily virtualizable instructions. One potential solution to address the security concern in VM/370 involves the implementation of para-virtualization. This approach entails the exclusion of privileged instructions from a VM. The VM could provide a distinct directive to be utilized by a guest OS that intends to execute an exclusive instruction. Implementing a specific directive would trigger a software interruption, transmitting details regarding the privileged directive the guest OS intended to execute to the VM OS (King & Chen, 2002). Subsequently, the VM OS would undertake the execution of the privileged directive on behalf of the guest OS. Distinct execution modes of the CPU are employed by the host OS, guest OS, and user processes to enable the host OS to differentiate between the utilization of the special instruction in the VM by a guest OS or a user process, with the latter being deemed impermissible. The utilization of paravirtualization has been employed as a means to improve the overall performance of a host OS.

In an OS, the kernel commonly places the CPU into an idle loop when there is no demand from any user processes within the OS to utilize the CPU (Li et al., 2010). The host machine's CPU may be utilized inefficiently when a guest OS enters an idle loop. Therefore, paravirtualization may be utilized to furnish a distinct directive within the VM, alerting the host OS of this circumstance.

This would enable the host OS to suspend the guest OS's CPU usage temporarily. The utilization of paravirtualization necessitates a distinction between the VM and the host machine, thereby requiring modifications to the code of a guest OS to prevent the use of nonvirtualizable instructions. The process of enabling a guest OS to function within the VM OS can be achieved through porting (Vaghani, 2010). An alternative approach to attain this objective involves the utilization of dynamic binary translation methodology for the guest OS's kernel. This technique involves substituting a segment of the kernel code that comprises non-virtualizable instructions with code that lacks such instructions. To minimize the additional computational burden of this configuration, the revised kernel code is stored in a cache, thereby obviating the need for frequent binary translation.

VMs are utilized for a variety of purposes, as follows:

1. To employ a pre-existing server for a novel application that necessitates the utilization of a distinct OS (Garfinkel et al., 2003).
2. To ensure the safety and dependability of applications with a common host and OS. This advantage is derived from the inherent limitation that VMs belonging to distinct applications cannot access one another's resources.
3. To conduct concurrent testing of a modified OS or an updated version of an application on a server while production runs of said OS are ongoing.
4. To facilitate disaster management by relocating a VM from a server that is compelled to shut down due to an emergency to an alternative server that is operational within the network (Whitaker et al., 2005).

The topic of discussion pertains to VMs for programming languages (PLs). As previously discussed, PLs have utilized VMs to acquire certain advantages. During the 1970s, the utilization of a VM was adopted by the Pascal PL as a means to ensure portability. The P-code instructions implemented by the VM were highly compatible with the execution of Pascal programs. The software incorporated an interpreter for P-code instructions as a means of implementation (Min et al., 2012). Converting a Pascal program into a series of P-code instructions by a compiler enables the execution of said instructions on any computer equipped with a P-code interpreter. The interpreter was highly portable due to the limited number of instructions in the VM. The availability of this feature in the 1970s contributed significantly to the widespread adoption of Pascal. Nonetheless, the utilization of the VM resulted in a significant reduction in performance due to the disparity in meaning between P-code instructions and instructions executed on the host computer.

Utilizing a VM is a fundamental aspect of the Java PL, which ensures both security and reliability. In the realm of Java programming, a program comprises distinct entities known as objects, which are defined by their respective classes and possess structural and behavioral characteristics. The process involves compiling every class into a bytecode representation consisting of a series of instructions for execution by the Java virtual machine (JVM) (Bhatt et al., 2018). When executing a Java application, the class loader is triggered each time a new class object is encountered. The process of loading a class involves retrieving its byte code representation from a library or the Internet, followed by a verification step to ensure that the class adheres to established security and reliability criteria (Zhao et al., 2013). This includes validating the class's digital signature and ensuring it does not employ pointer arithmetic or other disallowed features. If any of the checks fail, the application will be terminated. Utilizing the VM may result in a reduction in performance. However, incorporating the JVM into the hardware can compensate for this.

3.6. KERNEL-BASES OPERATING SYSTEMS (OSS)

The abstract representation of a kernel-based OS is depicted in Figure 3.5 (Härtig et al., 1997). The kernel serves as the fundamental component of the OS, offering a range of functions and services to facilitate diverse OS functionalities.

The remaining components of the OS are structured as a collection of non-kernel procedures that execute functions on processes and resources relevant to end-users, in addition to a graphical user interface (GUI). The kernel assumes control in response to an interrupt, such as a timer or I/O completion interrupt, which signals the occurrence of an event (Bershad, 1992). Alternatively, the kernel may take control when a system call is initiated through the execution of a software-interrupt instruction. Upon an interrupt, a routine responsible for servicing interrupts executes the function of saving the context and subsequently calls upon an event handler, a non-kernel OS routine.

The UI can initiate a system call to execute a user command, while a process can trigger a system call to access a service within the kernel. Additionally, a non-kernel routine can utilize a system call to activate a kernel function. If a user initiates a command to execute a program stored within a file, such as "file alpha," the UI will make a system call. Subsequently, the interrupt servicing routine will invoke a non-kernel routine to establish the execution of the program. The non-kernel procedure involves utilizing system calls to allocate memory for the program's execution, opening file alpha, and loading its contents into the allocated memory space. Subsequently, another system call is made to initiate the operation of the process that represents the program's execution (Malallah et al., 2021). If a process intends to generate a child process to execute the program stored in file alpha, it will likewise initiate a system call, and indistinguishable actions would ensue.

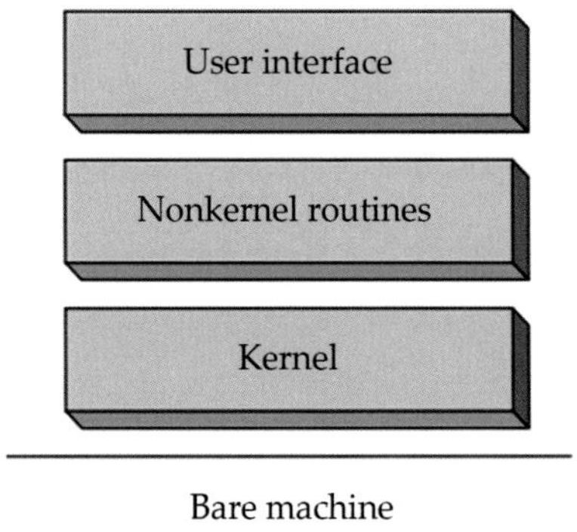

Figure 3.5. Structure of a kernel-based operating system.

Source: Engler D. R., Creative Commons License.

The kernel-based OS structure was historically motivated by the desire for enhanced portability of the OS and increased convenience in designing and writing non-kernel routines (Gien, 1990). The attainment of OS portability is accomplished by including architecture-specific components of OS code, which commonly comprise mechanisms, within the kernel while maintaining architecture-independent code outside of it. This approach restricts the porting endeavor solely to the kernel. The kernel is commonly designed as a monolithic entity within an OS to optimize performance. The remaining components of the OS, which are external to the kernel, may also adopt a monolithic architecture or may be organized into distinct layers (Hess & Paulson, 2010).

Table 3.3 presents a comprehensive list of the kernel's services and functions to facilitate diverse OS functionalities (Isohara et al., 2011). The functions above and services offer a collection of abstractions to non-kernel routines, thereby facilitating the design and coding process by minimizing the semantic gap they encounter. Table 3.3's I/O functions collectively implement the abstraction of virtual devices. The kernel offers an additional abstraction known as a "process."

The stratification issue observed in a layered OS design can also be encountered in a kernel-based design. This is due to an architecture-dependent component in the code responsible for executing an OS command, which is usually integrated into the kernel (Kalfa, 1992). Additionally, an architecture-independent component is present in a policy implementation that is typically located outside the kernel. The intercommunication between these components necessitates system calls, contributing to the OS's overhead due to the need to interrupt servicing operations. The act of commencing the execution of a program contained within a file named "alpha" should be considered. As previously mentioned, the non-kernel routine responsible for executing the command would necessitate four system calls. These calls would involve memory allocation, opening an alpha file, loading the program from the file into memory, and initiating program execution (Nikolaev & Back, 2013). The execution of these calls would result in significant overhead. Certain OS designs aim to minimize the OS's overhead by integrating the architecture-independent component of a function's code into the kernel.

Table 3.3. Typical Functions and Services Offered by the Kernel

OS Functionality	Examples of Kernel Functions and Services
Process management	The preservation of the context of an interrupted program, the dispatching of a process, and the manipulation of scheduling lists.
Process communication	The exchange of interprocess messages.
Memory management	Configure memory protection data, execute swap-in and swap-out operations and manage page fault occurrences.
I/O management	Trigger input/output operations, handle input/output completion interrupts, and address input/output errors.
File management	Open the file and then proceed to read from or write to it.
Security and protection	Implementing authentication protocols for a new user and ensuring the maintenance of file protection information.
Network management	The transmission and reception of data via a message.

Source: Garfinkel, Creative Commons License.

Consequently, the non-kernel procedure for commencing program execution would be integrated into the kernel. Additional instances include policies for process scheduling, device driver I/O scheduling, and memory management. The incorporation of these elements results in a decrease in OS overhead. Nonetheless, it also leads to a decrease in the OS's portability. The extensibility of kernel-based OSs is limited due to the need to modify the functions and services provided by the kernel to incorporate new OS functionalities.

3.7. MICROKERNEL-BASED OPERATING SYSTEMS (OSS)

Incorporating all architecture-specific OS codes within the kernel yields favorable portability. Nevertheless, kernels incorporate certain code that is not reliant on specific architectures in practical applications. This characteristic gives rise to various issues. The utilization of a sizable kernel size results in a reduction of portability, which is contrary to the intended objective. Incorporating new features may require kernel modification, resulting in limited extensibility. A kernel with a larger size is capable of accommodating a greater quantity of system calls (Kuz et al., 2007). Certain function calls may have infrequent usage, leading to inadequate testing of their implementations across various kernel versions. The compromise of the OS's reliability is evident.

In the early 1990s, the microkernel was created to address the issues surrounding kernels' portability, reliability, and extensibility issues. The microkernel is a fundamental component of OS code that comprises a limited set of mechanisms compared to a standard kernel (Daum et al., 2008). It facilitates a restricted range of system calls that undergo rigorous testing and frequent utilization. The inclusion of this particular feature serves to improve both the reliability and portability of the microkernel system.

The non-essential components of the OS's code are located outside the microkernel and rely on its services (Arlat et al., 2002). As a result, these components can be altered without impacting the kernel. In theory, these modifications can be implemented without requiring a system reboot. The microkernel's services are impartial towards any particular features or policies within an OS. This allows for incorporating novel features and functions into the OS to better accommodate specific operating environments.

The diagram depicted in Figure 3.6 provides a visual representation of an OS's architecture based on a microkernel (Stoess, 2007). The micro-kernel comprises functionalities for scheduling processes and memory management, but it lacks a scheduler or memory handler. The functions above are executed in the form of servers, which are essentially perpetual processes. The microkernel is an intermediary for communication between servers and user processes while primarily executing interrupt handling.

The compactness and adaptability of microkernels are advantageous attributes in the context of embedded systems, as OSs necessitate being concise and tailored to the specific demands of an embedded application. The extensibility of microkernels presents the possibility of utilizing a singular microkernel across a diverse range of computing systems, spanning from handheld devices to expansive parallel and distributed systems (Rawson, 1997). To a certain degree, this vision has been actualized. Various iterations of the Unix OS have been implemented utilizing the Mach microkernel. Amoeba, a distributed OS, employs a uniform micro-kernel across various computing devices, including workstations and large multiprocessors.

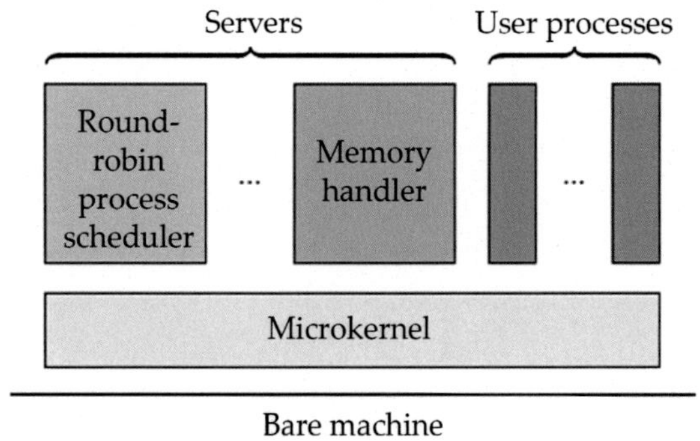

Figure 3.6. Structure of microkernel-based operating systems.

Source: Colin Drury, Creative Commons License.

The precise definition of the fundamental nucleus of OS code has been a topic of considerable discussion, leading to a significant degree of divergence in the range of services encompassed by a micro-kernel (Bruns et al., 2010). IBM's implementation of the Mach microkernel involves the exclusion of process scheduling policy and device drivers from the kernel, which are instead executed as servers. The QNX microkernel encompasses a range of fundamental system services, such as interrupt handling, process scheduling, interprocess communication (IPC), and core network functionality. The L4 microkernel incorporates memory management functionality and exclusively accommodates seven system calls. QNX and L4 have a size of 32 KB, with 1 KB being equivalent to 1,024 bytes (De Paoli et al., 1994).

Notwithstanding the variability above, one could posit that specific services necessitate provision by a microkernel. The functionalities mentioned earlier encompass assistance in memory management, facilitation of IPC, and handling interrupted servicing. Higher-level modules invoke memory management and IPC in the OS code, which are situated external to the microkernel (Marzi & Yang, 2012). The routine for servicing interrupts is designed to receive incoming interrupts and transmit them to superior-level modules for further processing.

OSs that employed first-generation microkernels experienced a reduction in throughput of up to 50% compared to OSs that did not utilize microkernels. The issue arises from partitioning certain features of a traditional kernel into a microkernel and an OS constructed through the utilization of said microkernel, thereby presenting the well-known problem of stratification (Nakajima &

Tokuda, 1998). As an illustration, a kernel encompasses the entirety of the process management function, which executes the tasks of creating, scheduling, and dispatching processes. Conversely, a microkernel may solely comprise the functions of process creation and dispatching, with process scheduling being executed as a server beneath the microkernel. To establish communication between the two entities, the utilization of the IPC mechanism would be necessary. The study revealed that a performance penalty of as much as 73% was attributed to IPC. The L4 microkernel, a subsequent iteration of microkernel architecture, optimized inter-process communication by defaulting to eliminate validity and rights checking and fine-tuning the microkernel to the specific hardware in use. The actions above resulted in a 20-fold increase in the speed of IPC as compared to the initial microkernel generation. The microkernel-based OS incorporated paging activities about virtual memory management, relocating them from the microkernel (Bershad, 1992). Following the implementation of these enhancements, it was observed that OSs based on microkernels experienced a mere 5% reduction in throughput as compared to their non-microkernel counterparts.

The Exokernel employs a distinct approach to organizing an OS to mitigate performance deterioration. The philosophy entails decentralizing resource management, allowing applications to perform it distributedly. The Exokernel is designed to optimize the allocation of hardware resources without offering any abstractions (Bricker et al., 1991). The application process perceives a resource within the computer system in its unprocessed state. The utilization of this methodology yields highly accelerated primitive operations, exhibiting a speed increase of 10 to 100 times compared to the utilization of a singular Unix kernel. As an illustration, the information retrieved from an input/output device is transmitted directly to the corresponding process that initiated the request, bypassing the Exokernel.

ACTIVITY 3.1:

Install and configure different types of operating systems on virtual machines or physical hardware and compare their performance and capabilities.

Conversely, if the Unix kernel were employed, the data would have traversed through it. As OS functionalities are conventionally executed at the application level, a library of OSs can be accessed by an application to choose and utilize an OS. The OS operates as a distinct process in the non-kernel mode and leverages the functionalities of the Exokernel.

3.8. SUMMARY

The concept of portability in OSs pertains to the convenience of the OS being executed on a computer with a distinct architecture. The extensibility of an OS pertains to its capacity to be conveniently modified or improved to suit a novel computing environment. The protracted life cycles of contemporary OSs have rendered portability and indispensable extensibility prerequisites. This chapter has explored various approaches to organizing OSs to fulfill these criteria. The functionality of an OS generally comprises a policy that outlines the guiding principle for executing the functionality, along with a set of mechanisms that execute actions that carry out the functionality. The code of mechanisms like dispatching and context save intrinsically relies on the computer's architecture, whereas policies are not architecture dependent. The extensibility and portability of an OS are contingent upon the structural organization of its policies and mechanisms.

REVIEW QUESTIONS

1. What are the main components of an operating system?
2. What is the function of kernel in an operating system?
3. What are the advantages and disadvantages of monolithic operating system structure?
4. How does a kernel-based operating system differ from a microkernel-based operating system?
5. What factors should be considered when choosing on operating system design approach for a specific system?

MULTIPLE CHOICE QUESTIONS

1. Which of the following is not a component of an operating system?

a. Applications
b. Compiler
c. Device drivers
d. Kernel

2. Which operating system design approach offer high performance and efficiency but can be difficult to maintain and modify?

a. Monolithic structure
b. Layered design
c. Kernel-based
d. None of the above

3. **Which operating system design approach offer modularity and flexibility but can suffer from inefficiencies due to excessive layering?**
   a. Monolithic structure
   b. Layered design
   c. Kernel-based
   d. None of the above
4. **What factors should be considered when choosing an operating system design approach?**
   a. Performance and efficiency
   b. Modularity and flexibility
   c. Maintainability and extensibility
   d. All of the above

Answers to Multiple Choice Questions

1. (b); 2. (a); 3. (b); 4. (d)

REFERENCES

1. Anderson, T. E., Levy, H. M., Bershad, B. N., & Lazowska, E. D., (1991). The interaction of architecture and operating system design. *ACM SIGPLAN Notices, 26*(4), 108–120.
2. Arlat, J., Fabre, J. C., & Rodríguez, M., (2002). Dependability of COTS microkernel-based systems. *IEEE Transactions on Computers, 51*(2), 138–163.
3. Auslander, M. A., Larkin, D. C., & Scherr, A. L., (1981). The evolution of the MVS operating system. *IBM Journal of Research and Development, 25*(5), 471–482.
4. Baumann, A., Heiser, G., Appavoo, J., Da Silva, D., Krieger, O., Wisniewski, R. W., & Kerr, J., (2005). Providing dynamic update in an operating system. In: *USENIX Annual Technical Conference, General Track* (Vol. 1, pp. 279–291).
5. Bershad, B. N., (1992). The increasing irrelevance of IPC performance for micro-kernel-based operating systems. In: *USENIX Workshop on Microkernels and Other Kernel Architectures* (Vol. 1, pp. 205–212).
6. Bhatt, M., Ahmed, I., & Lin, Z., (2018). Using virtual machine introspection for operating systems security education. In: *Proceedings of the 49th ACM Technical Symposium on Computer Science Education* (Vol. 1, pp. 396–401).
7. Biggs, S., Lee, D., & Heiser, G., (2018). The jury is in: Monolithic OS design is flawed. In: *Asia-Pacific Workshop on Systems (APSys). Korea: ACM SIGOPS* (Vol. 1, pp. 4–7).
8. Boos, K., Liyanage, N., Ijaz, R., & Zhong, L., (2020). Theseus: An experiment in

operating system structure and state management. In: *Proceedings of the 14th USENIX Conference on Operating Systems Design and Implementation* (Vol. 1, pp. 1–19).

9. Bricker, A., Gien, M., Guillemont, M., Lipkis, J., Orr, D., & Rozier, M., (1991). Architectural issues in microkernel-based operating systems: The CHORUS experience. *Computer Communications, 14*(6), 347–357.
10. Bruns, F., Traboulsi, S., Szczesny, D., Gonzalez, E., Xu, Y., & Bilgic, A., (2010). An evaluation of microkernel-based virtualization for embedded real-time systems. In: *2010 22nd Euromicro Conference on Real-Time System*s (Vol. 1, pp. 57–65). IEEE.
11. Casado, L., & Tsigas, P., (2009). Contikisec: A secure network layer for wireless sensor networks under the contiki operating system. In: *Identity and Privacy in the Internet Age: 14th Nordic Conference on Secure IT Systems, NordSec 2009, Oslo, Norway, 14–16 October 2009. Proceedings 14* (Vol. 1, pp. 133–147). Springer Berlin Heidelberg.
12. Chen, J. B., & Bershad, B. N., (1993). The impact of operating system structure on memory system performance. In: *Proceedings of the Fourteenth ACM Symposium on Operating Systems Principles* (Vol. 1, pp. 120–133).
13. Chen, J. B., Endo, Y., Chan, K., Mazieres, D., Dias, A., Seltzer, M., & Smith, M. D., (1996). The measured performance of personal computer operating systems. *ACM Transactions on Computer Systems (TOCS), 14*(1), 3–40.
14. Cheriton, D. R., & Duda, K. J., (1995). A caching model of operating system kernel functionality. *ACM SIGOPS Operating Systems Review, 29*(1), 83–86.
15. Christopher, W. A., Procter, S. J., & Anderson, T. E., (1993). The nachos instructional operating system. In: *USENIX Winter* (Vol. 1, pp. 481–488).
16. Coady, Y., Kiczales, G., Feeley, M., & Smolyn, G., (2001). Using aspectC to improve the modularity of path-specific customization in operating system code. In: *Proceedings of the 8th European Software Engineering Conference Held Jointly with 9th ACM SIGSOFT International Symposium on Foundations of Software Engineering* (Vol. 1, pp. 88–98).
17. Comer, D., (2011). *Operating System Design: The Xinu Approach, Linksys Version.* CRC Press.
18. Cook, D., (1979). In support of domain structure for operating systems. In: *Proceedings of the Seventh ACM Symposium on Operating Systems Principles* (Vol. 1, pp. 128–130).
19. Daum, M., Dörrenbächer, J., & Bogan, S., (2008). Model stack for the pervasive verification of a microkernel-based operating system. In: *5th International Verification Workshop (VERIFY'08)* (Vol. 372, pp. 56–70).
20. De Paoli, D., Hobbs, M., Wickham, G., & Goscinski, A., (1994). *RHODOS—A Microkernel Based Distributed Operating System: An Overview of the 1993 Version* (Vol. 1, pp. 3–7). Technical Report TR C94/04.
21. Dunlap, G. W., King, S. T., Cinar, S., Basrai, M. A., & Chen, P. M., (2002). ReVirt:

Enabling intrusion analysis through virtual-machine logging and replay. *ACM SIGOPS Operating Systems Review, 36(SI)*(1), 211–224.

22. Dutta, P., & Dunkels, A., (2012). Operating systems and network protocols for wireless sensor networks. *Philosophical Transactions of the Royal Society A: Mathematical, Physical and Engineering Sciences, 370*(1958), 68–84.
23. Farooq, M. O., & Kunz, T., (2011). Operating systems for wireless sensor networks: A survey. *Sensors, 11*(6), 5900–5930.
24. Feng, S., Da Xu, L., Tang, C., & Yang, S., (2003). An intelligent agent with layered architecture for operating systems resource management. *Expert Systems, 20*(4), 171–178.
25. Garfinkel, T., Pfaff, B., Chow, J., Rosenblum, M., & Boneh, D., (2003). Terra: A virtual machine-based platform for trusted computing. In: *Proceedings of the Nineteenth ACM Symposium on Operating Systems Principles* (Vol. 1, pp. 193–206).
26. Gien, M., (1990). Micro-kernel architecture key to modern operating systems design. *Unix Review, 8*(11), 58–60.
27. Gray, J., Lampson, B., Lindsay, B., & Sturgis, H., (1972). The control structure of an operating system. *IBM Research Rep. RC, 3949, 1*, 2–5.
28. Greenwald, M., & Cheriton, D., (1996). The synergy between non-blocking synchronization and operating system structure. In: *OSDI* (Vol. 96, pp. 123–136).
29. Härtig, H., Hohmuth, M., Liedtke, J., Schönberg, S., & Wolter, J., (1997). The performance of μ-kernel-based systems. *ACM SIGOPS Operating Systems Review, 31*(5), 66–77.
30. Hess, R., & Paulson, P., (2010). Linux kernel projects for an undergraduate operating systems course. In: *Proceedings of the 41st ACM Technical Symposium on Computer Science Education* (Vol. 1, pp. 485–489).
31. Isohara, T., Takemori, K., & Kubota, A., (2011). Kernel-based behavior analysis for android malware detection. In: *2011 Seventh International Conference on Computational Intelligence and Security* (Vol. 1, pp. 1011–1015). IEEE.
32. Jutla, D. N., (2010). Layering privacy on operating systems, social networks, and other platforms by design. *Identity in the Information Society, 3*(1), 319–341.
33. Kalfa, W., (1992). *Proposal of an External Processor Scheduling in Micro-Kernel Based Operating Systems* (Vol. 1, pp. 1–14). Technical Report, TR-92-028, ICSI, Berkeley.
34. Kapteijn, F., Nijhuis, T. A., Heiszwolf, J. J., & Moulijn, J. A., (2001). New non-traditional multiphase catalytic reactors based on monolithic structures. *Catalysis Today, 66*(2–4), 133–144.
35. King, S. T., & Chen, P. M., (2002). Operating system extensions to support host based virtual machines. *Computing, 23*(1), 18, 19.
36. King, S. T., Dunlap, G. W., & Chen, P. M., (2003). Operating system support for

virtual machines. In: *USENIX Annual Technical Conference, General Track* (Vol. 1, pp. 71–84).

37. King, S. T., Dunlap, G. W., & Chen, P. M., (2005). Debugging operating systems with time-traveling virtual machines. In: *Proceedings of the 2005 USENIX Technical Conference* (Vol. 1, pp. 1–15).
38. Kivity, A., Laor, D., Costa, G., Enberg, P., Har'El, N., Marti, D., & Zolotarov, V., (2014). OSv—Optimizing the operating system for virtual machines. In: *2014 {USENIX} Annual Technical Conference ({USENIX}{ATC} 14)* (Vol. 1, pp. 61–72).
39. Kuz, I., Liu, Y., Gorton, I., & Heiser, G., (2007). CAmkES: A component model for secure microkernel-based embedded systems. *Journal of Systems and Software, 80*(5), 687–699.
40. Lampson, B. W., & Sturgis, H. E., (1976). Reflections on an operating system design. *Communications of the ACM, 19*(5), 251–265.
41. Lauer, H. C., & Needham, R. M., (1979). On the duality of operating system structures. *ACM SIGOPS Operating Systems Review, 13*(2), 3–19.
42. Li, Y., Li, W., & Jiang, C., (2010). A survey of virtual machine system: Current technology and future trends. In: *2010 3rd International Symposium on Electronic Commerce and Security* (Vol. 1, pp. 332–336). IEEE.
43. Linden, T. A., (1976). Operating system structures to support security and reliable software. *ACM Computing Surveys (CSUR), 8*(4), 409–445.
44. Madnick, S. E., & Donovan, J. J., (1973). Application and analysis of the virtual machine approach to information system security and isolation. In: *Proceedings of the Workshop on Virtual Computer Systems* (Vol. 1, pp. 210–224).
45. Malallah, H., Zeebaree, S. R., Zebari, R. R., Sadeeq, M. A., Ageed, Z. S., Ibrahim, I. M., & Merceedi, K. J., (2021). A comprehensive study of kernel (issues and concepts) in different operating systems. *Asian Journal of Research in Computer Science, 8*(3), 16–31.
46. Martinović, G., Balen, J., & Rimac-Drlje, S., (2010). Impact of the host operating systems on virtual machine performance. In: *The 33rd International Convention MIPRO* (Vol. 1, pp. 613–618). IEEE.
47. Marzi, H., & Yang, Y., (2012). Microkernel based real-time embedded operating systems efficiency improvement. In: *2012 25th IEEE Canadian Conference on Electrical and Computer Engineering (CCECE)* (Vol. 1, pp. 1–4). IEEE.
48. Meyer, R. A., & Seawright, L. H., (1970). A virtual machine time-sharing system. *IBM Systems Journal, 9*(3), 199–218.
49. Min, C., Kim, I., Kim, T., & Eom, Y. I., (2012). VMMB: Virtual machine memory balancing for unmodified operating systems. *Journal of Grid Computing, 10*(1), 69–84.
50. Nakajima, T., & Tokuda, H., (1998). User-level real-time network system on microkernel-based operating systems. *Real-Time Systems, 14*(1), 45–60.
51. Nikolaev, R., & Back, G., (2013). VirtuOS: An operating system with kernel virtualization.

In: *Proceedings of the Twenty-Fourth ACM Symposium on Operating Systems Principles* (Vol. 1, pp. 116–132).

52. Ousterhout, J. K., Scelza, D. A., & Sindhu, P. S., (1980). Medusa: An experiment in distributed operating system structure. *Communications of the ACM, 23*(2), 92–105.
53. Payne, B. D., Sailer, R., Cáceres, R., Perez, R., & Lee, W., (2007). A layered approach to simplified access control in virtualized systems. *ACM SIGOPS Operating Systems Review, 41*(4), 12–19.
54. Rawson, F. L., (1997). Experience with the development of a microkernel-based, multiserver operating system. In: *Proceedings, The Sixth Workshop on Hot Topics in Operating Systems (Cat. No. 97TB100133)* (Vol. 1, pp. 2–7). IEEE.
55. Reed, D. P., (1976). *Processor Multiplexing in a Layered Operating System* (Vol. 1, pp. 5–9). Massachusetts Inst of Tech Cambridge Lab for Computer Science.
56. Robin, J. S., & Irvine, C. E., (2000). *Analysis of the Intel Pentium's Ability to Support a Secure Virtual Machine Monitor* (Vol. 1, pp. 2–6). Naval postgraduate school Monterey ca dept of computer science.
57. Stoess, J., (2007). Towards effective user-controlled scheduling for microkernel-based systems. *ACM SIGOPS Operating Systems Review, 41*(4), 59–68.
58. Stoy, J. E., & Strachey, C., (1972). OS6—An experimental operating system for a small computer. Part 1: General principles and structure. *The Computer Journal, 15*(2), 117–124.
59. Tanenbaum, A. S., & Woodhull, A. S., (1997). *Operating Systems: Design and Implementation* (Vol. 2, pp. 6–9). Englewood Cliffs: Prentice Hall.
60. Unrau, R. C., Krieger, O., Gamsa, B., & Stumm, M., (1995). Hierarchical clustering: A structure for scalable multiprocessor operating system design. *The Journal of Supercomputing, 9*(1), 105–134.
61. Vaghani, S. B., (2010). Virtual machine file system. *ACM SIGOPS Operating Systems Review, 44*(4), 57–70.
62. Vömel, S., & Freiling, F. C., (2011). A survey of main memory acquisition and analysis techniques for the windows operating system. *Digital Investigation, 8*(1), 3–22.
63. Watanabe, A., & Sakamura, K., (1995). Design fault tolerance in operating systems based on a standardization project. In: *25th International Symposium on Fault-Tolerant Computing. Digest of Papers* (Vol. 1, pp. 372–380). IEEE.
64. Watson, R. W., & Fletcher, J. G., (1980). An architecture for support of network operating system services. *Computer Networks (1976), 4*(1), 33–49.
65. Whitaker, A., Cox, R. S., Shaw, M., & Gribble, S. D., (2005). Rethinking the design of virtual machine monitors. *Computer, 38*(5), 57–62.
66. Xu, Z., & Zhu, Q., (2018). Cross-layer secure and resilient control of delay-sensitive networked robot operating systems. In: *2018 IEEE Conference on Control Technology and Applications* (CCTA) (Vol. 1, pp. 1712–1717). IEEE.

67. Yokote, Y., (1992). The Apertos reflective operating system: The concept and its implementation. *ACM SIGPLAN Notices, 27*(10), 414–434.
68. Zhao, X., Yin, J., Chen, Z., & He, S., (2013). Workload classification model for specializing virtual machine operating system. In: *2013 IEEE Sixth International Conference on Cloud Computing* (Vol. 1, pp. 343–350). IEEE.

CHAPTER 4

PROCESSES IN OPERATING SYSTEMS

UNIT INTRODUCTION

All contemporary computers frequently perform multiple tasks at once. A few instances may help to illustrate the issue because people accustomed to using computers might not be entirely aware of it. Think about a Web server first. There are requests for Web pages coming in from all over. When a request is received, the server determines if the requested page exists in the cache (Denning, 1976). If this is the case, it returns; if not, a disk demand to fetch it is launched. But from the CPU's point of view, disk requests take ages. Many additional requests might arrive while waiting for one to finish reading from the disk. If several disks are available, one or more recent ones can be transmitted to different disks until the initial request is fulfilled. There must be a mechanism to model and manage this concurrency. Here, processes (particularly threads) can be useful (Anagnoste, 2018).

Consider an individual PC next. Numerous processes are frequently launched, lacking the user's knowledge when the system begins. For example, a process could be initiated to monitor incoming emails. Periodically checking for updated pathogen definitions may supplement the antivirus software (Finkel, 2018). In addition, while a user browses the Internet, specific user processes such as printing files or backing up the customer's pictures to a USB drive may be operating. A multiprogramming system that supports multiple processes greatly assists in administering this activity.

The CPU swiftly changes between processes within any multiprogramming system, with each lasting for hundreds or even tens of milliseconds. While the CPU technically only runs one process at a time, which may operate on numerous of them within a second, creating the appearance of parallelism (Schlichting & Schneider, 1983). When discussing multiprocessor systems with multiple central processing units (CPUs) accessing the same physical memory, pseudo-parallelism is sometimes used to contrast it with actual hardware parallelism. People find it challenging to keep track of numerous concurrent activities. Because of this, operating system (OS) developers have developed a conceptual paradigm (sequential process) that makes dealing with parallelism easier over time (Namjoo & HcCluskey, 1995).

Learning Objectives

After the chapter, students will be able to understand the following:

- Understanding the basic concept of processes in an operating system;
- Learn about the model and creation of process;
- Understanding the termination of process in an operating system;
- Fundamental idea of process hierarchies;
- Implementation of processes in an operating system.

Key Terms

- Memory management
- Operating system
- Process hierarchy
- Process scheduling
- Processes
- Resource allocation
- System call
- User processes
- Virtual address space

4.1. THE PROCESS MODEL

In this architecture, every piece of computer-executable software, occasionally even the OS, is arranged as several linked or simple processes. A process is just a program component that runs, complete with the counter, registers, and variables at the time of execution. Each process theoretically has a virtual CPU (Johansen & Foss, 1997). Although the actual CPU changes back and forth between processes, it is much simpler to grasp the system when one imagines some processes operating in (pseudo) parallel rather than trying to keep track of the CPU's actual program switching patterns. Multiprogramming is the term for this quick switching back and forth (Lauer & Needham, 1979).

Did you Know?

The concept of processes was first introduced in the MULTICS operating system in the mid-1960s.

Figure 4.1(a) depicts a computer multiprogramming four distinct programs in memory. Figure 4.1(b) depicts four processes, each with its logical program counter. Since there is only one physical computer counter, the logical program counter for each process is loaded into the real program counter as each process executes. After completion, the physical program counts are temporarily stored in the transient logical program counter. Figure 4.1(c) demonstrates that, while the processes have progressed, only one phase is active at any given time (Chudnov et al., 2014).

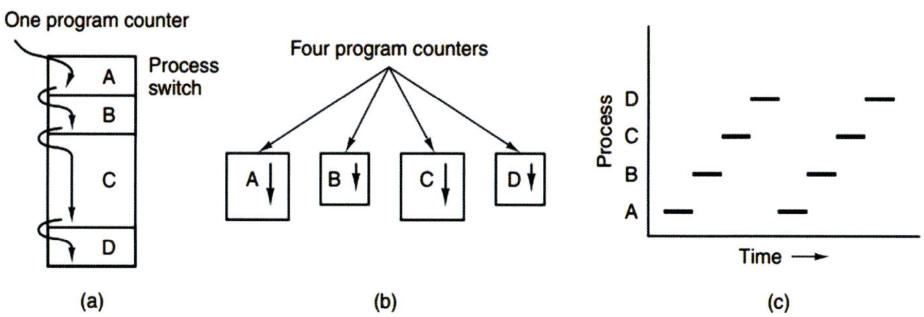

Source: Herbert Bos, Creative Commons License.

Figure 4.1. Illustration of (a) multiprogramming four programs; (b) conceptual model of four independent sequential processes; and (c) only one program is active at once.

Assume there is just one CPU throughout this chapter. Nevertheless, this presumption is no longer accurate as contemporary chips frequently have multicore architectures having two, four, or greater cores. Chapter 8 analyzes multicore chips and multiprocessor systems in general, but it is currently simpler to concentrate on a single CPU. Therefore, when there are a pair of cores (or CPUs), everyone can only carry out a single task at a moment since a CPU can only run a single program (Mohan & Lindsay, 1985).

Due to the CPU transitioning between processes, the rate at which a process accomplishes its computation will not be consistent and may not even be replicable if the same processes are run repeatedly (Harrison et al., 1976). Processes shouldn't, therefore, be programmed with time presumptions. Consider an audio process that plays music in the background of a high-definition video played by another device. It instructs the video servers to begin playing and then does a 10,000-time idle loop before streaming back the audio since it should begin a little later than the video. If the cycle is a dependable timer, video and audio will be irritatingly out of sync (Krohn & Tromer, 2009).

Remember

Processes can communicate with each other using a variety of mechanisms including, shared memory, message passing, and pipes.

Nevertheless, suppose the CPU transitions to another process where the idle loop is active. In that case, the audio process may not begin again until the related video frames have finished and disappeared. Special precautions must be taken to guarantee that certain events occur when a process has crucial immediate needs like this, which calls for specific events to occur within a predetermined number of milliseconds. However, most processes typically aren't impacted by the CPU's underlying multiprogramming or the relative speeds of several processes (Marquardt, 1996).

A process, as well as a program, differ in a modest but significant way. Here, an analogy might be useful. Think about a computer scientist who enjoys preparing cakes for his small daughter's birthday. He has a birthday cake recipe and a well-stocked kitchen using all the necessary ingredients, including flour, eggs, sugar, vanilla extract, etc. (Bogusch et al., 2001). In this comparison, the cake ingredients represent the input data, the computer scientists are the central processing unit (CPU), and a recipe is a program, an algorithm represented in proper syntax. Our baker's reading of the recipe, a gathering of the ingredients, and baking of the cake constitute the procedure (Solle et al., 2017).

Imagine that the son of the computer scientist bursts in, screaming like a little boy after getting stung by a bee. The computer scientist pulls out a first aid manual and starts by following its instructions after recording, and he exists in the process. Here, the processor switches from a lower-priority operation (baking) to a greater-priority process (providing medical treatment), each carried out by a distinct program. The computer scientist returns to his cake and picks off where he left off once the bee sting has been treated (Bassett et al., 1996). The main concept is that a procedure is a type of action. It has a state, an input, an output, and a program. Multiple processes may share a single processor, and a scheduling mechanism may be used to decide when to stop working on one process and start working on another. On the other hand, a program could be saved on a disk but does nothing (Cameron & Ingram, 2008).

Remembering that a program counts as two processes if it runs twice is important. For instance, if more than one printer is available, Printing two papers at once or operating a word processor several times is often feasible. It doesn't matter if two processes execute the same software simultaneously because they are independent. Even while the operating system (OS) may be able to split the code up so that only one copy remains in memory, such a technical capability does not impact the theoretical situation of two processes running simultaneously (Back et al., 1998).

4.2. PROCESS CREATION

OSs must support the formation of processes. In relatively simple systems or systems designed to run just one application, it can be possible to have every operation that will ever be needed available when the system starts up. General-purpose systems require a method for launching and quitting processes, though, as needed. We'll examine a few issues raised (De Paoli et al., 1996).

Four main things happen that lead to processes:

- Initializing the system;
- A running process calls a system call to create a new process;
- When a user is requested to launch a new process; and
- Beginning a batch task.

Usually, many processes are started once a computer's OS is booted. Several forefront processes work for and interact with users (humans). Others operate in the background, are not connected to specific users, but serve a particular purpose. For instance, one background process might be set up to receive an incoming email, resting most of the day but waking up once an email arrives (Mullender et al., 1990). When a request for a Web page hosted on that system is received, another background process could be set up to accept the request and wake up to handle it. Daemons are processes that run in the background to handle tasks like emails, Web pages, news, printing, and other activities. Numerous of them are frequently seen in large systems. The PS application in UNIX can show a list of active processes. The task manager is a Windows feature (Harrison et al., 1976).

New processes can be created later in addition to those created at boot time. To complete the tasks, a running process frequently makes system calls to start a few new processes. Developing new processes is especially beneficial when the job can be expressed in numerous connected but generally independent interacting processes (Cox et al., 1994). Assume, for instance, that a lot of data has been fetched across a network for processing later. In that situation, it might be practical to designate one process to gather and store the data in a shared buffer. A second process takes care of removing and processing the data items. Enabling each process to execute on a distinct CPU on a multiprocessor could also speed up the process (Irwansyah et al., 2018).

In interactive systems, users can launch a program by inputting a command and clicking an icon. Either of these operations launches a new process with the chosen program running inside. The newly begun process takes control of the window in command-based UNIX that runs X (Niermann et al., 2013). Windows processes begin without windows but can – and often do – generate them. Users may have several windows open simultaneously in both systems, each executing a different process. The user may choose a window and engage with the process using the mouse, for instance, by giving input as required (Tabata & Taniguchi, 2008).

Only the batch systems seen on huge mainframes are relevant to the last scenario whereby processes are created. Consider inventory management at a chain of businesses. Here, users can remotely (potentially) submit batch jobs into the system. The OS starts a new process and executes the subsequent job in the input queue when it determines that it still has enough resources to run another job (Suranauwarat & Taniguchi, 2001).

Technically, an entirely new process is formed in these situations by having an already-running process called a system call for process creation. It can be a batch management process, a user process already running, or a system process launched with the keyboard and mouse. To start the new process, that process performs a system call. This system calls the OS to start a new process and, indirectly or directly, specifies which application should run in it (Tabata et al., 2004).

Forking a new process in UNIX requires one system called: fork. This call duplicates the calling process exactly. The parent and child processes now share identical storage images, environmental strings, and view files as before the fork. There is nothing else. The child process typically calls an executive or a related system call to modify its memory image and launch a new application (Zarrabi et al., 2013). For instance, the shell forks away a child process and has the child run the command sort whenever a user types the command into the shell. This two-step procedure is necessary to enable the child to modify its file descriptor after the fork but before the executive performs standard input, standard output, and standard error redirection (Lang, 1999).

However, the process creation and program launch are handled by Windows' CreateProcess, just one Win32 method call. The program to be run, its command-line parameters, different security attributes, bits that control when open files get passed on, priority information, an explanation of the window that is going to be generated over the procedure (if any), and a link to a structure containing a pointer to data that explains the newly created activity while returns it to the caller are all included in this call's 10 parameters. In addition to CreateProcess, Win32 offers about 100 more functions for managing and synchronizing processes (Helmy & Jafri, 2006).

Once a process is created, parents and kids have separate address spaces in UNIX and Windows systems. A word in the address space of either process can be changed, but the other process is unaware of the change. In UNIX, two distinct address spaces are involved: no shared written memory and a duplicate of the parent's first address space in a child's first address space (Abe et al., 2008). In some UNIX implementations, the program text is shared between the two since it cannot be modified. The youngster could also recount the entirety of the parent's recall. The memory would nonetheless be shared copy-on-write in that scenario. To ensure the change occurred in a secret memory area, the section would be duplicated first when one of the two intendeds to modify a particular memory location. Again, there is no shared writable memory. A newly started process, however, could be able to lend some of its creator's other resources, including open files. Windows's parent and child address spaces are distinct from the beginning (Saraswat & Gupta, 2006).

4.3. PROCESS TERMINATION

A process is started, then it runs and performs its function. But nothing—not even processes—lasts forever (Cook et al., 2006). The new method will end eventually, usually as a result of the following circumstances:

- Regular (voluntary) exit;
- Voluntary exit due to error;
- An unintentional fatal error;
- Involuntary death caused by a different mechanism.

The majority of processes end because they have completed their tasks. A compiler makes a system function to notify the OS that it has completed compiling the program passed to it. In UNIX, this call represents an exit, whereas in Windows, it is an Exit Process (Lauer & Needham, 1979). Programs that focus on screens also allow for voluntary termination. The user can always click an icon or menu item in word processors, web browsers, and similar applications to instruct the process to close any open temporary files before terminating (Lau, 1984).

The second reason for termination is that the process discovers a fatal error.

For example, if someone types the command:

cc foo. c

and the compiler tries to build the program foo. c, but there is no such file. It simply reports this and exits. When provided with incorrect parameters, screen-oriented interactive processes typically do not terminate. Instead, a dialog window appears, asking the user to attempt again (Jefferson et al., 1987).

The third cause for terminating is a process error, frequently brought on by a programming flaw. Examples include using a forbidden instruction, referring to memory that doesn't exist, or dividing with zero (Richard III, 1998). A process can instruct the OS in some systems (like UNIX) that want to handle specific faults. In this instance, the process is notified (interrupted) rather than terminated if one of these errors occurs.

The fourth possible reason for a process to end is when it issues a system call instructing the OS to kill another process. UNIX calls this operation to kill. TerminateProcess is a Win32 function that is equivalent. In all situations, the murderer must consent to harm the killed. Some systems automatically destroy any processes that a process has launched when it terminates, whether the process did so intentionally or not. However, neither UNIX nor Windows operates this way (Tolga et al., 2005).

4.4. PROCESS HIERARCHIES

When one process generates another in some systems, the parent and child processes are still connected in specific ways. A process hierarchy can be formed by the child process by itself, producing further processes. Note that a process only has a single couple, unlike plants and animals that reproduce sexually. A process is, therefore, more akin to a hydra than a cow. A process group in UNIX comprises a process along with its offspring and future descendants (Parnas, 1978). All members of the procedure group currently connected to the keyboard—typically all active processes spawned in the current window—are sent the signal when a user sends one from the keyboard. Individually, each process has three options: respond to the signal, ignore its signal, or execute the fault action, which causes the signal to be killed (Roper-Lowe & Sharp, 1990).

Let's examine how UNIX sets up itself once it is started, immediately following the computer being booted, as another instance where the procedure hierarchy plays a crucial role. A unique process with the name in it is present in the boot image. It reads a file containing information about the number of terminals before it may run. A new process is then started for each terminal. These procedures hold off till a user logs in. When a login attempt is successful, a shell that can accept commands is launched. These commands might launch more processes, and so forth. As a result, the entire system's operations are connected by just one tree, with initialization at its base (Ballı & Korukoğlu, 2009).

Windows, in contrast, has no understanding of a procedure hierarchy. Every process is equivalent. The only indication of a procedure hierarchy is the special token (a handle) supplied to the parent whenever a process is established and may be used to manage the child. The hierarchy can be invalidated by freely passing this token to another process. In UNIX, processes cannot disinherit their offspring (Lu et al., 2000).

4.5. PROCESS STATES

Even though each process is autonomous and has its program counter, as well as interior state, connections to other processes, as well as interior state, connections to other processes are often needed. A single action can produce output used as input by another (Hays et al., 1990). The shell command is used to:

```
cat chapter1 chapter2 chapter3 | grep tree
```

Three files are concatenated and output by the first procedure, cat. The second stage, known as "grep in action," selects lines that include the word "tree." Grep can be prepared to execute but not have any input waiting for it, depending on the respective speed of both procedures (which rely on the varying levels of complexity of each application and how much CPU time each has got) (Giuffrida et al., 2013). After that, it must wait till there is input available.

It is logically impossible for a process to continue when it blocks, usually because it is awaiting input that has yet to be available. A program that is theoretically prepared and capable of running might also be terminated because the OS has chosen to provide the CPU with a different process temporarily. These two circumstances are entirely dissimilar. Because one can't process the user's command line till it has been input, the suspension occurs in the first scenario. The second instance involves system technicality (insufficient CPUs to give every process an individual private processor). Figure 4.2 displays a state diagram of the three possible states for a process (Smith, 1988):

- Running (currently making use of the CPU);
- Runnable; momentarily halted to permit the operation of another process; and
- Blocked (not able to operate unless a specific external event occurs).

The initial two states make sense together logically. The process is ready to run in both situations, but in the second scenario, there isn't a CPU accessible to it right now. The third stage differs significantly from the prior two because the process cannot operate even when the CPU is dormant and unoccupied.

Figure 4.2. Depiction of that process can be in the running, blocked, or ready state.

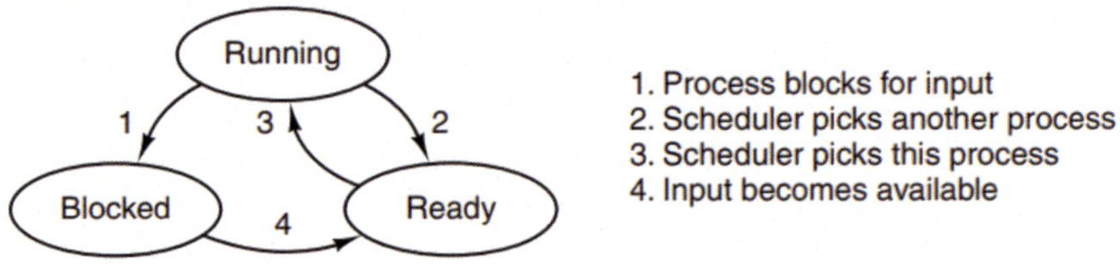

Source: Bob Lentz, Creative Commons License.

As illustrated, there are four conceivable transitions between these three phases. When the OS determines that an operation cannot proceed at this time, transition 1 takes place. In some systems, a system call like pause can be used by the process to enter a blocked state. Whenever a process is read from a pipe and a special file (such as a terminal) in another system, such as UNIX, but there isn't any input accessible, the process is instantly blocked (Krohn & Tromer, 2009).

The OS's process scheduler, responsible for transitions 2 and 3, initiates them without the process being aware. Transition 2 occurs when the scheduler decides that an operation has finished running and is ready to grant another procedure access to the CPU. Transition 3 occurs when the originating process is ready to resume using the CPU after all other processes have used their fair part of it. Scheduling is a critical issue addressed later in the section. Scheduling is deciding which process to execute, when, and for how long. Numerous algorithms have been developed to compromise the competing needs of system effectiveness and equitable access to individual operations (Denning, 1976).

When a process receives an external occurrence for which it had been awaiting (like the onset of some input), transition 4 takes place. Transition 3 will be initiated, and the process will start to run if no other processes are running at the time. If not, it may require a short while in the state of readiness before the CPU becomes available, and it can take a turn.

When using the process model, thinking about what is happening inside the system is considerably simpler. Certain processes execute software that executes user-typed commands. Other system-wide processes include processing requests to file services or controlling the specifics using a disk like a tape device. The system decides to terminate the active process and launch the blocked disk process while waiting for the disk interrupt when it happens. As a result, one can consider user processes, disk procedures, terminal processes, and additional processes instead of interruptions because these processes block while await for something to happen. The process awaiting it is unblocked and can resume running when the disk is being read, and the character has been inputted (Back et al., 1998).

The model depicted in Figure 4.3 results from this viewpoint. The scheduler, followed by several processes, is the OS's lowest level. What is referred to as the scheduler, although it is not much code, contains all the interruption handling information and the specifics of actually beginning and ending processes. The remainder of the OS is well organized regarding processes (Osman et al., 2002). However, few practical systems are as well-organized as this.

Did you Know?

The concept of processes is fundamental to modern computing and has enabled the development of complex systems that can run on a variety of hardware platforms.

Processes

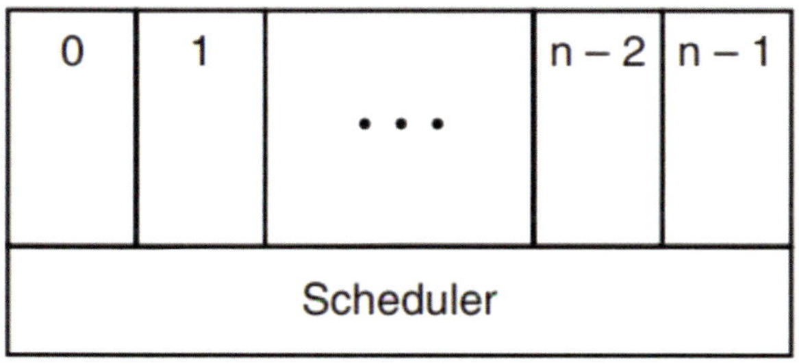

Figure 4.3. Representation of the lowest layer of a process-structured operating system that handles interrupts and scheduling.

Source: Joe Ruddick, Creative Commons License.

4.6. IMPLEMENTATION OF PROCESSES

The OS keeps a list named the process data table, having one entry per process, to carry out the process model. These items are sometimes referred to as process control blocks (PCBs). This entry contains crucial information about the state of the process, including the procedure counter, stack pointer, memory allocation, the status of all open files, calculating and scheduling information, and anything else that must be saved if the process changes from an operating state to a ready as well as blocked state so that it can later be activated as if it had not previously stopped (Young et al., 1997). Some of the important fields of a typical system are shown in Table 4.1. The first column's fields have to do with process management. The other two concerns, respectively, file management and memory management. It should be emphasized that the exact fields in this procedure table have depended greatly on the system. However, this figure provides an overview of the types of information required.

Being able to clarify a little a bit more about how the appearance of several sequential processes remains on one (or each) CPU after looking at the process table. Each I/O class has an area known as the interrupt vector, normally fixed and located towards the bottom of memory (Ousterhout et al., 1998). It includes the interrupt service procedure's advertisement. Suppose that a disk interrupt occurs when user processes 3 is active. The interrupt hardware pushes the program counter, program condition word, and occasionally one or more registers from User Process 3 onto the (current) stack. Following that, the computer goes to the address the interrupt vector indicates. All the gear can do is that. From this point forward, the software, specifically the interrupt service method, is responsible.

Table 4.1. Fields of a Typical Process-Table Entry

Process Management	Memory Management	File Management
Registers	Refers to text segment information	Root directory
Program counter	Data segment information pointer	Working directory
Program status word	Pointer to the information stack	File descriptors
Stack pointer	–	User ID
Process state	–	Group ID
Priority	–	–
Scheduling parameters	–	–
Process ID	–	–
Parent process	–	–
Process Group	–	–
Signals	–	–
The moment the process began	–	–
CPU time used	–	–
Kids' computer time	–	–
Next alarm time	–	–

Source: Andrew S. Tanenbaum, Creative Commons License.

All interruptions begin by storing the registers, frequently in an entry for the present process in the process table. The data that the interrupt then pushed into the stack is removed and the stack pointer is set to point to a temporary stack used by the process handler.

A tiny assembly-language routine is used to perform tasks like saving the registers or establishing the stack pointer because they cannot even be expressed using high-level languages like C. Since the task of preserving the registers is the same regardless of the reason for the interrupt, this routine is typically used for all interrupts (Ong et al., 2013).

ACTIVITY 4.1:

Experiment with different operating systems such a Linux or Windows to see how they manage processes. Try running multiple programs simultaneously and observe how the operating system allocates resources and schedules processes.

Following the completion of this function, a C procedure is called to complete the remaining tasks for this particular interrupt type. (Presumptively write the OS in C, the language of choice for all genuine OSs.) The scheduler is summoned to determine who should run next once it has completed its task and may have perhaps made some process ready. Control is then returned to the assembly language code, which begins executing by setting up its registers and memory map. It is important to note that the specifics differ slightly between systems.

The important concept is that after every interruption, the disrupted process returns to the same state preceding the interruption. A process could be interrupted many times during its execution.

4.7. SUMMARY

OSs offer a conceptual model comprising sequential activities executed in parallel to conceal the consequences of interruptions. Processes can be dynamically started and stopped (Rosen, 1972). The address space for each process is distinct. Processes can communicate with each other through inter-process communication mechanisms provided by the OSs. The OS manages processes by allocating resources, scheduling them for execution and providing mechanisms for synchronization and communication between processes. A process is an instance of a program that is being executed by OSs.

REVIEW QUESTIONS

1. What is a process in an operating system?
2. What are some of the resources that the operating system allocates to a process?
3. How is the virtual address space used by a process and why is it important for each process to have its own address space?
4. What are some of the challenges and limitations of process management in operating systems?
5. What is process scheduling?

MULTIPLE CHOICE QUESTIONS

1. What is the virtual address space used for by a process?

a. To store the program's executable code
b. To manage dynamically allocated memory
c. To manage the process's input and output data
d. All of the above

2. Which of the following resources can be allocated to a process by an operating system?

a. Memory
b. CPU Time
c. Input/output devices
d. All of the above

3. What is process synchronization?

a. The process of ensuring that each process has its own virtual address space
b. The process of ensuring that processes access shared resources in a safe and orderly manner
c. The process of allocating resources to a process

d. None of the above

4. Which of the following is a limitation of process management in operating systems?

a. Limited memory resources

b. Limited CPU resources

c. Limited input/output resources

d. All of the above

Answers to Multiple Choice Questions

1. (d); 2. (d); 3. (b); 4. (d)

REFERENCES

1. Abe, Y., Yamada, H., & Kono, K., (2008). Enforcing appropriate process execution for exploiting idle resources from outside operating systems. *ACM SIGOPS Operating Systems Review, 42*(4), 27–40.
2. Anagnoste, S., (2018). Robotic automation process–the operating system for the digital enterprise. In: *Proceedings of the International Conference on Business Excellence* (Vol. 12, No. 1, pp. 54–69).
3. Back, G., Tullmann, P., Stoller, L., Hsieh, W. C., & Lepreau, J., (1998). *Java Operating Systems: Design and Implementation*. Technical Report UUCS-98-015, 6.
4. Ballı, S., & Korukoğlu, S., (2009). Operating system selection using fuzzy AHP and TOPSIS methods. *Mathematical and Computational Applications, 14*(2), 119–130.
5. Bassett, M. H., Dave, P., Doyle, III. F. J., Kudva, G. K., Pekny, J. F., Reklaitis, G. V., & Zentner, M. G., (1996). Perspectives on model-based integration of process operations. *Computers & Chemical Engineering, 20*(6, 7), 821–844.
6. Bogusch, R., Lohmann, B., & Marquardt, W., (2001). Computer-aided process modeling with ModKit. *Computers & Chemical Engineering, 25*(7, 8), 963–995.
7. Cameron, I. T., & Ingram, G. D., (2008). A survey of industrial process modelling across the product and process lifecycle. *Computers & Chemical Engineering, 32*(3), 420–438.
8. Chudnov, A., Kuan, G., & Naumann, D. A., (2014). Information flow monitoring as abstract interpretation for relational logic. In: *2014 IEEE 27th Computer Security Foundations Symposium* (1(2), pp. 48–62).
9. Cook, B., Podelski, A., & Rybalchenko, A., (2006). Termination proofs for systems code. *ACM Sigplan Notices, 41*(6), 415–426.
10. Cox, A. L., Dwarkadas, S., Keleher, P., & Zwaenepoel, W., (1994). Treadmarks: Distributed shared memory on standard workstations and operating systems. In: *Proceedings of the Winter 94 Usenix Conference*, *1*(No. CONF).

11. De Paoli, D., Goscinski, A., Hobbs, M., & Joyce, P., (1996). Performance comparison of process migration with remote process creation mechanisms in RHODOS. In: *Proceedings of 16th International Conference on Distributed Computing Systems* (pp. 554–561).
12. Denning, P. J., (1976). Fault tolerant operating systems. *ACM Computing Surveys (CSUR), 8*(4), 359–389.
13. Finkel, R., (2018). Operating systems. In: *Computers, Software Engineering, and Digital Devices,* (pp. 1–18).
14. Giuffrida, C., Kuijsten, A., & Tanenbaum, A. S., (2013). Safe and automatic live update for operating systems. *ACM Sigplan Notices*, *48*(4), 279–292.
15. Harrison, M. A., Ruzzo, W. L., & Ullman, J. D., (1976). Protection in operating systems. *Communications of the ACM, 19*(8), 461–471.
16. Hays, J. H., Miller, L., Othmer, B., & Saeed, M., (1990). Simulation of process and resource management in a multiprogramming operating system. *ACM SIGCSE Bulletin, 22*(1), 125–128.
17. Helmy, T., & Jafri, S. S., (2006). Avoidance of priority inversion in real time systems based on resource restoration. *Int. J. Comput. Sci. Appl., 3*(1), 40–50.
18. Irwansyah, F. S., Yusuf, Y. M., Farida, I., & Ramdhani, M. A., (2018). Augmented reality (AR) technology on the android operating system in chemistry learning. In: *IOP Conference Series: Materials Science and Engineering* (Vol. 288, No. 1, p. 012068).
19. Jefferson, D., Beckman, B., Wieland, F., Blume, L., & DiLoreto, M., (1987). Time warp operating system. In: *Proceedings of the Eleventh ACM Symposium on Operating Systems Principles,* (Vol. 1, pp. 77–93).
20. Johansen, T. A., & Foss, B. A., (1997). Operating regime-based process modeling and identification. *Computers & Chemical Engineering, 21*(2), 159–176.
21. Krohn, M., & Tromer, E., (2009). Noninterference for a practical DIFC-based operating system. In: *2009 30th IEEE Symposium on Security and Privacy, 2(1),* 61–76.
22. Lang, S. D., (1999). An extended banker's algorithm for deadlock avoidance. *IEEE Transactions on Software Engineering, 25*(3), 428–432.
23. Lau, F. C., (1984). Two-part names and process termination. *ACM SIGOPS Operating Systems Review, 18*(3), 28–30.
24. Lauer, H. C., & Needham, R. M., (1979). On the duality of operating system structures. *ACM SIGOPS Operating Systems Review, 13*(2), 3–19.
25. Lu, Y. H., Benini, L., & DeMicheli, G., (2000). Operating-system directed power reduction. In: *Proceedings of the 2000 International Symposium on Low Power Electronics and Design*, 1, 37–42.
26. Marquardt, W., (1996). Trends in computer-aided process modeling. *Computers & Chemical Engineering, 20*(6, 7), 591–609.
27. Mohan, C., & Lindsay, B., (1985). Efficient commit protocols for the tree of processes

model of distributed transactions. *ACM SIGOPS Operating Systems Review, 19*(2), 40–52.

28. Mullender, S. J., Van, R. G., Tananbaum, A. S., Van, R. R., & VanStaveren, H., (1990). Amoeba: A distributed operating system for the 1990s. *Computer, 23*(5), 44–53.
29. Namjoo, M., & HcCluskey, E. J., (1995). Watchdog processors and capability checking. In: *Twenty-Fifth International Symposium on Fault-Tolerant Computing, 1995,'Highlights from Twenty-Five Years'* (p. 94-98). IEEE Computer Society.
30. Niermann, D., Doernbach, T., Petzoldt, C., Isken, M., & Freitag, M., (2023). Software framework concept with visual programming and digital twin for intuitive process creation with multiple robotic systems. *Robotics and Computer-Integrated Manufacturing, 82*, 102536.
31. Ong, S. E., Lee, S. C., Ali, N. B. Z., & Hussin, F. A. B., (2013). SEOS: Hardware implementation of real-time operating system for adaptability. In: *2013 First International Symposium on Computing and Networking* 1, pp. 612–616.
32. Osman, S., Subhraveti, D., Su, G., & Nieh, J., (2002). The design and implementation of zap: A system for migrating computing environments. *ACM SIGOPS Operating Systems Review, 36*(SI), 361–376.
33. Ousterhout, J. K., Cherenson, A. R., Douglis, F., Nelson, M. N., & Welch, B. B., (1988). The sprite network operating system. *Computer, 21*(2), 23–36.
34. Parnas, D. L., (1978). On a "buzzword": Hierarchical structure. *Programming Methodology: A Collection of Articles by Members of IFIP WG2* 3(2), pp. 335–342.
35. Richard, III. G. G., (1998). Efficient vector time with dynamic process creation and termination. *Journal of Parallel and Distributed Computing, 55*(1), 109–120.
36. Roper-Lowe, G. C., & Sharp, J. A., (1990). The analytic hierarchy process and its application to an information technology decision. *Journal of the Operational Research Society, 41*, 49–59.
37. Rosen, S., (1972). Programming systems and languages 1965–1975. *Communications of the ACM, 15*(7), 591–600.
38. Saraswat, P. K., & Gupta, P., (2006). Design and implementation of a process scheduler simulator and an improved process scheduling algorithm for multimedia operating systems. In: *2006 International Conference on Advanced Computing and Communications* (Vol. 1, pp. 513–517.
39. Schlichting, R. D., & Schneider, F. B., (1983). Fail-stop processors: An approach to designing fault-tolerant computing systems. *ACM Transactions on Computer Systems (TOCS), 1*(3), 222–238.
40. Smith, J. M., (1988). A survey of process migration mechanisms. *ACM SIGOPS Operating Systems Review, 22*(3), 28–40.
41. Solle, D., Hitzmann, B., Herwig, C., Pereira, R. M., Ulonska, S., Wuerth, L., & Steckenreiter, T., (2017). Between the poles of data□driven and mechanistic modeling for process operation. *Chemie Ingenieur Technik, 89*(5), 542–561.

42. Suranauwarat, S., & Taniguchi, H., (2001). The design, implementation and initial evaluation of an advanced knowledge-based process scheduler. *ACM SIGOPS Operating Systems Review*, *35*(4), 61–81.
43. Tabata, T., & Taniguchi, H., (2008). An improved recyclable resource management method for fast process creation and reduced memory consumption. *International Journal of Hybrid Information Technology*, *1*(1), 31–44.
44. Tabata, T., Nomura, Y., & Taniguchi, H., (2007). Mechanism of regulating execution performance for process group by execution resource on tender operating system. *Systems and Computers in Japan*, *38*(14), 63–78.
45. Tolga, E., Demircan, M. L., & Kahraman, C., (2005). Operating system selection using fuzzy replacement analysis and analytic hierarchy process. *International Journal of Production Economics*, *97*(1), 89–117.
46. Young, M., Tevanian, A., Rashid, R., Golub, D., & Eppinger, J., (1987). The duality of memory and communication in the implementation of a multiprocessor operating system. In: *Proceedings of the Eleventh ACM Symposium on Operating Systems Principles* (pp. 63–76).
47. Zarrabi, A., Samsudin, K., & Ziaei, A., (2013). Dynamic process migration framework. In: *2013 International Conference of Information and Communication Technology* 25(2), pp. 410–415.

CHAPTER 5

MEMORY MANAGEMENT

UNIT INTRODUCTION

The memory hierarchy comprises several components, including the memory management unit (MMU), the cache, RAM, referred to as memory in this chapter, and a disk. The present discourse is divided into two sections, wherein the first section pertains to optimizing memory usage techniques. In contrast, the subsequent section delves into the management of virtual memory. The latter is an integral component of the hierarchy of memory, encompassing the memory and the disk (Tofte & Talpin, 1997).

Memory binding refers to linking memory addresses with program instructions and data. A program undergoes multiple instances of memory binding to enhance convenience and flexibility. This process is carried out statically by the compiler and linker before the commencement of program execution, while the operating system (OS) performs it dynamically during the program's execution. The memory allocation model utilized by the kernel caters to the process's static and dynamic memory binding requirements (Morrisett et al., 1995).

The efficient utilization of memory and the speed of memory allocation are two primary considerations in developing a memory allocator. To optimize resource utilization, the kernel employs a mechanism whereby the memory a process has released is reallocated to other processes requiring it. Memory fragmentation is a prevalent issue during memory reuse, resulting in suboptimal utilization of memory resources (Gay & Aiken, 1998). The present discourse shall expound upon pragmatic methodologies to mitigate memory fragmentation in an OS. Specifically, the focus shall be non-linear memory allocation techniques, such as paging or segmentation (Nilakanta et al., 2006).

At a high frequency, the kernel generates and terminates data structures for storing control data, specifically diverse control blocks like PCBs. The data structures' sizes are predetermined, so the kernel utilizes various methods that leverage this foreknowledge to facilitate swift allocation, deallocation, and optimal memory utilization (Grossman et al., 2002).

Learning Objectives

After the chapter, students will be able to understand the following:

- Basic concept of memory management in operating systems;
- Learn about the hierarchy of memory in operating systems;
- Understanding static and dynamic allocation of memory in operating systems;
- Fundamental concept of memory allocation to a process in operating systems.

Key Terms

- Buffer
- Dynamic
- Memory allocation
- Memory management
- Memory protection
- Operating systems
- Performance
- Segmentation
- Static
- Virtual memory

5.1. MANAGING THE HIERARCHY OF MEMORY

The memory hierarchy consists of a disk, memory management unit (MMU), and multiple cache memories. These cache memories include the L1 and L3 caches and the memory and the disk. With the use of this technology, we hope to create the impression of a memory that is both fast and large while keeping the cost as cheap as possible. In the upper part of Figure 5.1, you can see a representation of the memory hierarchy (Liu et al., 2019) (Table 5.1).

Did you Know?

The first computer to use virtual memory was the Atlas computer in 1962.

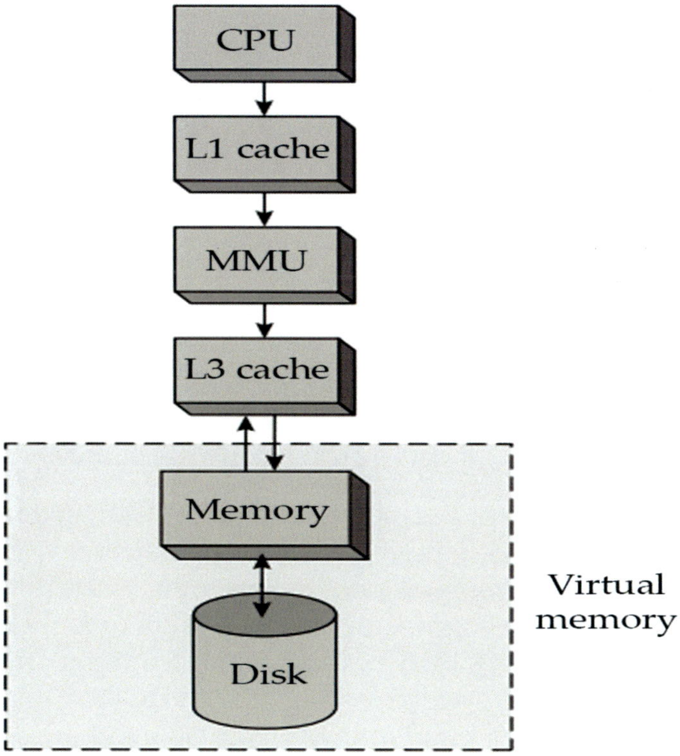

Source: Bohme, Creative Commons License.

Figure 5.1. Illustration of managing the memory hierarchy.

When the central processing unit (CPU) requires access to an instruction or data, it retrieves it from the cache, the swiftest form of memory. If the necessary instruction or data is not in the cache, it is retrieved from the subsequent lower tier in the memory hierarchy (Liu et al., 2016). This tier may consist of a slower cache, or RAM, referred to as memory within the context of this literature. If the necessary instruction or data is not present in the subsequent lower-level memory, it is retrieved from a lower-level memory, which is repeated as necessary. The efficacy of a process is contingent upon the hit ratios within the diverse levels of the memory hierarchy. The hit ratio within a given level denotes the proportion of instructions or data bytes sought in that level and successfully located (Fatahalian et al., 2006).

Table 5.1. Levels and Performance Issues of the Memory Hierarchy

Levels Description	Management	Performance Related Issues
Caches	The hardware manages its allocation and use.	To make sure high hit ratios.
Memory	Kernel manages the allocation.	To accommodate more process. In the memory and to ensure the high hit ratios.
Disk	The kernel manages the allocation and use.	Quickly store and load parts of the process.

Source: Bonwick, Creative Commons License.

The hardware solely carries out the management of caches. The kernel utilizes specific methodologies to ensure elevated cache hit ratios for a given process. The kernel utilizes thread switching within a process to optimize cache utilization. It implements affinitive scheduling in a multiprocessor environment to ensure a process is consistently scheduled on the same CPU, thereby increasing cache hit rates (Bamaqa et al., 2002).

The kernel and the run-time library of the computer language used in the process code work together to manage memory. The kernel gives users functions the memory they need. The main thing to consider regarding speed in this function is letting more user processes run in memory to improve system performance and user service. The kernel solves this problem by recycling memory when a task ends. During its processing, a process creates data structures in the memory space that the kernel has given it. The run-time library does this process. The method uses memory well by making and deleting data structures while the program runs. Because of this, the kernel and the run-time tools share some assumptions and ways of doing things (Ribeiro et al., 2009).

In keeping with the kernel's goal of letting many processes run in memory, the kernel may keep only a small part of each process's address area in memory. Virtual memory, which includes both memory and a disk (as shown in the dashed box in Figure 5.1), made this possible within the memory structure. When a process runs, the parts of its address space not currently in memory are loaded from the disk as needed. In this setup, the hit ratio of a process in memory tells us how well it works (Li et al., 2017). So, the kernel uses various ways to ensure that most processes work well. The kernel is the only one in charge of managing the disk for virtual memory. The kernel saves different parts of each process's address space on the hard drive to make accessing them faster. Its addition makes it easier for processes in a virtual memory system to run smoothly.

This chapter is about memory management, showing how to use memory best and speed up allocating and releasing memory (Liu et al., 2019).

5.2. STATIC AND DYNAMIC ALLOCATION OF MEMORY

Memory allocation is a part of the overarching binding process involved in the functioning of the software. In addition to binding, a program is associated with two more actions: loading and linking (Udayakumaran et al., 2006).

Each component of a software system, such as a function or a variable, maintains its unique collection of characters, and each individual byte in that collection has a predetermined monetary value. The process of defining the value of an attribute is referred to as the binding of that attribute. A variable in a program can have many different qualities, such as its name, type, dimensionality, scope, and memory address. These are only some of the attributes that a variable can have. In computer programming, a name binding refers to the specification of a variable's name, whereas a type binding refers to the specification of the variable's type (Deverge & Puaut, 2007). Memory binding is the process of specifying the memory address of a variable, which ultimately leads to the allocation of memory for the variable in question. This procedure is also known as "binding memory." Memory allocation refers to assigning memory addresses to store the instructions and data associated with a particular process (Evans, 1996).

Did you Know?

Early computers used punch cards for memory storage, and programs were physically loaded into memory using a loader.

Before making use of an entity's (a function or a variable's) attribute, you are free to do the action of binding that attribute at any time before making use of the attribute. Different approaches for binding carry out the binding process at varied periods. The timing of the binding process can affect the entity's ability to function effectively and adapt to changing circumstances. In general, one may differentiate between early and late binding by looking at when the binding occurs (Lee & Chang, 2003). Utilizing late binding is beneficial in situations in which the operating system (OS) or run-time library obtains additional knowledge about an entity at a later moment, which could potentially result in a binding of greater quality. As an illustration, it might enhance the usage of resources such as memory. The two basic binding methods, namely static binding and dynamic binding, respectively embody the ideas of early binding and late binding (Budzinski & Davidson, 1981).

A loader, a linker, or a compiler can be the one to do static memory allocation in the course of a program's preparation for execution. During the course of the execution of a program, the procedure of dynamic memory allocation is carried out in a postponed fashion. To be more specific, memory is not allotted to a function or variable until it has been accessed for the first time (Truong et al., 1998).

The feasibility of allocating static memory to a process is contingent upon the foreknowledge of the sizes of its data structures before the commencement of its execution. In cases where sizes are unknown, estimation is necessary. Incorrect estimations may result in memory wastage and limited adaptability. An illustrative instance involves an array whose magnitude remains indeterminate at compilation. Overestimating the size of an array can result in a waste of memory, while underestimating its size can lead to incorrect operation of the process (Jomier, 1981). The utilization of dynamic memory allocation can circumvent the issues above by assigning a memory region whose dimensions correspond to the precise size of the array. This value can be determined at the moment of the allocation. The system can allow dynamic modification of the array size while the process is in operation. Dynamic memory allocation, though useful, results in the additional cost of memory allocation operations that are executed during the course of a process (Bovet & Estrin, 1970).

OSs employ static and dynamic memory allocation techniques in varying situations to achieve an optimal balance between execution efficiency and memory efficiency. In cases with adequate information regarding memory requirements, the kernel or run-time library renders static memory allocation decisions, ensuring optimal execution efficiency. In cases where limited information is available beforehand, dynamic memory allocation is employed to make memory allocation decisions. This approach results in increased overhead, but it guarantees optimal memory utilization. In certain scenarios, the information at hand is utilized to make determinations regarding memory allocation statically to minimize the burden of dynamic memory allocation (Bovet & Estrin, 1970).

5.3. EXECUTION OF PROGRAMS

Before execution, a program denoted as P and authored in a particular programming language (PL), L, necessitates a transformation process. Several of these transformations execute memory binding, associating the program's instructions and data with a fresh set of addresses. The schematic diagram in Figure 5.2 illustrates three transformations carried out on program P before loading into memory for execution (King, 1976).

Compilation or assembly – generally, "translator" refers to a compiler or an assembler. The process involves the translation of program P into an object module form that is equivalent in functionality. The present software comprises directives written in the computer's machine language (Kiriansky et al., 2002). Upon invocation of the translator, the user must specify the program's origin, denoting the address of its initial instruction or byte. Failure to do so will result in the translator assuming a default address, commonly set at 0. The start addresses of a program, also known as the execution, start address, refers to the memory location of the first instruction that initiates its execution. The program's source may either coincide with its origin or diverge from it (Biswas & Mall, 1999).

The designations allocated by the translator are commonly referred to as *translated addresses*. The program P's instructions and data are bound to translated addresses by the translator. The object module specifies the translated source of the program, along with its translated starting address and dimensions (Redelinghuys et al., 2002).

Program P can invoke other programs, such as mathematical libraries' functions while executing it. This process is commonly referred to as *linking*. It is recommended that the program incorporates these functions and utilizes their respective start addresses in the function call instructions within P. Connecting or associating different elements or components is commonly referred to as linking (Magdalenić et al., 2013).

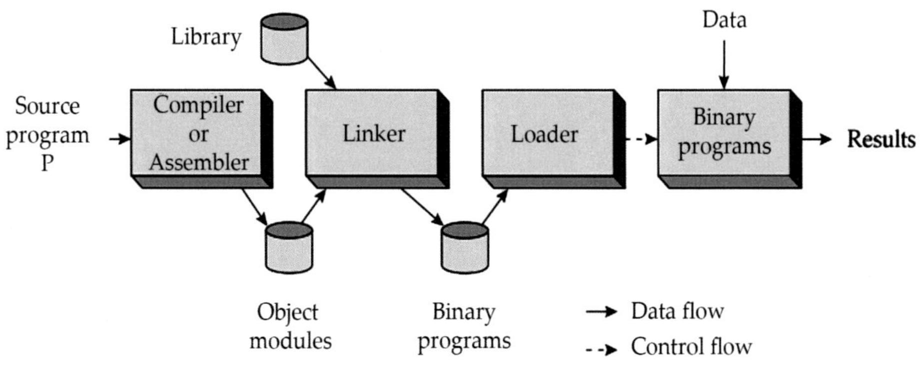

Figure 5.2. Schematic of the transformation followed by the execution of a program.

Source: Dhananjay, Creative Commons License.

The relocation process may result in conflicting translated time addresses between program P and certain object module(s) that have been merged with it. Resolving this conflict involves altering the memory binding of the object module(s), commonly called the relocation of object modules. The process entails modifying the addresses of operands utilized in their respective instructions

(Steinhöfel & Hähnle, 2019). The program is responsible for executing the relocation and linking functions and is commonly referred to as a linker. The designations allocated by the system are commonly referred to as linked addresses. Without a specified linked origin, the linker assumes that the linked origin corresponds to the translated origin (Larus, 1990). The linker performs the task of binding the instructions and data of a program to a specific set of linked addresses to avoid any potential address conflicts that may arise due to the program's origin and relocation requirements. Upon completion, the resultant program, which exists in a compiled binary format, is archived within a designated repository. The library directory contains information about its nomenclature, associated source, magnitude, and initial linkage address (Prywes & Pnueli, 1983).

Did you Know?

The term garbage collection was coined by John McCarthy in 1959.

For a binary program to be executed, it must first be loaded into memory. The loader is responsible for executing this operation. Suppose the load origin, referring to the starting address of the memory region designated for program loading, deviates from the program's linked origin. In that case, the loader must modify its memory binding again. A loader that exhibits the ability to relocate is referred to as a relocating loader, while a loader that lacks this ability is known as an absolute loader. It should be noted that translators, linkers, and loaders are not considered integral components of the OS (Ko et al., 1997).

This section delves into various program types and their characteristics regarding memory bindings, linker processing, and memory demands during runtime. The relocation and linking actions executed by the linker are demonstrated through programs composed in a basic hypothetical assembly language (Puschner & Koza, 1989).

An elementary form of PL known as Assembly Language. The format of an assembly language statement is as follows:

[Label] <Opcode> <operand spec>, <operand spec>

The initial parameter is consistently a general-purpose register (GPR), specifically AREG, BREG, CREG, or DREG. The second operand can be identified as a General-Purpose Register (GPR), or a symbolic name related to a memory byte. Arithmetic operations are designated through the utilization of self-explanatory opcodes such as ADD and MULT. The MOVER instruction facilitates the transfer of a value from a memory operand to a register operand, while the MOVEM instruction performs the reverse operation.

Arithmetic operations are executed within a register and result in the establishment of a condition code. The condition code's evaluation may be performed using a branch-on-condition, BC, instruction. The format of the assembly statement associated with it is as follows (King, 1976):

BC <condition code spec>, <instruction address>

The BC instruction facilitates the transfer of control to the instruction located at the address specified by <instruction address> if the present value of the condition code corresponds to <condition code spec>. For the sake of ease, it is assumed that all addresses and constants are expressed in decimal format and that each instruction takes up a total of 4 bytes. The signage does not constitute an element of an instructional directive (Boyer et al., 1975).

5.3.1. Relocation

The assembly program P and its corresponding generated code are depicted in Figure 5.3. The ENTRY and EXTRN statements hold importance in the context of linking. The DS statement functions to allocate a specified number of bytes as indicated by its operand.

```
        Assembly statement                  Generated code
                                          Address     Code

        START   500
        ENTRY   TOTAL
        EXTRN   MAX, ALPHA
        READ     A                         500)   + 09 0 540
LOOP                                       504)
          :
        MOVER   AREG, ALPHA                516)   + 04 1 000
        BC       ANY, MAX                  520)   + 06 6 000
          :
        BC       LT, LOOP                  532)   + 06 1 504
        STOP                               536)   + 00 0 000
A       DS       1                         540)
TOTAL   DS       3                         541)
        END
```

Figure 5.3. Representation of assembly program P and generated code.

Source: Denning, Creative Commons License.

The instruction "START 500" denotes that the relocated address of the program should be set to 500. Consequently, the address of LOOP after translation is 504. A's location is identified as 540.

Addresses 532 and 500 are utilized by the instructions to refer to LOOP and A correspondingly (Götz et al., 2009). The determination of these addresses is contingent upon the program's source in a self-evident manner. Instructions that utilize specific addresses are referred to as address-sensitive instructions in academic discourse. For a program with address-sensitive instructions to execute accurately, it must be loaded into the memory region that aligns with the program's origin. If execution is required in a different memory region, appropriate modifications must be made to addresses in instructions that are sensitive to address. Moving from one place to another is commonly referred to as relocation. Proficiency in translated and linked origins and familiarity with address-sensitive instructions are prerequisites. The following example demonstrates the relocation of P (Scott & Davidson, 2002).

5.3.1.1. Static and Dynamic Relocation of Programs

Upon execution of a program, the kernel assigns a memory region of sufficient size to accommodate it. It initiates the loader with the program's name and load origin as arguments. The loader is responsible for loading a program into its designated memory space, performing relocation if necessary due to a mismatch between the linked origin and load origin, and transferring control to initiate program execution (McGee, 1965). The relocation being discussed is classified as static relocation, given that it is executed before the commencement of program execution. At a certain point during program execution, the kernel may require modification of the allocated memory area to accommodate other programs in memory. The relocation process must be executed during program execution, thus qualifying as dynamic relocation.

The process of dynamic relocation involves temporarily halting a program's execution, implementing the previously outlined relocation procedure, and resuming its execution. The program's execution necessitates the availability of information about the translated origin and address-sensitive instructions. Additionally, it would result in the memory above and processing expenses. Certain computer architectures offer a relocation register to facilitate dynamic relocation (Ryder, 1974). The relocation register is a distinctive register located within the CPU utilized to augment the memory address of each instruction executed during program execution. The outcome corresponds to an additional memory location effectively employed for memory referencing. Therefore, the effective memory address = the memory address utilized in the current instruction + the contents of the relocation register (Hatfield et al., 1971).

5.3.2. Linking

Linking means associating an external reference with the relevant linked site. At first, the linker looks through all the object modules that will be linked and collect the names of every entry point and the linked addresses that correspond to them (Cowan et al., 1996). The data described above is kept in a tabular format for purposes unrelated to the public. After that, the computer program assesses each external reference by first locating the appropriate linked address of the external symbol in its table and then adding that address into the instruction containing the external reference. This step completes the evaluation of the external reference. Clearing up an issue with an external reference is usually known as "resolution" (Ramakrishnan & Lancaster, 1993).

5.3.2.1. Static and Dynamic Linking/Loading

In contemporary OSs, there has been a blurring of the differentiation between the concepts of linking and loading. The terminology is utilized subsequently: The linking process combines individual modules to create a cohesive and functional executable program. This is accomplished through the use of a linker. A loader is responsible for loading a program or a portion thereof into memory to facilitate its execution (Gao et al., 2009).

Static linking involves the linking of all program modules by the linker before program execution, resulting in the creation of a binary program that lacks any unresolved references (external). If multiple programs utilize a common module from a library, each program will receive an individualized instance of the module (Drossopoulou et al., 2006). This may result in multiple copies of the module in memory if the programs utilizing the module are executed concurrently.

The dynamic linking process is carried out at runtime of a compiled binary program. The linker is activated in the event of an unaddressed external reference during its runtime. Upon encountering an external reference, the linker proceeds to resolve it and subsequently allows for the program's execution to continue. The configuration above presents various advantages regarding utilizing, disseminating, and modifying library components (Rossberg et al., 2004). Modules that are not utilized during the execution of a program are not required to be linked to it. Suppose a program references a module linked to another program currently in execution. In that case, it is possible for the same instance of the module to be linked to the program, as mentioned earlier, resulting in a conservation of memory resources. Dynamic linking confers a notable advantage when a library of modules is updated. A program that calls upon a library module will automatically utilize the updated version. DLLs leverage certain features to their benefit (Siefers et al., 2010).

The initial step involves subjecting each program to static linking to enable dynamic linking. The process of linking external references in a program involves the static linker associating each reference with a module that serves the sole purpose of invoking the dynamic linker and transmitting the corresponding external symbol's name (Subramonian et al., 2007). Upon encountering an external reference during program execution, the dynamic linker is triggered. The system records the various entry points and their corresponding load addresses within a table. If the table contains the external symbol, the external reference's resolution is accomplished by utilizing the symbol's load address.

5.3.2.1.1. Program Forms Employed in OSs

Two program features have an impact on the way an OS provides service to it (Brega et al., 2000):

i. Is the program capable of being executed in any memory location, or is it restricted to a particular memory region?
ii. Is it possible for multiple users to concurrently access and utilize the program's code?

If the load origin of the concerned program does not align with the commencement address of the memory region, it is necessary to relocate the program before its execution (Yuanfang et al., 1999). This incurs a high cost. A program capable of executing in any memory location holds an advantageous position within this particular context. The significance of program shareability arises when multiple users may require simultaneous access to the program. In cases where a program lacks shareability, it necessitates that each user possesses an individual copy of the program, resulting in multiple instances of the program being stored in memory concurrently (He & Wang, 2009).

Table 5.2. Program Forms Employed in Operating Systems

Program Form	**Features**
Object module	This document comprises the guidelines and data necessary for the execution of a program, along with the pertinent details essential for its relocation and linking.
Binary program	The executable form of a program.
Dynamically linked program	Lazy linking occurs when a program references a symbol from an object module.
Self-relocating program	The program can dynamically transfer its code to operate within any given memory location.
Reentrant program	The software application can run multiple data sets simultaneously.

Source: Dhananjay, Creative Commons License.

Table 5.2 presents a summary of significant programs utilized in OSs. A linker can relocate the program form of an object module, whereas a linker cannot relocate a binary program. Utilizing a dynamically linked program form results in memory conservation as it solely links the object modules referred to during its execution (Na et al., 2003). The three program forms were previously discussed in earlier sections. A program capable of relocating itself can be executed in any memory location. The significance of the program form diminishes in the presence of a relocation register or virtual memory support provided by a computer system. Utilizing the reentrant program form obviates the necessity of maintaining multiple program instances in the memory. The subsequent sections will elaborate on the two forms of programs being referred to (Lin & Zhu, 2010).

5.3.2.2. Self-Relocating Programs

When you relocate a program, you must change the address-sensitive instructions within the program to run correctly from the new memory location. For a linker to successfully relocate a program, the program's object module form must be present, which in turn causes a significant amount of unnecessary overhead. The self-relocating program form was developed to overcome these constraints by relocating itself on its own will to fit into the memory space allotted to it (Sayapin, 2021).

A program that can relocate itself is aware of its own translated origin and the translated addresses of any address-sensitive connected instructions. The preceding entity also contains a relocating logic, indicating that the code can relocate. The logic that relocates data takes control of the starting address of the program's execution, which identifies the beginning of the data. As a result, the loading of the program in preparation for execution sets off the logic for relocation. The procedure begins by calling a placeholder function to get things started. When you call this function, it will generate an address, which will correspond to the position of the next instruction. By using this address, one can determine the region in memory where the program is loaded for execution, which is sometimes referred to as the program's load origin (Zhang & Xia, 2012).

5.3.2.3. Reentrant Programs

Software applications can be distributed through static as well as dynamic methods. Let us consider two programs, A and B, which depend on program C. A and B are designated as programs that share, while C is identified as the shared program (Bobrow, 1980). The process of performing static sharing of the PL C involves the utilization of static linking. Consequently, the code and data about C are incorporated in both A and B, resulting in the loss of

C's identity within the binary programs generated by the linker. In the event of concurrent execution of programs, A and B, it can be observed that two instances of C will be present in the memory, as depicted in Figure 5.4(a). The implementation of static program sharing is straightforward. However, it has the potential to result in memory wastage (Liu et al., 2018).

Dynamic sharing involves loading a singular instance of a shared program's code into memory, which is subsequently utilized by all executing sharing programs. The implementation of dynamic sharing is achieved through the utilization of dynamic linking. The kernel maintains records of shared programs residing in the memory (Pan et al., 2005). Upon the request of a program to utilize a shared program, the kernel proceeds to dynamically establish a link between the program and the corresponding copy of the shared program that is currently stored in memory. The dynamic sharing phenomenon is depicted in Figure 5.4(b). When program A requires shared access to program C, the kernel identifies that program C is not currently in memory (Samreen & Alalfi, 2020).

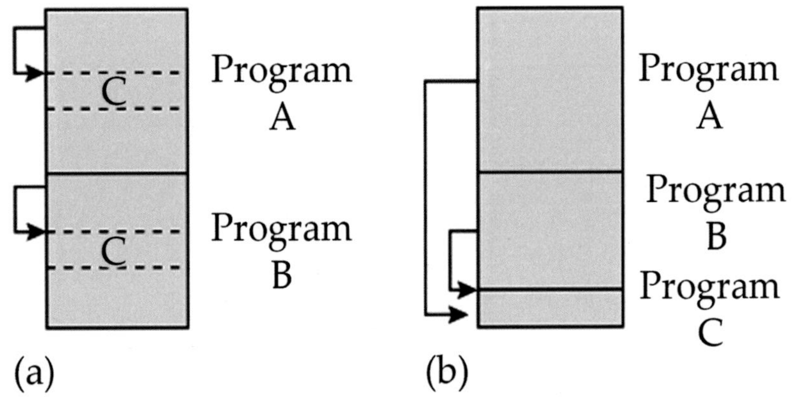

Figure 5.4. Sharing of the program "C" by A and B: (a) static and (b) dynamic sharing.

Source: Peterson, Creative Commons License.

Consequently, it allocates a duplicate of the PL C in the computer's memory and establishes a dynamic connection between it and program A. The linkage between A and C is illustrated in Figure 5.4(b) through an arrow pointing from A to C. In cases where program B necessitates the utilization of program C, the kernel identifies the presence of an extant instance of C in the memory. Subsequently, it establishes a linkage between B and the existing copy of C. The approach above obviates the necessity of maintaining numerous program duplicates in the memory. However, it is imperative to guarantee that simultaneous program executions do not impede each other (Szabo & Babuška, 1988).

The execution of program C, coded as a reentrant program, is depicted in Figure 5.5. The PL C is designed assuming that AREG is directed towards initiating its data region, as Figure 5.5(a) depicts. The retrieval of data elements within this domain involves the utilization of distinct offsets derived from the address stored in AREG. Upon invocation by program A, C reserves a designated data space for its use. Figure 5.5(b) portrays the representation as Data (CA) Suppose the execution of process A is interrupted. In that case, the data contained within AREG is saved within A's process control block (PCB) and restored to AREG upon A's next scheduled execution. Upon invocation of C by B, an allocation of a data area known as Data (CB) takes place, with AREG being configured to indicate the beginning of this region (*refer* Figure 5.5(c)). Consequently, the executions of programs A and B do not impede each other (Agre & Tripathi, 1982).

Remember

In the early days of computing, memory management was not considered a critical issue because memory was relatively cheap and abundant.

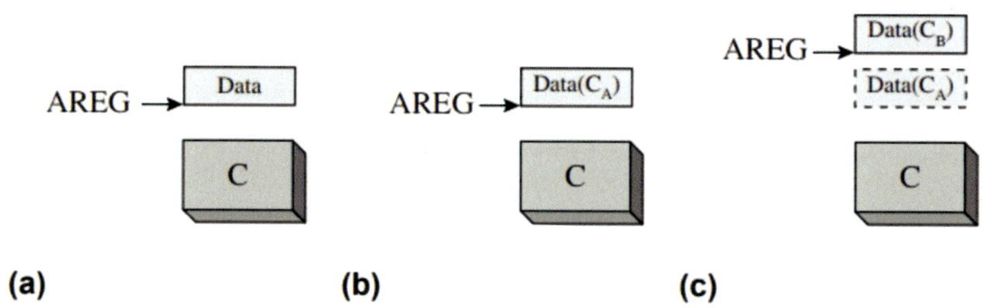

Figure 5.5. (a) The structure of a re-entrant program; (b) and (c) simultaneous invocations of the program.

Source: Russinovich, Creative Commons License.

5.4. MEMORY ALLOCATION TO A PROCESS

5.4.1. Stacks and Heaps

The PL's compiler produces program code and assigns static data allocation. The process generates an object module for the program. The linking process involves connecting a program with the necessary library functions and runtime support of the PL. This creates an executable form of the program, which is then saved in a file. A file's directory entry contains the recorded information regarding the program's size (Braden et al., 2003).

During program execution, the run-time support allocates two distinct types of data. The initial type of data pertains to variables that possess a scope linked to functions, procedures, or program blocks, as well as parameters of function or procedure invocations. The data above is assigned upon entering a function, procedure, or block and released upon exit. The data is allocated on the stack due to the last-in, first-out (LIFO) nature of the allocation and deallocation process. The second data type is generated dynamically by a program utilizing language features such as the new statement in Pascal, C++, or Java or the malloc and calloc statements in C. The term used to denote this information type is program-controlled dynamic data (PCD Data). The allocation of PCD data is accomplished by utilizing a data structure called a heap (Levy et al., 2017).

5.4.1.1. Stack

A stack is a data structure that follows the LIFO principle for allocating and deallocating elements. It is assumed that every item within the stack conforms to a uniform size, typically denoted as l bytes. At any given moment, solely the final element of the stack is retrievable. A contiguous block of memory is allocated to serve as the stack. The stack base (SB) is a pointer that indicates the initial entry of the stack, whereas the top of the stack (TOS) is a pointer that indicates the most recently allocated entry in the stack. The convention adopted in this context is that the stack exhibits a growth pattern towards the lower end of memory. This growth pattern is visually represented as upward growth in the figures (Yang et al., 2014).

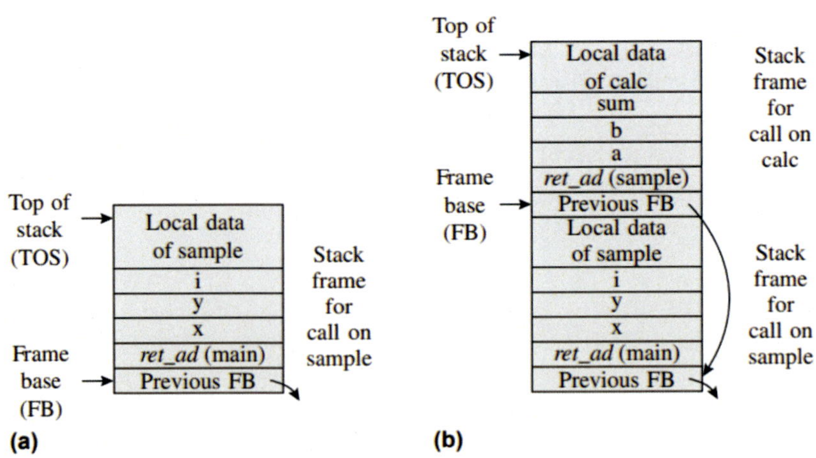

Figure 5.6. Illustration of the stack after (a) the main calls sample; and (b) the sample calls the calc.

Source: Vahalia, Creative Commons License.

During program execution, a stack is employed to facilitate function calls. In compiler terminology, a stack frame, an activation record, refers to the stack entries relevant to a particular function call. When a function is invoked, a stack frame is pushed onto the stack. The stack frame initially comprises the function's parameters' values or addresses and the return address, which denotes the instruction's address to which control must be transferred upon completion. During function execution, the PL's run-time support generates function-specific local data within the stack frame (Kc & Keromytis, 2005). This data is created by the language in which the program is written. Upon the conclusion of the function's execution, the complete stack frame is removed from the stack, and the return address enclosed within it is utilized to transfer control back to the invoking program (Figure 5.6).

5.4.1.2. Heap

A heap data structure enables the allocation and deallocation of memory in a non-sequential manner. Upon submitting an allocation request, a process is provided with a pointer to the allocated memory area in a heap. Subsequently, the process interacts exclusively with the allocated memory area through the pointer above. To deallocate memory, it is necessary for the deallocation request to include a pointer to the specific memory area that is to be deallocated. The following example demonstrates the utilization of a heap to manage the PCD (process control data) of a given process. As depicted in the illustration, gaps emerge in the memory allocation during the creation and deallocation of data structures. The heap allocator must effectively recycle available memory regions to satisfy forthcoming memory requirements (Fadel et al., 1999).

5.4.2. The Memory Allocation Model

Upon receiving a command to execute a program, the kernel initiates creating a new process. Currently, there is a need to determine the appropriate amount of memory allocation for the subsequent components (Figure 5.7):

- The program's code and static data;
- Stack;
- Program-controlled dynamic data (PCD Data).

The program's dimensions can be acquired by examining its directory entry. The dynamic nature of program execution results in varying stack sizes and PCD data, challenging the kernel to determine the appropriate memory allocation for these components. The program can predict the upper bounds of the stack and heap growth and assign appropriate memory allocation. Nonetheless, this constitutes a static allocation characterized by an adaptability deficiency (Hudak, 1983).

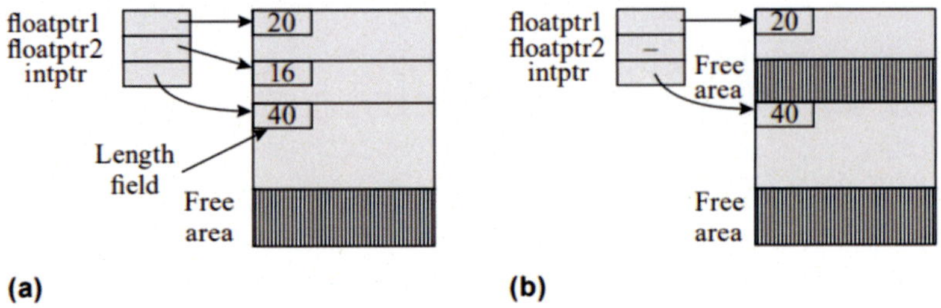

Figure 5.7. Illustration of (a) the heap; and (b) a hole occurring in the allocation on the deallocated memory.

Source: Randell, Creative Commons License.

To mitigate the challenges associated with managing the components above separately, OSs employ the memory allocation framework depicted in Figure 5.8. The program's code and static data components are allocated memory areas that precisely correspond to their respective sizes. The PCD information and the stack exhibit a mutually exclusive relationship in memory allocation. They share a singular, expansive memory space yet expand in opposing directions upon allocating new data. The allocation of PCD data commences from the lower end of the specified region, whereas the stack allocation is initiated from the upper end of the same region. The memory allocated between these two components is unoccupied. The creation of novel data is feasible in either of the components. The present model does not impose specific size limitations on the stack and PCD data constituents (Soto et al., 2012).

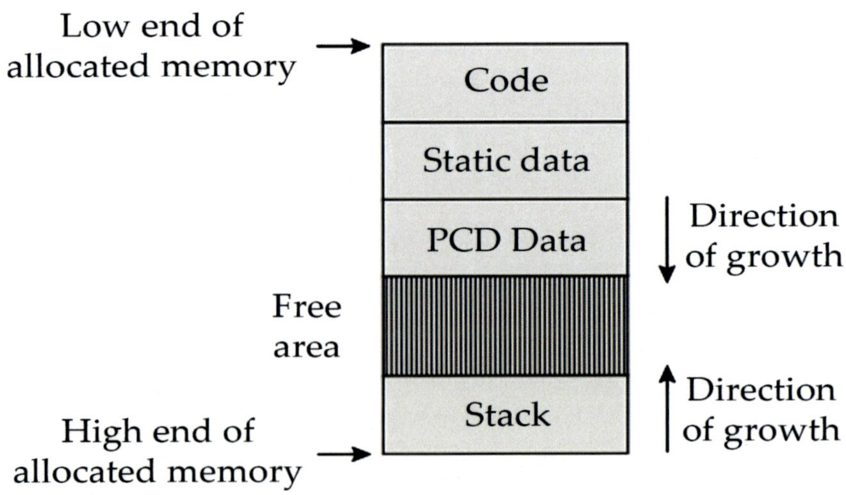

Figure 5.8. Depiction of memory allocation model for a process.

Source: McDougall, Creative Commons License.

5.4.3. Memory Protection

Memory protection is implemented using a duo of control registers, namely the base register and the size register, housed within the CPU. The registers, as mentioned earlier, hold the initial memory location assigned to a given process and its corresponding memory capacity. In the context of computer systems, it is common for memory protection hardware to trigger an interrupt related to memory protection violation. This occurs when the memory address utilized in the current process instruction falls beyond the range of addresses specified by the base and size registers. Upon processing the interrupt, the kernel terminates the faulty process. The program status word (PSW) contains the memory protection information (MPI) field, which comprises the base and size registers. During the process scheduling, the kernel loads suitable values into the registers (Witchel et al., 2005).

ACTIVITY 5.1:

Design and implement a simple memory management system, including memory allocation, de-allocation, and garbage collection.

A process initiated by a user, and executed in the user mode of the CPU, cannot modify the contents of the registers in question. This is because the instructions for loading and saving these registers are considered privileged and, therefore, inaccessible to user-level processes. Utilizing a relocation register results in streamlined memory protection verifications, provided each program possesses a linked origin of 0. The hardware responsible for memory protection compares the address and the size register's contents to determine if the former is smaller. The relocation and size register combination now comprise the Machine Status Word's Memory Protection Key Identifier fields (Feng et al., 2021).

5.5. SUMMARY

The chapter dug into the methods for effectively managing memory, which included the prompt allocation and deallocation of memory to processes and optimizing memory utilization to enable the simultaneous accommodation of many processes. During the coding and compilation processes, the memory allocation used for program execution is not preset. Nevertheless, the employment of memory locations is required for its operands due to the directives that it contains. The problem described earlier can now be solved as follows: The generation of an object module is the end product of the compilation process, which begins with the premise that a program will use a specific amount of memory space. A linker is a system software that modifies the operand addresses included in a program's instructions using the relocation mechanism (Doudalis et al., 2010). Due to this adjustment, the software can carry out its instructions correctly inside the allotted memory space. The linker enables the production of an executable program by facilitating the connection between a program and the necessary library functions and making this connection easier. Programs that can relocate themselves can carry out their relocation process. The relocation register in the CPU is a specialized register that dynamically makes it easier to relocate programs to different hardware. This feature allows the kernel to change the memory region currently being used by a running program.

Memory allocation can be carried through using either of two distinct approaches. Pre-execution When using static memory allocation, it is necessary to understand the required quantity accurately, as memory might be wasted if allocated in excess. During the course of the execution of the program, the procedure of dynamic memory allocation takes place, which increases the amount of memory management overhead. Conversely, this method makes the most efficient use of memory by assigning only the required quantity. The kernel uses a model of memory allocation for a process that contains a statically allocated component for the code and data of the program, and dynamically allocated components for the stack, and for the heap in which a program can dynamically allocate memory through statements such as new or alloc (Huffmire et al., 2006).

REVIEW QUESTIONS

1. What is memory management and why is it important in operating systems?
2. How is memory divided in an operating system?
3. What are the main techniques used by operating system to manage memory and how do they work?
4. What are some common issues and challenges associated with memory management in modern operating systems?
5. How do operating systems optimize memory usage to improve system performance and stability?

MULTIPLE CHOICE QUESTIONS

1. What is the primary goal of memory management in operating systems?

a. To allocate the maximum amount of memory to each process

b. To prevent memory-related errors and ensure each process has the required amount of memory

c. To provide equal memory access to all processes

d. None of the above

2. Which of the following is not a memory area in operating systems?

a. Kernel

b. User space

c. Stack

d. Shared memory

3. What is the primary purpose of paging in memory management?

a. To divide memory into fixed-size blocks

b. To allow operating system to use more memory than physically available

c. To transfer less used data from RAM to the hard disk

d. To swap memory between the hard disk and RAM

4. Which of the following is not a common memory allocation algorithm used in operating systems?

a. First-fit

b. Best-fit

c. Worst-fit

d. Round-robin

5. What is the purpose of virtual memory?

a. To reduce overall memory consumption in the system

b. To divide memory into fixed-size blocks

c. To prevent memory-related errors in the systems

d. To allow the operating system to use more memory than physically available

Answers to Multiple Choice Questions

1. (b); 2. (c); 3. (d); 4. (d); 5. (d)

REFERENCES

1. Agre, J. R., & Tripathi, S. K., (1982). Modeling reentrant and nonreentrant software. *ACM SIGMETRICS Performance Evaluation Review, 11*(4), 163–178.
2. Bamaqa, A., Sedky, M., & Bastaki, B., (2022). Reactive and proactive anomaly detection in crowd management using hierarchical temporal memory. *International Journal of Machine Learning and Computing (IJMLC), 12*(1), 7–16.
3. Biswas, B., & Mall, R., (1999). Reverse execution of programs. *ACM SIGPLAN Notices, 34*(4), 61–69.
4. Bobrow, D. G., (1980). Managing reentrant structures using reference counts. *ACM Transactions on Programming Languages and Systems (TOPLAS), 2*(3), 269–273.
5. Bovet, D. P., & Estrin, G., (1970). A dynamic memory allocation algorithm. *IEEE Transactions on Computers, 100*(5), 403–411.
6. Bovet, D. P., & Estrin, G., (1970). On static memory allocation in computer systems. *IEEE Transactions on Computers, 100*(6), 492–503.
7. Boyer, R. S., Elspas, B., & Levitt, K. N., (1975). SELECT—A formal system for testing and debugging programs by symbolic execution. *ACM SigPlan Notices, 10*(6), 234–245.
8. Braden, R., Faber, T., & Handley, M., (2003). From protocol stack to protocol heap: Role-based architecture. *ACM SIGCOMM Computer Communication Review, 33*(1), 17–22.
9. Brega, R., Tomatis, N., & Arras, K. O., (2000). The need for autonomy and real-time in mobile robotics: A case study of XO/2 and pygmalion. In: *Proceedings. 2000 IEEE/RSJ International Conference on Intelligent Robots and Systems,* (Vol. 2, pp. 1422–1427).
10. Budzinski, R. L., & Davidson, E. S., (1981). A comparison of dynamic and static virtual memory allocation algorithms. *IEEE Transactions on Software Engineering,* (1), 122–131.
11. Cowan, C., Autrey, T., Krasic, C., Pu, C., & Walpole, J., (1996). Fast concurrent dynamic linking for an adaptive operating system. In: *Proceedings of International Conference on Configurable Distributed Systems* 1, pp. 108–115.
12. Deverge, J. F., & Puaut, I., (2007). WCET-directed dynamic scratchpad memory allocation of data. In: *19th Euromicro Conference on Real-Time Systems* (Vol. 7, pp. 179–190).
13. Doudalis, I., Clause, J., Venkataramani, G., Prvulovic, M., & Orso, A., (2010). Effective and efficient memory protection using dynamic tainting. *IEEE Transactions on Computers, 61*(1), 87–100.
14. Drossopoulou, S., Lagorio, G., & Eisenbach, S., (2006). A flexible model for dynamic linking in java and C. *Theoretical Computer Science*, *368*(1, 2), 1–29.

15. Evans, D., (1996). Static detection of dynamic memory errors. *ACM SIGPLAN Notices, 31*(5), 44–53.
16. Fadel, R., Jakobsen, K. V., Katajainen, J., & Teuhola, J., (1999). Heaps and heapsort on secondary storage. *Theoretical Computer Science, 220*(2), 345–362.
17. Fatahalian, K., Horn, D. R., Knight, T. J., Leem, L., Houston, M., Park, J. Y., & Hanrahan, P., (2006). Sequoia: Programming the memory hierarchy. In: *Proceedings of the 2006 ACM/IEEE Conference on Supercomputing,* (p. 83-es).
18. Feng, E., Lu, X., Du, D., Yang, B., Jiang, X., Xia, Y., & Chen, H., (2021). Scalable memory protection in the PENGLAI enclave. In: *OSDI* (Vol. 1, pp. 275–294).
19. Gao, X., Ma, Z. T., & Liu, Y., (2009). Research of DSO application in PKI system. In: *2009 Asia-Pacific Conference on Computational Intelligence and Industrial Applications* (Vol. 1, pp. 116–118).
20. Gay, D., & Aiken, A., (1998). Memory management with explicit regions. In: *Proceedings of the ACM SIGPLAN 1998 Conference on Programming Language Design and Implementation* (pp. 313–323).
21. Götz, M., Dittmann, F., & Xie, T., (2009). Dynamic relocation of hybrid tasks: Strategies and methodologies. *Microprocessors and Microsystems, 33*(1), 81–90.
22. Grossman, D., Morrisett, G., Jim, T., Hicks, M., Wang, Y., & Cheney, J., (2002). Region-based memory management in cyclone. In: *Proceedings of the ACM SIGPLAN 2002 Conference on Programming Language Design and Implementation* 47(2), pp. 282–293.
23. Hatfield, D. J., & Gerald, J., (1971). Program restructuring for virtual memory. *IBM Systems Journal, 10*(3), 168–192.
24. He, H., & Wang, J., (2009). The software design of embedded control system based on DSP. In: *2009 International Conference on Future Computer and Communication* pp. 603–606.
25. Hudak, P., (1983). Distributed task and memory management. In: *Proceedings of the Second Annual ACM Symposium on Principles of Distributed Computing* 92, pp. 277–289.
26. Huffmire, T., Prasad, S., Sherwood, T., & Kastner, R., (2006). Policy-driven memory protection for reconfigurable hardware. In: *Computer Security–ESORICS 2006: 11th European Symposium on Research in Computer Security, Hamburg, Germany, September 18–20, 2006. Proceedings 11* (pp. 461–478).
27. Jomier, G., (1981). A mathematical model for the comparison of static and dynamic memory allocation in a paged system. *IEEE Transactions on Software Engineering,* (4)375–385.
28. Kc, G. S., & Keromytis, A. D., (2005). e-NeXSH: Achieving an effectively non-executable stack and heap via system-call policing. In: *21st Annual Computer Security Applications Conference,* 5(2), p. 15.

29. King, J. C., (1976). Symbolic execution and program testing. *Communications of the ACM, 19*(7), 385–394.
30. Kiriansky, V., Bruening, D., & Amarasinghe, S. P., (2002). Secure execution via program shepherding. In: *USENIX Security Symposium* (Vol. 92, p. 84).
31. Ko, C., Ruschitzka, M., & Levitt, K., (1997). Execution monitoring of security-critical programs in distributed systems: A specification-based approach. In: *Proceedings. 1997 IEEE Symposium on Security and Privacy* (Vol. 1, pp. 175–187).
32. Larus, J. R., (1990). Abstract execution: A technique for efficiently tracing programs. *Software: Practice and Experience, 20*(12), 1241–1258.
33. Lee, H. G., & Chang, N., (2003). Energy-aware memory allocation in heterogeneous non-volatile memory systems. In: *Proceedings of the 2003 International Symposium on Low Power Electronics and Design* (Vol. 1, pp. 420–423).
34. Levy, A., Campbell, B., Ghena, B., Giffin, D. B., Pannuto, P., Dutta, P., & Levis, P., (2017). Multiprogramming a 64kb computer safely and efficiently. In: *Proceedings of the 26th Symposium on Operating Systems Principles* (Vol. 1, pp. 234–251).
35. Li, Y., Ghose, S., Choi, J., Sun, J., Wang, H., & Mutlu, O., (2017). Utility-based hybrid memory management. In: *2017 IEEE International Conference on Cluster Computing,* (pp. 152–165).
36. Lin, Y., & Zhu, X., (2010). Design and research of the intelligent front-end based on the DCS configuration software. In: *2010 International Conference on Web Information Systems and Mining* (Vol. 1, pp. 425–428).
37. Liu, C., Liu, H., Cao, Z., Chen, Z., Chen, B., & Roscoe, B., (2018). Reguard: Finding reentrancy bugs in smart contracts. In: *Proceedings of the 40th International Conference on Software Engineering: Companion Proceedings* (pp. 65–68).
38. Liu, L., Yang, H., Li, Y., Xie, M., Li, L., & Wu, C., (2016). Memos: A full hierarchy hybrid memory management framework. In: *2016 IEEE 34th International Conference on Computer Design (ICCD),* (pp. 368–371).
39. Liu, L., Yang, S., Peng, L., & Li, X., (2019). Hierarchical hybrid memory management in OS for tiered memory systems. *IEEE Transactions on Parallel and Distributed Systems, 30*(10), 2223–2236.
40. Magdalenić, I., Radošević, D., & Orehovački, T., (2013). Autogenerator: Generation and execution of programming code on demand. *Expert Systems with Applications, 40*(8), 2845–2857.
41. McGee, W. C., (1965). On dynamic program relocation. *IBM Systems Journal, 4*(3), 184–199.
42. Morrisett, G., Felleisen, M., & Harper, R., (1995). Abstract models of memory management. In: *Proceedings of the Seventh International Conference on Functional Programming Languages and Computer Architecture* 95, pp. 66–77.
43. Na, S., & Oh, S., (2003). Design and implementation of sync engine for automatic installation system of PDA application programs. In: *Proceedings 2003 IEEE*

International Symposium on Computational Intelligence in Robotics and Automation; Computational Intelligence in Robotics and Automation for the New Millennium (Vol. 1, pp. 372–377).

44. Nilakanta, S., Miller, L. L., & Zhu, D., (2006). Organizational memory management: Technological and research issues. *Journal of Database Management (JDM), 17*(1), 85–94.
45. Pan, J. C. H., & Chen, J. S., (2005). Mixed binary integer programming formulations for the reentrant job shop scheduling problem. *Computers & Operations Research, 32*(5), 1197–1212.
46. Prywes, N. S., & Pnueli, A., (1983). Compilation of nonprocedural specifications into computer programs. *IEEE Transactions on Software Engineering*, (3), 267–279.
47. Puschner, P., & Koza, C., (1989). Calculating the maximum execution time of real-time programs. *Real-Time Systems, 1*(2), 159–176.
48. Ramakrishnan, S., & Lancaster, A. M., (1993). Operating systems projects: Linking theory, practice and use. In: *Proceedings of the Twenty-Fourth SIGCSE Technical Symposium on Computer Science Education* 4(3), pp. 256–260.
49. Redelinghuys, G., Visser, W., & Geldenhuys, J., (2012). Symbolic execution of programs with strings. In: *Proceedings of the South African Institute for Computer Scientists and Information Technologists Conference* (pp. 139–148).
50. Ribeiro, C. P., Méhaut, J. F., Carissimi, A., Castro, M., & Fernandes, L. G., (2009). Memory affinity for hierarchical shared memory multiprocessors. In: *2009 21st International Symposium on Computer Architecture and High-Performance Computing* (pp. 59–66).
51. Rossberg, A., Le Botlan, D., Tack, G., Brunklaus, T., & Smolka, G., (2004). Alice through the looking glass. *Trends in Functional Programming, 5*, 79–96.
52. Ryder, K. D., (1974). Optimizing program placement in virtual systems. *IBM Systems Journal, 13*(4), 292–306.
53. Samreen, N. F., & Alalfi, M. H., (2020). Reentrancy vulnerability identification in Ethereum smart contracts. In: *2020 IEEE International Workshop on Blockchain Oriented Software Engineering (IWBOSE)* 1, pp. 22–29.
54. Sayapin, S. N., (2021). Decision-making by the autonomous symbiotic self-relocating massage robot "triangel" based on SEMS after the fall of patient on surface. *Smart Electromechanical Systems: Behavioral Decision Making* (Vol. 1, pp. 37–52).
55. Scott, K., & Davidson, J., (2002). Safe virtual execution using software dynamic translation. In: *18th Annual Computer Security Applications Conference* 1, pp. 209–218.
56. Siefers, J., Tan, G., & Morrisett, G., (2010). Robusta: Taming the native beast of the JVM. In: *Proceedings of the 17th ACM Conference on Computer and Communications Security* 1, pp. 201–211.
57. Soto, M., Rossi, A., Sevaux, M., Laurent, J., & Jussien, N., (2012). Dynamic memory allocation problem. *Memory Allocation Problems in Embedded Systems*, 109–130.

58. Steinhöfel, D., & Hähnle, R., (2019). Abstract execution. In: *Formal Methods–The Next 30 Years: Third World Congress, FM 2019, Porto, Portugal, October 7–11, 2019, Proceedings 3* (pp. 319–336).
59. Subramonian, V., Deng, G., Gill, C., Balasubramanian, J., Shen, L. J., Otte, W., & Wang, N., (2007). The design and performance of component middleware for QoS-enabled deployment and configuration of DRE systems. *Journal of Systems and Software, 80*(5), 668–677.
60. Szabo, B. A., & Babuška, I., (1988). Computation of the amplitude of stress singular terms for cracks and reentrant corners. In: *Fracture Mechanics: Nineteenth Symposium, ASTM STP* (Vol. 969, pp. 101–124).
61. Tofte, M., & Talpin, J. P., (1997). Region-based memory management. *Information and Computation*, *132*(2), 109–176.
62. Truong, D. N., Bodin, F., & Seznec, A., (1998). Improving cache behavior of dynamically allocated data structures. In: *Proceedings. 1998 International Conference on Parallel Architectures and Compilation Techniques* 1, pp. 322–329.
63. Udayakumaran, S., Dominguez, A., & Barua, R., (2006). Dynamic allocation for scratch-pad memory using compile-time decisions. *ACM Transactions on Embedded Computing Systems (TECS), 5*(2), 472–511.
64. Witchel, E., Rhee, J., & Asanović, K., (2005). Mondrix: Memory isolation for Linux using mondriaan memory protection. In: *Proceedings of the Twentieth ACM Symposium on Operating Systems Principles* 1, pp. 31–44.
65. Yang, S., Kwon, D., Yi, H., Cho, Y., Kwon, Y., & Paek, Y., (2014). Techniques to minimize state transfer costs for dynamic execution offloading in mobile cloud computing. *IEEE Transactions on Mobile Computing, 13*(11), 2648–2660.
66. Yuanfang, H., Suqin, Z., & Weidu, J., (1999). Applying object-oriented method to CSIE system. In: *Proceedings Technology of Object-Oriented Languages and Systems* 3(2), pp. 484–491.
67. Zhang, Y., & Xia, F., (2012). A self-relocation-based method for malware detection. In: *Applied Mechanics and Materials* (Vol. 220, pp. 2688–2693).

CHAPTER 6

FILE SYSTEMS

UNIT INTRODUCTION

One of the fundamental roles of an operating system (OS) is to facilitate the storage and retrieval of data on a computer or any other electronic device. The data in question may encompass various forms, such as textual correspondence, analytical documents, electronic spreadsheets, preferred musical compositions, or photographic representations of one's kin. A file system facilitates managing, storing, and retrieving crucial data (Levy & Silberschatz, 1990). From a certain perspective, a file system can be likened to a personal aide, effectively storing and monitoring the whereabouts of significant information. The file system's primary functions are allocating storage locations on a disk and maintaining a record of the corresponding information's location. Upon needing information, the file system references its records to ascertain the location and retrieves the requisite data. Certain file systems incorporate recovery mechanisms in the event of disk area corruption or unforeseen OS shutdowns, such as those that may occur during power outages (Satyanarayanan, 1990).

To carry out various functions, the file systems utilized by computer operating systems execute the subsequent overarching tasks:

- A user-friendly interface that facilitates the opening and saving of files for users and applications is essential (Thanh et al., 2008).

- A hierarchical structure can be utilized to arrange files.
- The storage system retains file metadata to furnish comprehensive details regarding the files.
- The process of arranging and managing the storage space allocation on a given storage device (Gifford et al., 1991).

Learning Objectives

After the chapter, students will be able to understand the following:

- Basic concept of file system in an operating system;
- Understanding the functions of file systems in operating systems;
- Learn about the concept of file metadata;
- Fundamental idea of Window file systems.

Key Terms

- Directory
- Ext4
- FAT32
- File system
- Formatting
- Fragmentation
- Metadata
- NTFS
- Partitioning
- Storage device
- ZFS

6.1. UNDERSTANDING FILE SYSTEM FUNCTIONS

6.1.1. User Interface (UI)

Upon a user's double-click on a file, the user interface (UI) initiates a request to the file system to open the file. The determination of the file opening process is contingent upon the file type (Wang et al., 2009). If the file is classified as an application, it is subsequently loaded into the computer's memory and executed by the central processing unit (CPU). If the file in question is a document, the program that corresponds with the type of document is launched into memory and subsequently initiates the opening of the file. In the case of Windows operating systems (OSs), double-clicking on the Budget.xls file results in loading the Excel application into the computer's memory, which subsequently proceeds to open the file above. When a user generates or modifies a file and intends to preserve it, the application invokes the file system to retain the updated or novel file on the disk. Most OS users engage with the file system by utilizing a file managers application, such as File Explorer on Windows or Files on the GNOME desktop in Linux (Korn & Krell, 1990). To excel as a network or computer professional, it is imperative to possess a comprehensive comprehension of the inner workings of a file system. This knowledge will enable to make well-informed decisions when installing or resolving file system-related issues.

Did you Know?

The FAT (file allocation table) file system was first introduced in 1977 and is still used in many embedded systems.

6.1.2. Hierarchical Structure

The primary objective of a file system is to establish a framework for organizing and storing data. A hierarchical arrangement of file cabinets, folders, and drawers is the commonly employed analogy to depict a file system. The computer may be conceptualized as a storage unit, with the disk drives serving as compartments. The storage system comprises manila folders, hanging folders, and individual documents (files) that are systematically arranged within each drawer (drive), as depicted in Figure 6.1 (Mothukuri et al., 2021). A file is a collection of information organized coherently, designated with a specific identifier, and saved onto a storage device. Upon storage, the file system documents the file's location on the disk to facilitate subsequent retrieval (Hanson & Serebnick, 1986). Upon request of the filename, the OS proceeds to retrieve the data contained within the file on the disk.

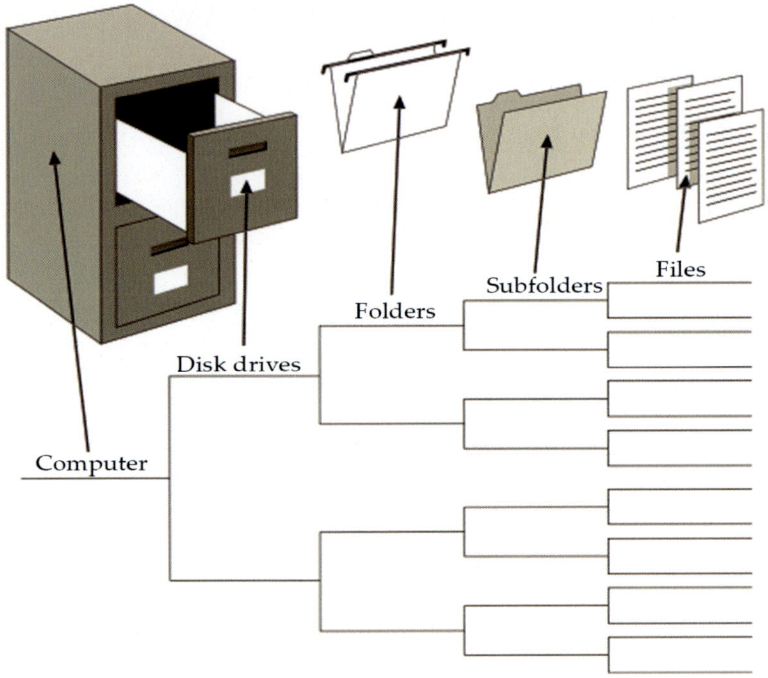

Figure 6.1. Illustration of a file system.

Source: Greg Tomsho, Creative Commons License.

Files may contain various data types, such as text, images, video, music, sounds, or Web pages. Regardless of the nature of the data stored within the file system, it is imperative to convert it into a digital format comprising a sequence of binary digits, namely 1s and 0s, which are understandable to the computer. The OS performs the function of transforming data into digital form for the computer and subsequently into the end-user format, such as text or pictures, and the applications utilized for typing graphics and other purposes (Bouqata et al., 2003).

In addition, it is imperative to establish a mechanism for recording digital data onto a storage medium, monitoring its location, revising it as needed, and retrieving it upon request by the user or a program under user control. To accomplish this task, the OS commonly coherently organizes file data, generates documentation of this arrangement, and constructs a directory or folder to monitor the classification of data contained within each file. A directory of folders is a hierarchical arrangement encompassing files and potentially subfolders within its structure (Fu et al., 2002). The directory facilitates the association between names and files on the disk, simplifying accessing the appropriate data for users and programs. The terminology employed by Windows OSs is characterized by the use of the terms "folder" and "subfolder," whereas Linux/UNIX systems have traditionally utilized the terms "directory" and "subdirectory."

6.1.2.1. Designing a Folder Structure

The capacity to store data in a structured manner facilitated by utilizing directories is a crucial aspect of a file system for end-users (Olivier et al., 2014). As an illustration, within Windows OSs, the arrangement of system files takes place in the designated \Windows directory. The /etc. The directory in UNIX and the System directory in Mac OS X are where numerous system files are stored, including critical system files in Mac OS X.

> **Remember**
>
> In operating systems such as Linux, it is possible to switch between different file systems without having to reformat the storage device.

It is possible to arrange folders hierarchically that resemble a tree-like structure. The Windows 10 OS comprises a directory named \Windows, which encompasses several subfolders, including \Windows\AppPatch, \Windows\Help, \Windows\Boot, \Windows\Media, \Windows\System32, and \Windows\System. The folder system exhibits a hierarchical structure resembling a tree, with numerous subfolders containing further subfolders, including the restore and spool subfolders located within the System32 subfolder (Hedges et al., 2005). The /etc. Directory in various Linux versions, such as Red Hat Enterprise Linux and Fedora, contains numerous subdirectories, including but not limited to /etc/cron.d, /etc/fonts, /etc/java, /etc/security, and /etc/sysconfig. Creating a hierarchical structure of directories and subdirectories allows for a systematic approach to organizing files and folders, resulting in enhanced accessibility and usability of the information.

In the absence of a meticulously planned hierarchy of folders, it is a prevalent occurrence for a hard drive to become inundated with an abundance of files and software applications, leading to disorder and disarray. Certain computer users tend to store most of their files in their computer's primary or root folder (Asaad et al., 2020). In contrast, others install every application program into a solitary folder. Certain application software programs employ an automated configuration as a partial remedy. They propose directories for novel programs, such as establishing fresh subdirectories beneath the Program Files directory in numerous Windows systems.

Nevertheless, certain users encounter challenges in effectively arranging their files. An unorganized file system can pose challenges in executing or uninstalling software applications and identifying the most up-to-date iterations (Cai et al., 2019). Moreover, it results in users investing unproductive time searching for particular files.

To prevent potential disorientation, it is advisable to meticulously plan and construct the arrangement of files and folders from the outset, especially on servers that multiple users frequently access. The proposed plan involves devising a folder hierarchy that is in harmony with the pre-existing structure of the OS (Kim et al., 2019). Additionally, the implementation of access controls is recommended to restrict unauthorized users from circumventing the established hierarchy. The default configuration of the OS framework, in conjunction with any additional modifications made by the user, may comprise directories designated for the subsequent purposes:

- The operating system commonly establishes operating system files.
- Software applications are commonly established by both the operating system and the installed software applications. The decisions made regarding installing these applications can also impact their setup (Wang et al., 2004).
- The user and applications such as Microsoft Word establish work files, including graphics, word-processing, spreadsheet, and database files.
- Public files that are shared over a network, which the user has established.
- The operating system, utilities applications, and user-selected installation preferences establish the utility files.
- The OS establishes temporary files, applications that utilize such files, and user determinations regarding the location of temporary files (Kazar et al., 1990).

It is advisable to adhere to established conventions when determining the allocation of folders for particular kinds of files. For example, it is advisable to avoid overcrowding the root directory with excessive directories or files. It is recommended that each software application be assigned a separate folder or subfolder to facilitate efficient administration of updates and software removal (Padioleau & Ridoux, 2005). It is advisable to group analogous information, such as accounting programs or workplace efficiency software, to facilitate access control. Maintaining distinct and secure storage for OS files is recommended to prevent users' accidental deletion of critical files. Certain essential files on Windows OSs are concealed from ordinary users and designated as system files to prevent accidental removal.

Furthermore, the majority of OS files are safeguarded by access control mechanisms. It is recommended that directories and folders be named in a manner that accurately and unambiguously reflects their intended functions. An illustration of this scenario involves a law office administrator who utilizes legal time-accounting software, Microsoft Office, legal forms software, confidential and shared worksheets, and Word files on a computer operating on the Windows 10 platform. The office administrator is responsible for maintaining specialized web pages on the law firm's website (Devarakonda et al., 1995). The hierarchical arrangement of folders starting from the root directory could potentially be structured in the following manner:

- The default directory structure established by the operating system is called Windows for the system files.
- The default folder established by the OS is designated for general programs and utilities and is commonly referred to as program files (Zadok & Badulescu, 1999).
- The default folder set up by the computer's OS, known as "Documents and Settings," is utilized for work files, including documents written in Word and confidential spreadsheets.
- The folder suggested for sharing spreadsheets over a network is a sample folder the user can establish (Schleier-Smith et al., 2020). Alternatively, the standard Public Documents folder the operating system provides can also be utilized for this purpose, as mentioned below.
- The folder designated as a sample folder by the user may contain forms tailored for specific purposes and utilized by the legal documentation software.
- Inetpub is a folder that can be created with the set-up of web design software, specifically for hosting web pages. The files or software applications are categorized through subfolders within each major folder (Zhao et al., 2010).

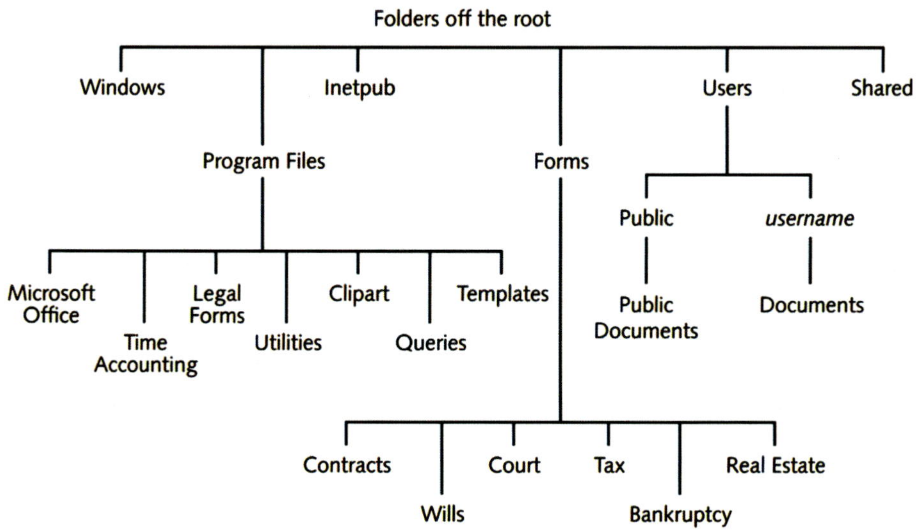

Figure 6.2. Representation of sample folder structure for the Windows-based system.

Source: Kristin McNary, Creative Commons License.

The program files directory comprises subdirectories for distinct software packages, such as \Program Files\Microsoft Office for the

Microsoft Office software and \Program Files\ for others. This document pertains to the legal time-accounting software folder and its time-accounting features. The Users directory would include a subdirectory named Documents, which would serve as a repository for sensitive spreadsheets and Word documents. In contrast, communal spreadsheets would be stored in the Public Documents directory. The folder structure is depicted in Figure 6.2 (Hertel, 2004).

In the context of Linux systems, such as Red Hat Enterprise Linux or Fedora, a customary directory arrangement that is pre-existing within the OS is outlined as follows:

- The bin directory serves as a location for storing binary files, including user programs and utilities.
- The directory "sbin" contains system administration utilities and binary files for managing the system (Le et al., 2012).
- The "lib" refers to the runtime library files that are required by programs stored in the "/bin" and "/sbin" directories.
- The "usr" directory is designated for storing user files and programs.
- The term "v." is commonly used to refer to files that exhibit variable content or are utilized for temporary purposes.
- The abbreviation "tmp" refers to files utilized exclusively for temporary purposes.
- The development of software for electronic devices (Griffioen & Appleton, 1994).
- int for DVD/CD-ROM drives, flash drives, and other removable media
- The topic of discussion pertains to the treatment of system and configuration files.
- The "oot" refers to files utilized by the root account.
- The directory labeled "home" is designated for the storage of individual user directories, which are usually organized as subfolders named after each respective user.
- The procedure for tracking system resources (Prabhakaran et al., 2005).
- The default folder structure generated by the Mac OS X operating system at the root level comprises:
- Applications for software designed for the Mac OS X operating system;
- The system files for Mac OS X are organized in a specific manner;
- The library designated for storing library files, including fonts, is paramount;
- Creating user accounts is recommended, along with allocating subfolders for each user account to facilitate the storage of files;

- The documentation required for the submission (Ridge et al., 2015).

6.1.3. File Metadata

Folders and files can contain metadata pertaining to their respective contents or attributes and their names and storage locations on the disk. The term used to describe this data is metadata. Metadata refers to descriptive information that characterizes data but does not constitute it. The vocabulary of a document is classified as metadata, along with the details enumerated in the subsequent inventory:

- The date and time of the creation of the folder or file.
- The date and time of the last modification of the folder or file. The date and time of the last access to a folder or file. The topic of interest pertains to the size of folders or files (Lu et al., 2014).
- The attributes of a folder or file, including security details and backup status, are noteworthy considerations.
- The compression or encryption status of the data contained within a folder or file.

Figure 6.3 depicts a portion of the metadata retained for a file within the Windows 10 OS. The metadata above can be exhibited through the utilization of File Explorer (Agrawal et al., 2008).

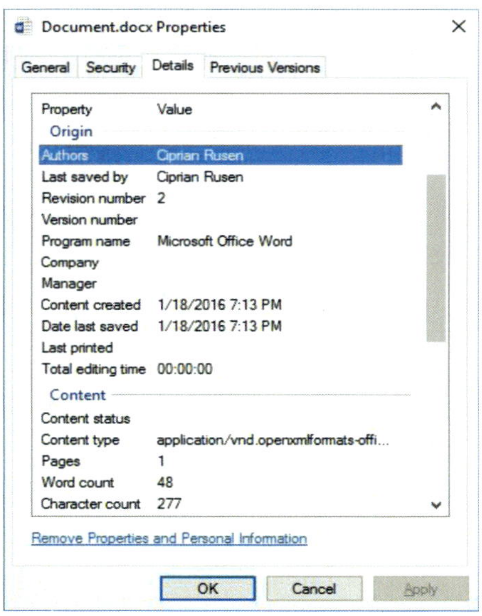

Figure 6.3. Image of Windows file metadata.

Source: Ciprian Adrian Rusen, Creative Commons License.

6.1.4. Storage Device Space Organization

The present section pertains to storage within the mechanical hard disk drives (HDDs) framework. Notably, the principles and methodologies remain consistent for solid-state drives (SSDs). The dissimilarities between them are predominantly rooted in their physiological attributes (Carniel & de Aguiar, 2023). In contrast to HDDs, SSDs lack platters and read/write heads.

Upon delivery from the manufacturer, a hard disk undergoes low-level formatting. The low-level formatting process involves utilizing software to designate the precise locations of disk tracks and sectors. Each disk is partitioned into tracks, resembling multiple concentric circles on the disk's surface. The quantity of tracks on a hard disk is contingent upon the size and producer of the disk. Each track's division is accomplished by partitioning equal-sized portions known as sectors. The diagram depicted in Figure 6.4 showcases a hard disk partitioned into distinct tracks and sectors on a platter (Casadei & Viroli, 2019).

Figure 6.4. Illustration of disk tracks and sectors on a platter.

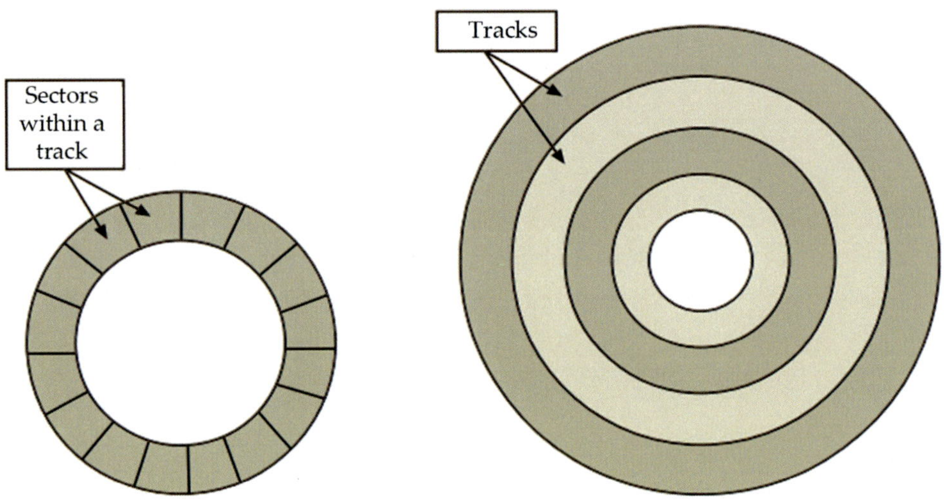

Source: Brooke Greenhouse, Creative Commons License.

6.1.4.1. Block Allocation

The present publication examines OSs that employ block allocation to monitor the location of particular files on the disk. The process of block allocation involves the partitioning of a disk into clusters or allocation units in Windows OSs. These clusters are then mapped to a set of sectors on the disk (Dirik & Jacob, 2009).

One of the two techniques involves storing block allocation data on the disk. A particular method involves utilizing a static disk segment to retain this information. An instance of this is the file allocation table (FAT) file system, originally executed in MS-DOS and is compatible with all iterations of Windows and most other OSs. An alternative method involves utilizing diverse disk locations to house a distinct file type to allocate folders and files. Illustrative instances encompass the new technology file system (NTFS) and the file systems of UNIX/Linux (Case, 1991). The master file table (MFT) is the allocation table utilized on disks formatted with NTFS, as elaborated upon in a subsequent section of this chapter. The sectors of the disk that contain the allocation and folder information are crucial for accessing the files on the system. In their absence, specialized disk repair tools would be required to gain access to the files (Huang et al., 2006).

Did you Know?

The choice of a file system can have a significant impact on system performance and some file systems are better suited for certain types of workloads than others.

When a system utilizes a designated region or multiple regions on the disk to retain file allocation data, it is apparent that the disk area is accessed frequently. Numerous difficulties in accessing disk files can be attributed to FATs and folder information issues. The separation of data storage from the actual file implies that discrepancies may arise between the folder or allocation data and the data stored on the disk in the event of disk malfunctions (Morenoff & McLean, 1967). Although infrequent in contemporary times, it is crucial to exercise appropriate caution when handling disks to mitigate such issues.

6.1.4.2. Partitions

The process of partitioning and formatting a hard disk is a prerequisite for installing a file system. Partitioning refers to reserving a set of tracks and sectors for the exclusive use of a specific file system, such as FAT or NTFS (Sarawagi & Stonebraker, 1994). Upon partitioning a disk, it is necessary to perform high-level or simple formatting to establish the disk's divisions and patterns essential for a specific OS to facilitate file storage. In light of the advancements in contemporary technology that facilitate the creation of disks with larger storage capacity, and the increasing employment of disks in a wider range of applications, it may be advantageous to incorporate multiple file systems on a single disk. This can be achieved by allocating a partition for each respective file system. In certain scenarios, installing Windows 10 alongside Windows 7 or the co-installation of Red Hat Enterprise Linux and Windows 10 on a single computer may necessitate utilizing multiple file systems

(Tian et al., 2011). To cater to specific applications designed for Linux and Windows 10, installing multiple OSs on a single system may be necessary.

It is possible to partition the disk to accommodate multiple file systems on a single disk, thereby enabling the installation of distinct file systems on separate disk partitions. It is possible to generate partitions within an OS, thereby dividing a solitary physical drive, such as a computer's hard disk, into numerous logical volumes. These volumes can be allocated unique drive letters for differentiation purposes. Parting a hard disk into multiple logical drives is a valuable method for arranging file storage and was a requisite for earlier OSs, such as MS-DOS and Windows 3.1, that were incapable of recognizing exceedingly large hard drives (Shao et al., 2004).

6.1.4.3. Formatting

Once a disk has been partitioned, the subsequent step involves the implementation of formatting to establish a file system on the partition. Upon installing a Windows OS, the system will autonomously generate and configure the requisite partitions, as previously indicated. Alternatively, the user may opt to generate and configure the partitions manually.

Subsequently, the installation procedure generates the directory hierarchy and inscribes the OS files onto the storage medium. One may utilize the Disk Management tool to generate supplementary volumes upon successfully installing the OS. An alternative approach to formatting a hard disk involves utilizing the format command within the Command Prompt window. The instruction above is responsible for persisting the entire file system architecture onto the disk (Ghosh, 1974).

Like numerous commands at the system level, the format command encompasses various supplementary switches that alter the specific operation of the program. The Command Prompt window provides access to a list of switches that can be viewed by typing "format /?" in the window above. Please refer to Table 6.1 for a comprehensive enumeration of format switches.

Formatting disk results in the complete erasure of all previously stored data. The format command is responsible for inscribing fresh sectors and track markers on disks without any formatting process. The /q (quick format) option can be utilized on previously utilized disks (Chen et al., 1995). The command above instructs the format to forego the disk check process and solely generate a fresh root directory alongside either a FAT or MFT. The utilization of the /q switch expedites the format operation. However, it omits the exhaustive examination of the disk, potentially resulting in complications in the future if an application endeavors to inscribe data to a defective disk location.

Table 6.1. Different Format Command Switches and Their Functions

Switch	Function
/v:label	Specifies the volume label.
/q	Uses a quick format technique that does not check the disk for damaged clusters or bad spots.
/f:size	Specifies the size of the floppy disk to format (such as 160, 180, 320, 360, 720, 1.2, 1.44, or 2.88, where the file sizes are in KB or MB).
/fs:filesystem	Specifies whether to format for FAT16, FAT32, or NTFS.
/t:tracks	Designates the number of tracks on a side (disks can be formatted on both sides).
/n:sectors	Designates how many sectors are in a track.
/c	NTFS only: this causes files created on the volume to be compressed.
/p:count	The count parameter dictates the frequency with which zeros are to be inscribed in each sector of the given number. This feature entails the complete erasure of all data stored on the disk by replacing it with 0 bits. This measure aims to enhance security by preventing any possibility of data recovery. The usage of the /q switch is invalid.
/X	Forces the volume to dismount first, if necessary.
/R:revision	UDF only: forces a specific UDF format revision.
/L	NTFS only: use large file records.
/A:size	Overrides the default allocation unit (cluster) size.
/N:sectors	Specifies the number of sectors per track.
/S:state	Specifies support for short filenames. The state is either enable or disable. Short names are disabled by default.
/I:state	The option to enable integrity on the new volume is exclusively limited to ReFS. The state can be either enabled or disabled. By default, data redundancy supporting storage is equipped with integrity.

Source: GregTomson, Creative Commons License.

6.2. WINDOWS FILE SYSTEMS

The OSs from Windows XP to Windows Server 2008 R2 are compatible with three distinct file systems: extended FAT16, FAT32, and NTFS. ReFS is also supported by Windows 8, Microsoft Server 2012, and subsequent versions.

These OSs can support file systems designed for DVD/CD-ROM drives and portable storage devices such as flash drives.

6.2.1. FAT16 and Extended FAT16

The FAT16 file system extension in Windows has developed from the original FAT16 system utilized in the initial releases of MS-DOS and Windows (3.x/95/98/Me). It is possible to partition an extended file system into several distinct logical files. The FAT is a data structure utilized for storing directory information about files, including but not limited to file names, file features, and file location. The nomenclature "FAT16" denotes the utilization of 16-bit records in the file distribution table and the allocation of 216 clusters in this file system. Clusters refer to contiguous blocks of storage space on a disk that is comprised of one or more sectors.

The extended version of the file allocation table 16 (FAT16) file system has a volume size limit of 4 GB and a file size limit of 2 GB (Rimer, 1999). The utilization of the extended FAT16 file system offers a benefit in that it has a long-standing history, and it is compatible with non-Windows OS, such as UNIX/Linux, enabling the reading of disks written in FAT16 format. Moreover, its simplicity makes the file system less prone to errors, rendering it a dependable file system.

The FAT16 file system initially employed filenames with a maximum length of eight characters, followed by a period and a three-character extension, commonly referred to as "8.3" filenames. An example of such a filename is "Filename.ext." Various file extensions are utilized to distinguish between different types of files. For instance, text files are denoted by .txt, .doc, or .docx, representing word-processing files, and Excel spreadsheets are indicated by .xls or .xlsx, among others. The constraints inherent in the naming convention played a role in the emergence and adoption of extended FAT16's long filenames (LFNs).

- A long file name (LFN) can accommodate up to 255 characters;
- The system is insensitive to letter cases;
- It is impossible to utilize characters such as /, \, [,], :, ;, and = in both 8.3 filenames and LFNs (Awan & Khiyal, 2004).

The feasibility of utilizing most permissible characters in Windows filenames is facilitated by storing LFN characters in Unicode. This coding system enables the representation of any character in any language. However, it is noteworthy that certain exceptions exist, as outlined in the preceding bulleted list. One of the benefits of utilizing LFNs and Unicode is their cross-platform compatibility, as LFNs can be accessed by different OS, including Mac OS and UNIX/Linux systems. This is particularly useful when a Windows 2008 server is equipped with file services catering to Mac OS and UNIX/Linux clients (Braam et al.,

1999). In the past, ASCII (American Standard Code for Information Interchange, pronounced as-key) values were utilized to represent letters and digits. The limitation of the standard above lies in its utilization of a complete byte to represent individual characters, thereby restricting the range of characters that can be symbolized to a maximum of 255. The current character capacity is insufficient to accommodate the diverse characters required to represent global languages, which employ multiple distinct alphabets, such as Greek, Japanese, Russian, and Hindi. ASCII addresses the issue at hand by utilizing diverse character sets, which are contingent upon the specific characters being depicted (Volos et al., 2014). The Unicode Consortium is a non-profit entity that proposes an alternative approach wherein a solitary and distinct code is assigned to every conceivable character in any language. The initial 128 characters within the Unicode character encoding system correspond to the 128 characters within the ASCII character set. The Unicode standard enables the definition of more than 1 million characters. The character codes encompass contemporary languages and ancient scripts, such as Egyptian hieroglyphs. Implementing Unicode may not yield a significant impact for individuals who predominantly utilize the English language for communication purposes. However, in the current era of globalized communication, utilizing Unicode has become an essential requirement.

6.2.2. FAT32

Since the release of Windows 95 Release 2, all subsequent versions of Windows have provided support for FAT32 (Ji et al., 2000). The FAT32 file system was developed to accommodate disks with larger capacities than those supported by the FAT16 file system while also addressing the issue of cluster size limitations. The length of a FAT entry in the FAT32 file system is 32 bits. It is noteworthy that FAT32 can support up to 228 clusters, although it is important to note that this value is not raised to the 32nd power because additional space is reserved for the OS. The FAT32 file system allows the root directory to be positioned at any location on the volume rather than solely at the outset. FAT32 can utilize disk space more efficiently than FAT16 due to its capacity to employ smaller cluster sizes (Carvey, 2005). Theoretically, FAT32 partitions can accommodate a size of 2 terabytes (TB). However, it is noteworthy that the maximum volume that can be formatted is 32 GB, which is significantly larger than the maximum volume that can be formatted using FAT16. The upper limit of file size in the FAT32 file system has been increased to 4 gigabytes.

The FAT32 file system exhibits similarities to the extended version of FAT16, including the presence of a dual FAT configuration at the onset of a partition to ensure resilience against errors and the utilization of LFNs and Unicode (Boukhobza & Timsit, 2005).

Occasionally, users opt to utilize extended FAT16 or FAT32 file systems due to their familiarity with these systems or the presence of dual-boot systems, such as a system featuring both Windows XP and the older Windows 98. Extended FAT16 or FAT32 file systems are advantageous because they provide rapid response times on smaller partitions, typically ranging from 1 to 2 GB in size.

6.2.3. FAT64

The file system known as FAT64, or exFAT, is proprietary. Microsoft developed this technology to cater to the storage requirements of individuals on mobile devices, particularly for managing sizable data files. The expansion in the dimensions of images, videos, and other media formats has led to significant deliberation on the file size restrictions of FAT16 and FAT32 (Lee et al., 2019). The maximum storage capacity for the FAT16 file system is 2 gigabytes, with an additional byte subtracted from the total. In contrast, the FAT32 file system has a maximum storage capacity of 4 gigabytes, with an additional byte subtracted from the total. The FAT64 file system, which has a maximum capacity of 16 exabytes, is a suitable option for USB flash drives intended to store sizable files.

The availability of FAT64 commences with the release of Service Pack 1 for the Windows Vista OS. Additionally, it can be obtained for Linux through a third-party source. In late 2010, Mac OS X Snow Leopard was updated to include support from Apple.

6.2.4. NTFS

The NTFS file system is the principal file system for all Windows OSs, from Windows NT 3.1 (Lina et al., 2006). The system in question has been specifically designed to cater to the requirements of a networked environment in contemporary times.

The methodology employed by NTFS for file and cluster management differs slightly from that of FAT file systems. In contrast to the utilization of a framework comprising of FATs and directories, the NTFS employs an MFT. Similar to the FATs and directories, this table can be found at the partition's start. The boot sector's location is situated before the MFT (Soules et al., 2002). Following the MFT, the file system utilizes several system files to facilitate the full functionality of NTFS.

It should be noted that the MFT is simply a file located within the file system, similar to other system files. A duplicate of the initial three entries of the MFT is stored as the second file within the disk (Gifford et al., 1991). This measure guarantees that it can be reconstructed in the event of MFT corruption.

File number five, denoted as $, comprises the entries in the root folder. On the other hand, file number six, referred to as $Bitmap, contains information regarding the clusters currently in use on the disk. Typically, during the initial formatting of a disk, the MFT and its associated files occupy approximately 1 megabyte of disk space.

Upon creation of a file in NTFS, a corresponding entry is appended to the MFT. The document encompasses customary data, including file name, magnitude, dates, and timestamps (Roselli et al., 2000). The item above also encompasses supplementary characteristics, including but not limited to security configurations, proprietorship, and authorizations. In cases where the MFT record lacks sufficient space to accommodate security settings, the excess settings are relocated to an alternate cluster located elsewhere on the disk. The MFT record subsequently establishes a reference to this relocated information. When a file is of diminutive size, it may be feasible to accommodate the file data within the MFT record. In cases where the available space is insufficient, the system proceeds to assign clusters to alternative locations on the disk. It is possible to have a variety of security attributes consecutively assigned to distinct users. The technique of hard linking enables the existence of multiple filenames that pertain to a single file. The characteristic above, which can also be found in UNIX/Linux file systems, is occasionally utilized to enable the presentation of a single file in numerous directories while avoiding the need to allocate additional disk space for the file (Almedia, 1998) (Table 6.2).

Table 6.2. Different NTFS Version

Official Version Number	Generally Accepted Version Number	Windows Operating System
1.0	NTFS	–
1.1	NTFS	–
1.2	NTFS 4	Windows NT 3.51 and NT 4.0
3.0	NTFS 5.0	Windows 2000
3.1	NTFS 5.1/5.2	Windows XP/Windows Server 2003/ Windows Server 2008/Vista
3.1	NTFS 6.0	Windows Server 2008 R2/Windows 7 and later

Source: Kristin McNary, Creative Commons License.

NTFS includes several fundamental features, such as:

- Long filenames.
- Inherent security functionalities.

- The file compression of the system in question surpasses that of the FAT system.
- The capacity to utilize disks and files of larger sizes compared to the FAT system.
- Implementing file activity tracking can improve recovery and stability compared to the FAT system.
- The provision of support for the portable operating system interface for UNIX (POSIX).
- Volume striping and volume extensions.
- The disk fragmentation level in the file system is lower than in FAT (Bolosky et al., 2000).

NTFS is a comprehensive network file system endowed with security features compliant with the C2 security specifications of the United States government. C2 security pertains to stringent and confidential protocols for safeguarding data, conducting system audits, and regulating system entry, as mandated by select governmental entities. A security measure involves the capability to determine the level of access permitted for users to folders and files contained within said folders (Blaze, 1993). Customization of file and folder access can be customized to meet an enterprise's specific needs. The protection of system files on a server can be implemented in a manner that restricts access solely to the server administrator. It is possible to secure a collection of databases by restricting access to read-only while prohibiting any modifications to the data. Additionally, a shared folder may be configured to allow users within a specified group to view and edit files but not to remove them.

The process of file compression involves the reduction of a file's size through the removal of unused space or the utilization of compression algorithms. Certain files can potentially undergo compression exceeding 40%, conserving significant disk space for alternative storage requirements (Leung et al., 2008). This feature proves to be particularly advantageous for files that are not frequently accessed. The NTFS file system offers the capability to compress files as required.

The NTFS file system can expand to support exceedingly large files, specifically in the context of database implementations (Bettany et al., 2015). For instance, a database file in Microsoft SQL Server could be 20 GB or more. This implies that a given entity can store various types of multimedia, such as photographs, digitized images, and audio recordings, within a unified database. In theory, the NTFS system can accommodate files of up to 264 bytes.

One of the features of NTFS is journaling, which refers to the capacity to maintain a record or chronicle of the activities within the file system. This process is of utmost importance in a power outage or a hard disk failure

(Muthitacharoen et al., 2001). Significant data can be retrieved and restored in such circumstances. The FAT does not provide this functionality.

The NTFS file system facilitates adherence to POSIX standards, enabling applications to be transferred across different computer systems. Initially conceived as a standard for UNIX, POSIX was created to ensure the seamless transferability of applications across diverse versions of UNIX. Other OSs have adopted POSIX and file systems beyond UNIX. The NTFS adheres to the POSIX 1 convention, encompassing the utilization of case-sensitive filenames and the incorporation of multiple filenames, also known as hard links, which will be elaborated upon in subsequent sections of this chapter. In the context of file management, it is noteworthy that the files "Myfile.doc" and "MYFile.doc" are distinct entities unless one is utilizing the File Explorer or the Command Prompt window (Wolthusen, 2001).

The NTFS file system possesses a significant capability in managing volumes, which involves the creation of extensions on a pre-existing volume, particularly in cases where additional disk storage is introduced. Volume striping is a technique involving uniform file content distribution across multiple volumes (Agrawal et al., 2007). This approach prolongs the lifespan of disks, facilitates fault tolerance capabilities, and optimizes disk performance by balancing the disk load.

Due to its hotfix capability, NTFS is comparatively less susceptible to file corruption than FAT. This implies that in case of detection of a bad disk area, NTFS automatically transfers the information from the damaged area to another disk area that is not affected (Zhang et al., 2020).

In addition to the features above of NTFS 4, NTFS 5 incorporates several supplementary features:

- The capacity to apply encryption to files;
- The absence of a necessity to reboot the system after establishing an extended volume;
- The capacity to decrease drive designations;
- Indexing is a technique used to achieve fast access to data (Berghel et al., 2008).

The capacity to preserve shortcuts and other file attributes when transferring files and folders across different volumes. In the context of Windows OSs, a shortcut refers to a graphical representation, typically in the form of an icon or link, which enables the user to initiate software either in its original location or in an alternate location with a single or double-click of the mouse.

NTFS 6 incorporates several novel functionalities as follows:

- Transactional NTFS;

- The process of adjusting the size of a partition;
- Self-healing (Vogels, 1999).

Transactional NTFS is a mechanism that executes operations on an NTFS volume in transaction mode. This implies that all designated file system transactions are either executed in their entirety or not executed at all. It is possible to bundle registry and file system operations into a transactional unit, thereby ensuring that all operations are executed, or none are successful. In the event of a failure in any file system operations, the entire process is terminated, and no further actions are executed. The utilization of Transactional NTFS is prevalent in the Windows Server 2008 OS (Douceur & Bolosky, 1999).

Since the release of Windows Vista, Microsoft has implemented a feature that enables the resizing of partitions. This allows for the modification of the volume's storage capacity without necessitating the deletion of the partition or reformatting of the disk. The current capacity remains restricted, and there exist alternative third-party offerings that exhibit greater proficiency and resilience.

ACTIVITY 6.1:

Use command-line tools to create and manage files and directories on a storage device with different files systems.

6.2.5. Resilient File System (ReFS)

The ReFS file system was introduced with the release of Windows Server 2012 (Bettany et al., 2015). Resilient file system (ReFS) is primarily utilized in scenarios involving extensive file-sharing applications, wherein the management of volumes is facilitated by Storage Spaces. While ReFS maintains some backward compatibility with NTFS, it lacks support for features such as file compression, disk quotas, and EFS (encrypting file system) (Prade et al., 2020). Booting Windows from a volume formatted with the ReFS is impossible. The ReFS can autonomously rectify minor file system issues and accommodate volume capacities of up to 1 yottabyte (YB), equivalent to one trillion TB. The ReFS collaborates with Storage Spaces to rectify disk malfunction resulting from corruption, whether from software or hardware-related issues (Nordvik et al., 2019).

In contrast to alternative fault-tolerant disk solutions, such as RAID 1 and RAID 5, which solely facilitate failure recovery, ReFS can rectify certain forms of data corruption autonomously. The utilization of this particular capability, in conjunction with Storage Spaces, facilitates the development of disk systems that are both highly dependable and expandable, all while avoiding the use of RAID disk controllers and the potentially inefficient disk allocation schemes that are often associated with RAID configurations (Groß et al., 2022). Due to the absence of certain functionalities, ReFS is not designed to substitute NTFS. ReFS is an optimal choice for facilitating volumes intended for high-availability applications that operate with exceedingly large files while not necessitating user-specific functionalities, such as disk quotas and EFS.

6.2.6. CDFS and UDF

Windows OSs can identify supplementary file systems utilized by peripheral storage technologies, starting from Windows 2000. Three entities are referenced within this context. The support for CD-ROM file systems (CDFS) enables the read and write operations of files to DVD/CD-ROM drives by OSs. The ability to utilize DVD/CD-ROM technology is crucial for loading OSs and facilitating the sharing of DVD/CD-ROM drives across a network. The universal disk format (UDF) file system is utilized in DVD/CD-ROMs to enable the storage of larger files, which is particularly useful for accommodating movies and games (Kellermann et al., 2004).

6.3. SUMMARY

One of the fundamental roles of an OS is to facilitate the storage and retrieval of data on a computer or other digital apparatus. A file system facilitates this data's management, storage, and retrieval. The file system executes various functions, such as furnishing a user-friendly interface, establishing a hierarchical arrangement, preserving metadata, arranging storage space on a storage device, and delivering tools to sustain and govern the file system. In addition to the primary functions of file creation and modification, the file system should provide supplementary features such as file defragmentation, compression of file contents, maintenance of file and data integrity, implementation of file security measures, and management of removable storage media. Before installing a file system onto a hard disk, it is necessary to partition and format the disk. Partitioning refers to reserving a set of tracks and sectors for a specific file system, such as FAT or NTFS. Since the release of Windows 2000, the primary file systems utilized in the Windows OS have been the extended versions of FAT16, FAT32, and NTFS. The file system generates a FAT in FAT16 and FAT32 to retain data about files. The FAT32 file system exhibits greater resilience than its predecessor, FAT16, and enables the utilization of more clusters and larger partitions. Various UNIX/Linux distributions employ distinct file systems utilities, such as disk and format, to partition and format disks. The Mac OS X OS provides two significant disk tools: Disk Utility and Disk First Aid.

REVIEW QUESTIONS

1. What is the file system and why is it important in operating systems?
2. What are the different types of file systems that can be used by an operating system?
3. How do file systems manage permission for files and directories?
4. What factors should be considered when choosing a file system for a particular storage device or operating system?
5. What how file fragmentation affects file system performance and how can it be addressed?

MULTIPLE CHOICE QUESTIONS

1. What is a file system?

a. A method of organizing and storing files on a storage device
b. A type of operating system
c. A program used for formatting hard drives
d. None of the above

2. Which of the following is not a type of the file system?

a. FAT32
b. HFS+
c. ZIP
d. Ext4

3. What is a file system's primary function?

a. To manage permissions for files and directories
b. To improve system performance and reliability
c. To organize and store files on a storage device
d. To control access to the internet

4. What is file fragmentation?

a. A feature of file systems that compresses files to save storage space
b. A technique used to encrypt files on a storage device
c. A problem that occurs when files are stored in non-contiguous blocks on a storage device
d. None of the above

Answers to Multiple Choice Questions

1. (a); 2. (c); 3. (c); 4. (d)

REFERENCES

1. Agrawal, N., Arpaci-Dusseau, A. C., & Arpaci-Dusseau, R. H., (2008). Towards realistic file-system benchmarks with codemri. *ACM SIGMETRICS Performance Evaluation Review, 36*(2), 52–57.
2. Agrawal, N., Bolosky, W. J., Douceur, J. R., & Lorch, J. R., (2007). A five-year study of file-system metadata. *ACM Transactions on Storage (TOS), 3*(3), 9–10.
3. Almedia, D., (1998). *Framework for Implementing File Systems in Windows NT* (Vol. 1, pp. 4–8). Doctoral dissertation, Massachusetts Institute of Technology.
4. Asaad, R. R., Ahmad, H. B., & Ali, R. I., (2020). A review: big data technologies with Hadoop distributed filesystem and implementing M/R. *Academic Journal of Nawroz University, 9*(1), 25–33.
5. Awan, M. A., & Khiyal, S. H., (2004). Stackably extensible template layer for file system development under windows NT (family). In: *E-Tech 2004* (Vol. 1, pp. 74–82). IEEE.
6. Berghel, H., Hoelzer, D., & Sthultz, M., (2008). Data hiding tactics for windows and Unix file systems. *Advances in Computers, 74*(1), 1–17.

7. Bettany, A., Halsey, M., Halsey, M., & Bettany, A., (2015). Understanding windows file systems. *Windows File System Troubleshooting, 1,* 13–30.
8. Blaze, M., (1993). A cryptographic file system for UNIX. In: *Proceedings of the 1st ACM Conference on Computer and Communications Security* (Vol. 1, pp. 9–16).
9. Bolosky, W. J., Corbin, S., Goebel, D., & Douceur, J. R., (2000). Single instance storage in Windows 2000. In: *Proceedings of the 4th USENIX Windows Systems Symposium* (Vol. 1, pp. 13–24).
10. Boukhobza, J., & Timsit, C., (2005). On windows file access modes: A performance study. In: *Proceedings of the 4th International Symposium on Information and Communication Technologies* (Vol. 1, pp. 44–49).
11. Bouqata, B., Carothers, C. D., Szymanski, B. K., & Zaki, M. J., (2003). Understanding filesystem performance for data mining applications. In: *Proceedings of the 6th International Workshop on High Performance Data Mining: Pervasive and Data Stream Mining (HPDM: PDS '03)* (Vol. 1, pp. 4–7).
12. Braam, P. J., Callahan, M. J., Satyanarayanan, M., & Schnieder, M., (1999). Porting the coda file system to windows. In: *USENIX Annual Technical Conference, FREENIX Track* (Vol. 1, pp. 69–74).
13. Cai, M., Huang, H., & Huang, J., (2019). Understanding security vulnerabilities in file systems. In: *Proceedings of the 10th ACM SIGOPS Asia-Pacific Workshop on Systems* (Vol., pp. 8–15).
14. Carniel, A. C., & De Aguiar, C. D., (2023). Spatial index structures for modern storage devices: A survey. *IEEE Transactions on Knowledge and Data Engineering, 3*(1), 4–9.
15. Carvey, H., (2005). The windows registry as a forensic resource. *Digital Investigation, 2*(3), 201–205.
16. Casadei, R., & Viroli, M., (2019). Coordinating computation at the edge: A decentralized, self-organizing, spatial approach. In: *2019 Fourth International Conference on Fog and Mobile Edge Computing (FMEC)* (Vol. 1, pp. 60–67). IEEE.
17. Case, D. O., (1991). Conceptual organization and retrieval of text by historians: The role of memory and metaphor. *Journal of the American Society for Information Science, 42*(9), 657–668.
18. Chen, L. T., Drach, R., Keating, M., Louis, S., Rotem, D., & Shoshani, A., (1995). Efficient organization and access of multi-dimensional datasets on tertiary storage systems. *Information Systems, 20*(2), 155–183.
19. Devarakonda, M. V., Mohindra, A., Simoneaux, J., & Tetzlaff, W. H., (1995). Evaluation of design alternatives for a cluster file system. In: *USENIX* (Vol. 1, pp. 35–46).
20. Dirik, C., & Jacob, B., (2009). The performance of PC solid-state disks (SSDs) as a function of bandwidth, concurrency, device architecture, and system organization. *ACM SIGARCH Computer Architecture News, 37*(3), 279–289.
21. Douceur, J. R., & Bolosky, W. J., (1999). A large-scale study of file-system contents. *ACM SIGMETRICS Performance Evaluation Review, 27*(1), 59–70.

22. Fu, K., Kaashoek, M. F., & Mazieres, D., (2002). Fast and secure distributed read-only file system. *ACM Transactions on Computer Systems (TOCS), 20*(1), 1–24.
23. Ghosh, S. P., (1974). File organization: Consecutive storage of relevant records on drum-type storage. *Information and Control, 25*(2), 145–165.
24. Gifford, D. K., Jouvelot, P., Sheldon, M. A., & O'Toole, Jr. J. W., (1991). Semantic file systems. *ACM SIGOPS Operating Systems Review, 25*(5), 16–25.
25. Griffioen, J., & Appleton, R., (1994). Reducing file system latency using a predictive approach. In: *USENIX Summer* (Vol. 1, pp. 197–207).
26. Groß, T., Schleier, T., & Müller, T., (2022). ReFuzz-structure aware fuzzing of the resilient file system (ReFS). In: *Proceedings of the 2022 ACM on Asia Conference on Computer and Communications Security* (Vol. 1, pp. 589–601).
27. Hanson, E., & Serebnick, J., (1986). Evaluation of the public service functions of serial file systems. *College & Research Libraries, 47*(6), 575–586.
28. Hedges, R., Loewe, B., McLarty, T., & Morrone, C., (2005). Parallel file system testing for the lunatic fringe: The care and feeding of restless I/O power users. In: *22nd IEEE/13th NASA Goddard Conference on Mass Storage Systems and Technologies (MSST'05)* (Vol. 1, pp. 3–17). IEEE.
29. Hertel, C. R., (2004). *Implementing CIFS: The Common Internet File System* (Vol. 1, pp. 5–10). Prentice Hall Professional.
30. Huang, H. H., Karpovich, J. F., & Grimshaw, A. S., (2006). A feasibility study of a virtual storage system for large organizations. In: *First International Workshop on Virtualization Technology in Distributed Computing (VTDC 2006)* (Vol. 1, p. 9-11). IEEE.
31. Ji, M., Felten, E. W., Wang, R., & Singh, J. P., (2000). Archipelago: An island-based file system for highly available and scalable internet services. In: *Proceedings of 4th USENIX Windows Systems Symposium* (Vol. 1, pp. 4–7).
32. Kazar, M. L., Leverett, B. W., Anderson, O. T., Apostolides, V., Bottos, B. A., Chutani, S., & Zayas, E. R., (1990). DEcorum file system architectural overview. In: *USENIX Summer* (Vol. 90, pp. 151–163).
33. Kellermann, K. I., Fomalont, E. B., Kelly, J., Shaver, P., Rosati, P., Tozzi, P., & Mainieri, V., (2004). VLA observations of the CDFS and hubble UDF. In: *American Astronomical Society Meeting Abstracts* (Vol. 205, pp. 155–158).
34. Kim, J., Kim, Y., Khan, A., & Park, S., (2019). Understanding the performance of storage class memory file systems in the NUMA architecture. *Cluster Computing, 22*(1), 347–360.
35. Korn, D. G., & Krell, E., (1990). A new dimension for the Unix® file system. *Software: Practice and Experience, 20*(S1), S19–S34.
36. Le, D., Huang, H., & Wang, H., (2012). Understanding performance implications of nested file systems in a virtualized environment. In: *FAST* (Vol. 8, pp. 5–10).

37. Lee, W. Y., Kim, K. H., & Lee, H., (2019). Extraction of creation-time for recovered files on windows FAT32 file system. *Applied Sciences, 9*(24), 5522.
38. Leung, A. W., Pasupathy, S., Goodson, G. R., & Miller, E. L., (2008). Measurement and analysis of large-scale network file system workloads. In: *USENIX Annual Technical Conference* (Vol. 1, No. 2, pp. 5–2).
39. Levy, E., & Silberschatz, A., (1990). Distributed file systems: Concepts and examples. *ACM Computing Surveys (CSUR), 22*(4), 321–374.
40. Lina, W., Chi, G., Dejun, W., & Qin, Z., (2006). Building hot snapshot copy based on windows file system. *Wuhan University Journal of Natural Sciences, 11*(6), 1503–1506.
41. Lu, L., Arpaci-Dusseau, A. C., Arpaci-Dusseau, R. H., & Lu, S., (2014). A study of Linux file system evolution. *ACM Transactions on Storage (TOS), 10*(1), 1–32.
42. Morenoff, E., & McLean, J. B., (1967). Application of level changing to a multilevel storage organization. *Communications of the ACM, 10*(3), 149–154.
43. Mothukuri, V., Cheerla, S. S., Parizi, R. M., Zhang, Q., & Choo, K. K. R., (2021). BlockHDFS: Blockchain-integrated Hadoop distributed file system for secure provenance traceability. *Blockchain: Research and Applications, 2*(4), 100032.
44. Muthitacharoen, A., Chen, B., & Mazieres, D., (2001). A low-bandwidth network file system. In: *Proceedings of the Eighteenth ACM Symposium on Operating Systems Principles* (Vol. 1, pp. 174–187).
45. Nordvik, R., Georges, H., Toolan, F., & Axelsson, S., (2019). Reverse engineering of ReFS. *Digital Investigation, 30*(1), 127–147.
46. Olivier, P., Boukhobza, J., Soula, M., Grand, M. L., Draa, I. C., & Senn, E., (2014). A tracing toolset for embedded Linux flash file system. In: *Proceedings of the 8th International Conference on Performance Evaluation Methodologies and Tools* (Vol. 1, pp. 153–158).
47. Padioleau, Y., & Ridoux, O., (2005). A parts-of-file system. In: *USENIX 2005 Annual Technical Conference, General Track* (Vol. 1, pp. 4–7).
48. Prabhakaran, V., Arpaci-Dusseau, A. C., & Arpaci-Dusseau, R. H., (2005). Analysis and evolution of journaling file systems. In: *USENIX Annual Technical Conference, General Track* (Vol. 194, pp. 196–215).
49. Prade, P., Groβ, T., & Dewald, A., (2020). Forensic analysis of the resilient file system (refs) version 3.4. *Forensic Science International: Digital Investigation, 32*(1), 300–915.
50. Ridge, T., Sheets, D., Tuerk, T., Giugliano, A., Madhavapeddy, A., & Sewell, P., (2015). SibylFS: Formal specification and oracle-based testing for POSIX and real-world file systems. In: *Proceedings of the 25th Symposium on Operating Systems Principles* (Vol. 1, pp. 38–53).
51. Rimer, M. S., (1999). *The Secure File System Under Windows NT* (Vol. 1, pp. 5–7). Doctoral dissertation, Massachusetts Institute of Technology.

52. Roselli, D. S., Lorch, J. R., & Anderson, T. E., (2000). A comparison of file system workloads. In: *USENIX Annual Technical Conference, General Track* (Vol. 1, pp. 41–54).
53. Sarawagi, S., & Stonebraker, M., (1994). Efficient organization of large multidimensional arrays. In: *Proceedings of 1994 IEEE 10th International Conference on Data Engineering* (Vol. 1, pp. 328–336). IEEE.
54. Satyanarayanan, M., (1990). A survey of distributed file systems. *Annual Review of Computer Science, 4*(1), 73–104.
55. Schleier-Smith, J., Holz, L., Pemberton, N., & Hellerstein, J. M., (2020). *A FaaS File System for Serverless Computing, 1,* 4–6.
56. Shao, M., Schindler, J., Schlosser, S. W., Ailamaki, A., & Ganger, G. R., (2004). Clotho: Decoupling memory page layout from storage organization. In: *Proceedings of the Thirtieth International Conference on Very Large Data Bases* (Vol. 1, 30, pp. 696–707).
57. Soules, C. A., Goodson, G. R., Strunk, J. D., & Ganger, G. R., (2002). *Metadata Efficiency in a Comprehensive Versioning File System* (Vol. 1, pp. 5–7). Carnegie-Mellon Univ Pittsburgh Pa School of Computer Science.
58. Thanh, T. D., Mohan, S., Choi, E., Kim, S., & Kim, P., (2008). A taxonomy and survey on distributed file systems. In: *2008 Fourth International Conference on Networked Computing and Advanced Information Management* (Vol. 1, pp. 144–149). IEEE.
59. Tian, Y., Klasky, S., Abbasi, H., Lofstead, J., Grout, R., Podhorszki, N., & Yu, W., (2011). EDO: Improving read performance for scientific applications through elastic data organization. In: *2011 IEEE International Conference on Cluster Computing* (Vol. 1, pp. 93–102). IEEE.
60. Vogels, W., (1999). File system usage in Windows NT 4.0. *ACM SIGOPS Operating Systems Review, 33*(5), 93–109.
61. Volos, H., Nalli, S., Panneerselvam, S., Varadarajan, V., Saxena, P., & Swift, M. M., (2014). Aerie: Flexible file-system interfaces to storage-class memory. In: *Proceedings of the Ninth European Conference on Computer* Systems (Vol. 1, pp. 1–14).
62. Wang, F., Oral, S., Shipman, G., Drokin, O., Wang, T., & Huang, I., (2009). *Understanding Lustre Filesystem Internals* (Vol. 120, No. 1, pp. 3–7). Oak Ridge National Laboratory, National Center for Computational Sciences, Tech. Rep.
63. Wang, F., Xin, Q., Hong, B., Brandt, S. A., Miller, E. L., & Long, D., (2004). *File System Workload Analysis for Large Scale Scientific Computing Applications, 1,* 2–6.
64. Wolthusen, S. D., (2001). Security policy enforcement at the file system level in the windows NT operating system family. In: *17th Annual Computer Security Applications Conference* (Vol. 1, pp. 55–63). IEEE.
65. Zadok, E., & Badulescu, I., (1999). A stackable file system interface for Linux. In: *LinuxExpo Conference Proceedings* (Vol. 94, p. 10).
66. Zhang, N., Jiang, Y., & Wang, J., (2020). The research of data recovery on Windows

file systems. In: *2020 International Conference on Intelligent Transportation, Big Data & Smart City (ICITBS)* (Vol. 1, pp. 644–647). IEEE.

67. Zhao, T., March, V., Dong, S., & See, S., (2010). Evaluation of a performance model of lustre file system. In: *2010 15th Annual ChinaGrid Conference* (Vol. 1, pp. 191–196). IEEE.

CHAPTER 7

MOBILE OPERATING SYSTEMS

UNIT INTRODUCTION

An operating system (OS) specifically designed for mobile devices, such as mobile phones, cell phones, personal digital assistants (PDAs), tablet computers, and other electronic mobile devices, is referred to as a mobile operating system (mobile OS). This OS type is also widely called a mobile OS (Okediran et al., 2014). Modern mobile OSs combine the capabilities of a personal computer OS with those of cell phones, touchscreen, Wi-Fi, Bluetooth, GPS smartphone navigation, digital cameras, recordings camera, recognition of speech, sound recorder, audio player, PDA, and other comparable features (Ali, 2014).

A portable version of the OS often found in desktop computers is provided by the mobile OS, a software system developed specifically for mobile devices. A mobile OS is a software framework that allows other programs to run on mobile devices (Ivanov et al., 2018). This is analogous to how the Linux or Windows OS rules a laptop or desktop computer. The following is an exhaustive listing of the prevalent OSs that are frequently utilized in mobile devices like smartphones, along with the makers of those mobile devices:

- Nokia is responsible for developing the mobile operating system, the Symbian OS, used in Nokia cell phones (Ying et al., 2018).
- Google built the Android operating system, a mobile platform that is open-source and free to use.

- The iPhone Operating System, usually called iOS, was developed by Apple and is a mobile operating system (Nosrati et al., 2012).
- BlackBerry OS is a mobile operating system exclusive to research in motion's smartphones and was created by RIM, particularly for those devices. Microsoft has produced a mobile operating system known as Windows Phone 7, formerly Windows Mobile.
- Palm is responsible for developing its own mobile operating system, referred to as the Palm OS and the Garnet OS (Kamboj & Gupta, 2012).
- HP and Palm have collaborated to create a mobile operating system called Palm webOS.
- Samsung Electronics is responsible for developing the mobile operating system known as Bada.
- Nokia is the company that developed the Maemo operating system, which is free to use and available to the public under the GPL license. In a similar vein, the MeeGo operating system is a joint project between Nokia and Intel (Tilson et al., 2012). Like Linux, it is free and open-source software distributed under the GPL license.

Learning Objectives

After the chapter, students will be able to understand the following:

- Basic concept of mobile operating systems;
- Learn about different types of mobile operating systems;
- Understanding significance and applications of mobile operating systems;
- Comparison of android operating system with other MOS;
- Security concerns associated with mobile operating systems.

Key Terms

- Accessibility
- Android
- Bada
- Black Berry OS
- Integration
- iOS
- Market share
- Symbian
- Updates
- Windows phones

7.1. MOBILE OPERATING SYSTEMS (OSS)

A mobile operating system (OS), commonly referred to as a mobile OS, mobile platform, or handheld OS, is responsible for managing and controlling the operations of a mobile device. It functions similarly to a desktop computer's OS, such as Linux or Windows. Presently, these technologies focus primarily on broadband wireless and local connection, mobile multimedia content, and diverse input methods, albeit relatively uncomplicated.

A mobile OS is an OS specifically engineered to function on mobile devices, including but not limited to cell phones, mobile devices, PDAs, tablet computers, and other handheld devices. The OS is accountable for ascertaining the functionalities and attributes accessible on the device, including thumbwheel, synchronization with applications, keyboards, WAP, text messaging, email, and other features. The mobile OS is crucial in determining the compatibility of third-party mobile applications (apps) with a device (Figure 7.1).

Did you Know?

The first mobile operating system was developed by IBM in 1980 and was called the IBM Simon.

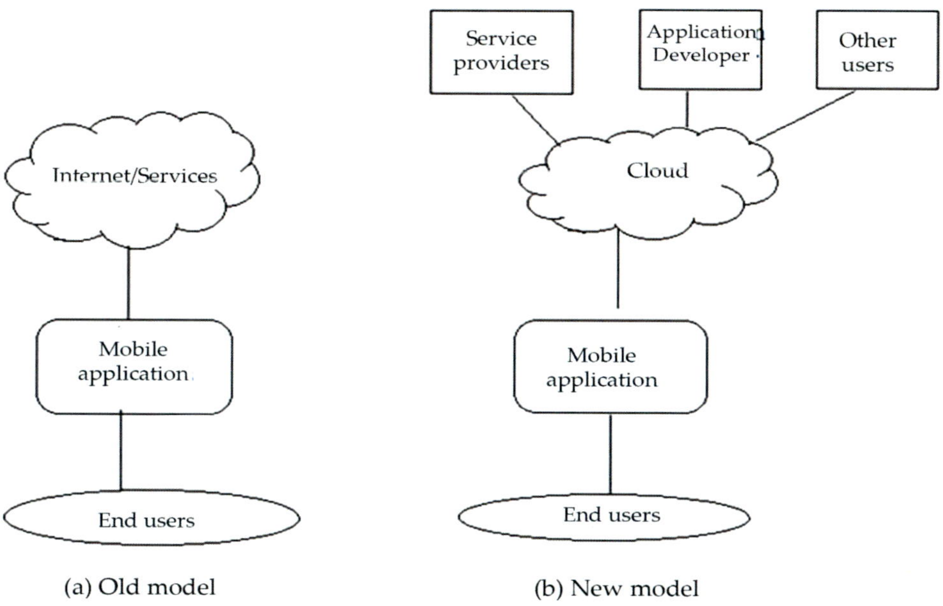

Figure 7.1. Architecture of mobile operating system.

Source: Ques10, Creative Commons License.

7.2. TYPES OF MOBILE OPERATING SYSTEMS (OSS)

Upon purchasing a mobile device, its maker will have deliberately selected the OS to be installed on the said device. It is frequently advisable to acquire knowledge regarding the mobile OS before procuring a device to ascertain its suitability and support for the desired mobile applications. The subsequent are the prevalent classifications of mobile OSs.

7.2.1. Android OS (Google Inc.)

> **Did you Know?**
>
> Android's operating system was initially designed to be used in digital cameras before being adapted for use in smartphones.

Android is a complete software stack that was developed specifically for mobile devices. It consists of an OS, core application software, and middleware (Okediran et al., 2014). In 2005, Google Inc. bought out Android Inc., which had initially developed the software. Android's mobile OS is built on a customized Linux kernel version, which serves as the system's foundation. Google and the other companies who are part of the Open Handset Alliance worked together on creating and distributing the Android OS. The android open-source project (AOSP) maintains the Android OS and ensures that it continues to grow in functionality (Nosrati et al., 2012). Currently, the Android OS is the mobile device platform that is being used on most smartphones worldwide.

The Android OS boasts a substantial cohort of developers who create applications, commonly called "apps," which enhance the devices' capabilities. At present, the number of Android applications available exceeds 1,50,000. The Android Market is an internet-based platform for distributing mobile applications managed by Google (Jindal & Jain, 2012). However, it is worth noting that applications can also be obtained from alternative sources. Developers predominantly utilize the Java language to write code, enabling them to manage the device through Java libraries developed by Google. The most recent iteration of the Android OS includes Android 2.3, colloquially referred to as Gingerbread and designed for use on smartphones. Android 3.0, known as Honeycomb, is optimized for tablet devices (Delac et al., 2011).

7.2.2. Bada (Samsung Electronics)

Bada is a proprietary OS developed by Samsung that was initially released in 2010 for deployment on cell phones and low-end smartphones. The most recent iteration of this software is version 2 (Lin et al., 2014).

The mobile OS was initially introduced in the Samsung Wave, marking its debut in the smartphone market. Bada offers a range of mobile functionalities, including but not limited to multipoint-touch, 3D graphics, and application downloading and installation. The design encompasses a spectrum of mobile devices, ranging from basic feature phones to advanced smartphones (Raggo & Hosmer, 2012). According to Samsung, Bada is poised to supplant its in-house feature phone platform, transforming feature phones into smartphones at a swift pace.

7.2.3. BlackBerry OS (Research in Motion)

The BlackBerry OS is a mobile OS that is proprietary and has been created by research in motion. It is intended for use on the company's widely used BlackBerry handheld devices. The BlackBerry platform is widely utilized by corporate clientele due to its capability to synchronize with various business software such as Lotus Domino, Microsoft Exchange, and Novell GroupWise email, among others, provided that it is used in conjunction with the BlackBerry Enterprise Server (Schilit et al., 1993).

7.2.4. iPhone OS/iOS (Apple)

Apple first developed the iPhone OS for the company's iPhone hardware. iOS is the name of the modern mobile OS, and it is compatible with various Apple devices, including the iPhone, the iPad and iPad-2, and iPod Touch. Apple does not grant licenses for its iOS mobile OS to be utilized on hardware produced by companies that are not affiliated with the company (Li et al., 2019). As a result, the iOS mobile OS is only available on devices that Apple creates. Apple first developed the Mac X OS, which served as a basis for creating iOS, Apple's mobile OS.

Did you Know?

Apple's iOS operating system was originally called "iPhone OS."

7.2.5. Palm OS (Garnet OS)

The Palm OS is a mobile OS that is proprietary and is specifically designed for PDAs (Novac et al., 2017). It was initially launched in 1996 on the Pilot 1000 portable device. Recent iterations of the Palm OS have incorporated expanded backing for expansion ports, advanced processors, enhanced security, memory cards, and compatibility with ARM processors and cellphones. Garnet OS is an extension of Palm OS 5 that offers expanded support for various display resolutions, wireless connectivity options, and advanced multimedia features.

7.2.6. Symbian OS (Nokia)

Symbian is a software platform and open-source OS specifically developed for smartphones. At present, it is being maintained by Nokia. The Symbian OS is categorized into distinct series, namely series 40, series 60, series 80, and series 90 (Tilson et al., 2011). The most recent iteration within the Symbian platform is the Symbian^3 OS. The smartphone platform was developed to be a more advanced and innovative iteration. The introduction of Symbian^3 brought forth novel functionalities such as an updated 3D and 2D graphic infrastructure, enhancements to the user interface (UI), and the provision of compatibility with external displays through HDMI.

Did you Know?

Nokia's Symbian operating system was once the most popular mobile operating system in the worlds, with a market share of over 50% in 2009.

7.2.7. WebOS (Palm/HP)

WebOS is a Linux kernel-based mobile OS. Palm created the WebOS platform to replace its Palm OS mobile OS (Johansen et al., 1995). The aforementioned Mobile OS is a proprietary OS that was subsequently procured by HP and is currently denoted as webOS (with a lowercase "w") in HP's written materials. HP utilizes WebOS across various devices, such as smartphones and the HP TouchPad.

HP has targeted the mobile enterprise market by enhancing safety features and management capabilities by introducing webOS 3.x. HP has disclosed its intention to release a webOS iteration that can operate within the Microsoft Windows OS and will be integrated into all HP laptops and desktops by 2012.

7.2.8. Maemo

Nokia has created the Maemo platform to cater to the needs of cell phones and Internet tablet computers. The underlying foundation of this system is rooted in the Linux distribution known as Debian. The platform comprises the Maemo OS and the Maemo software development kit (SDK) (Palmieri et al., 2012).

The Maemo OS has been primarily constructed using open-source code. It was created by Maemo Devices, a division of Nokia, in partnership with various open-source initiatives, including Debian, Linux kernel, and GNOME. Maemo is a Debian GNU/Linux-based OS that heavily relies on the graphical user interface (GUI), frameworks, and libraries developed by the GNOME project

(Wessel et al., 2015). The OS employs the Matchbox window manager and the GTK-based Hildon as its GUI and application framework (Figure 7.2).

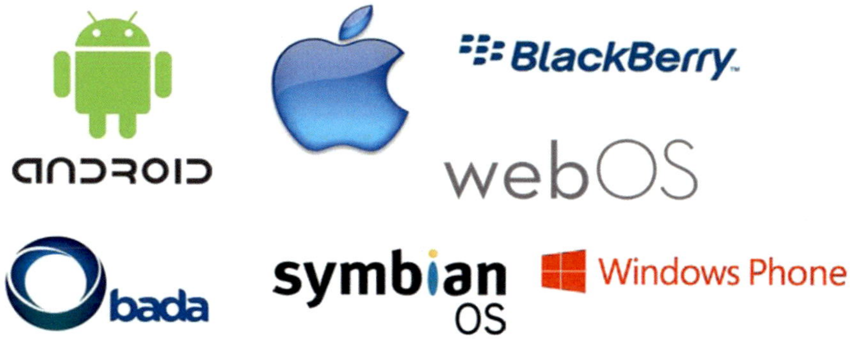

Figure 7.2. Types of mobile operating systems.

Source: Harinarayana Gundapau, Creative Commons License.

7.3. IMPORTANCE AND APPLICATIONS OF MOBILE OPERATING SYSTEMS (OSS)

A mobile OS is an intermediary layer that facilitates communication and interaction between the underlying hardware components and the end user (Böhm et al., 2015). The utilization of mobile devices is facilitated without the requirement of programming knowledge. OSs offer various services to users.

The Android platform offers an expanding array of third-party applications that end-users can obtain via app distribution channels such as the Google Play store or the Appstore on Amazon. The Play Store application facilitates users in exploring, acquiring, and upgrading applications that Google and other independent developers' release. The Java programming language (PL) is utilized to develop applications through the Android SDK.

The most recent applications of Bada OS comprise Chat On, an online platform designed to facilitate improved social connections among users and their friends or groups via the Internet (Xuan et al., 2014). The vocal mimicry tool is designed to imitate human speech playfully and humorously. It can capture and reproduce audio recordings of spoken language with a distinctive and unconventional vocal inflection. Other available features include a magic torch, the ability to type while walking, and a special effects camera. The Blackberry device boasts a wide range of carrier compatibility, with over 475 carriers worldwide supporting its use. It is available in five distinct form factors, including small and large keyboard options, flip phone, no keyboard, and candy-bar designs (Joseph & Shinto Kurian, 2013). Additionally, the device features a removable and expandable battery and supports multitasking capabilities for various programs. It is possible to synchronize Blackberry devices with multiple computers concurrently, provided multiple computers are available.

The OS utilized by iPhones, known as iPhone OS, features a home screen that includes a set of pre-installed applications (Lin & Ye, 2009). Certain applications are concealed by default and can be accessed by the user via the Settings application or an alternative approach. For instance, Nike+iPod is enabled through the Settings application. Several applications, including Safari, YouTube, and the App Store, can be deactivated in the Restrictions segment of the Settings application.

The Palm OS has standard applications: address, memo pad, preferences, date book, toDos list, security, and notepad (Murmann & Rossnagel, 2005). Blazer is a web browser designed for handheld devices running the Palm OS. The Symbian OS is widely utilized for various applications, including but not limited to the Google search client, Fring, Nokia email service, Nokia podcasting, Joiku, Qik, Google Maps, Handy Taskman, Opera Mini, and Agile Messenger.

WebOS is a widely used OS that supports applications such as Facebook for Palm, Weatherman 2.0, Tweed, Flight Track, pReader, Trapster, DrPodder, Evernote, and Grooveshark.

The Maemo OS has a range of applications, such as gPodder for podcast streaming, Maemo mapper, which incorporates GPS functionality, media support, FBReader for e-book reading, rhapsody for subscription-based music (available only in the US), ScummVM for game emulation, and many others (Ivanov et al., 2018).

7.4. COMPARISON OF ANDROID WITH OTHER MOBILE OPERATING SYSTEMS (OSS)

Table 7.1 presents a comparative analysis of the Android OS about the iOS and Windows OSes. This section provides a discussion on both the benefits and drawbacks of Android (Sharma et al., 2013).

Table 7.1. Comparison of Android and Other Operating Systems

Android OS	iOS	Windows OS
• Very customizable. Open-source operating systems can be modified, hacked, and molded to suit specific needs. • Found on all systems at all rates based on hardware and software version. • Second-largest app marketplace. Replace the battery.	• Screen pixel density is the highest. • Apple-specific hardware cannot be altered. • Largest app marketplace. • iPhone accessories range from timers to docking stations to stun weapons. • Due to manufacturer interest, only the iPhone can use accessories. • · The smartphone inspired other manufacturers to build cell phones that functioned for business and enjoyment.	• Mixed closed-open source. • App functionality must be designed for the user. • Programs are alphabetized. • When a letter is tapped, the alphabet appears, which means one can tap Y for YouTube to go to the app. • Windows Phone requires a 30-second boot time. • · Microsoft-specified hardware must be used.

Source: Raghav Arora, Creative Commons License.

7.4.1. Advantages of Android

- Android is considered an open platform due to its foundation in the Linux operating system, which is open-source software. This allows for the possibility of development by any interested party (Adekotujo et al., 2020).
- One of the advantages of owning an Android device is the convenient accessibility to the Android Application Market. This platform, provided by Google, offers many free. Applications that cater to the diverse interests of Android users keen on exploring their devices' full potential.
- The populist operating system, Android, is distinct from iOS, which is exclusively designed for Apple's iPhone (Shaw et al., 2016). On the other hand, Android is available on various devices from various

manufacturers, including HTC and Samsung, each with its flagship gadget.

- The USB provides comprehensive facilities. It is possible to substitute the battery and storage capacity of the DiskDrive and enable USB tethering (Sheikh et al., 2013).
- The operating system can provide notifications for various events, such as the receipt of a new SMS, Email, or the latest articles from an RSS Reader, thereby ensuring ease of access for the user.
- The Android operating system supports a wide range of Google services, including but not limited to Gmail and Google Reader. It is possible to access all Google services by utilizing a singular operating system, specifically Android.
- The installation of ROM modifications on Android phones offers a variety of custom ROM options that do not pose any potential harm to the device (Bala et al., 2015).

7.4.2. Disadvantages of Android

- Android requires an active connection to the internet to function properly. A GPRS web connection must be available in the vicinity to enable the device to connect to the internet and fulfill our requirements (Wukkadada et al., 2015).
- Device manufacturers sometimes release a certified version of the Android operating system customized for their device and may exhibit slower performance.
- The Android Market exhibits lower managerial control and may occasionally harbor malicious software (Götz et al., 2017).
- As end-users who engage in direct service provision, individuals may encounter challenges connecting with Google.
- Occasionally, advertisements are present on the platform due to its convenience and no cost, resulting in frequent and abundant advertising. The visual presentation of the application's interface does not impede its operational efficacy, as it may be situated at its upper or lower extremities.
- The topic of discussion is wasteful batteries. The rapid depletion of the battery can be attributed to the multitude of background processes that the operating system executes (Ahmad et al., 2013) (Figure 7.3).

Figure 7.3. Illustration of different version of android operating system.

Source: Shrey Jakhetia, Creative Commons License.

7.5. SECURITY CONCERNS ASSOCIATED WITH MOBILE OPERATING SYSTEMS (OSS)

The risks frequently linked with mobility in the business world are significant. These risks include:

- Illicit access to company data, networks, and applications due to lost or stolen devices (Khan et al., 2015).
- Confidential data breaches can occur when handheld devices fall into inappropriate hands, even if it is only temporarily (Armando et al., 2014).
- Compromised devices can also be a vector for getting into or assault against enterprise assets.
- A lack of insight into activity or security posture makes it difficult to prove compliance with regulations (Weichbroth & Łysik, 2020).

Mobile security controls can effectively manage these risks. The range of controls that are accessible is contingent upon the type of mobile device, OS, and make/model. Therefore, a comprehensive evaluation of mobility should encompass the potential hazards associated with all devices recognized in the workplace and authorized by the mobility policy.

Mobile devices such as smartphones and tablets frequently operate on one of four mobile OSs: The mobile OSs currently available in the market include Apple iOS, Google Android, RIM

BlackBerry OS, and Windows Phone (Wu et al., 2014). Various OSs employ distinct methods to ensure the security of mobile devices about their security features (Delac et al., 2011). Currently, a variety of security concerns exist. The issues above arise within mobile OSs due to insufficient consideration during the design phase. Certain individuals identify and exploit vulnerabilities to target mobile devices for various objectives. Various methods exist for unauthorized access to sensitive information, including theft of network data, personal data, and saved login credentials on mobile devices. Certain applications are specifically designed to target particular OS attacks on mobile devices. Typically, these refer to applications developed by external parties. At times, these applications modify the system files or default settings of the system, which significantly impacts the security of our mobile devices.

ACTIVITY 7.1

- Evaluate the security features of popular mobile operating systems and identify any vulnerability
- Analyze the impact of updates and upgrades to mobile operating systems on users and devices

7.6. SUMMARY

Mobile OSs are software platforms that are designed to run on mobile devices such as smartphones, tablets, and other portable devices. These OSs are responsible for managing the hardware and software resources of mobile device and provide a UI and other essential functions to allow users to interact with the device. There are several mobile OSs in use today including Android, iOS, windows phone and Black Berry OS. Each OS has its unique features and capabilities, which are designed to cater to the needs of different users. This chapter provides a comparison of android OS with the other mobile OSs and discusses its benefits and drawbacks. Security concerns related associated with mobile OSs are also part of this chapter. Overall, mobile OSs play a crucial role in the functionality and usability of mobile devices and are constantly evolving to meet the changing needs of users.

REVIEW QUESTIONS

1. What are the key features of popular mobile operating systems?
2. How does the design of mobile operating system affect user experience?
3. Explain the types of mobile operating systems?
4. What are the benefits and drawbacks of android operating system?
5. What are some of the security concerns associated with mobile operating systems?

MULTIPLE CHOICE QUESTIONS

1. Which mobile operating system is developed by Google?

a. iOS
b. Android
c. Black Berry OS
d. Windows phone

2. Which mobile operating system is known for its stability and security?

a. iOS
b. Android
c. Black Berry OS
d. Windows phone

3. Which mobile operating system is used by Samsung for some of its smart watches and other IoT devices?

a. KaiOS
b. Tizen

c. Android

d. None of the above

4. Which mobile operating system is known for its strong security features and messaging capabilities?

a. iOS

b. Android

c. Black Berry OS

d. Windows phone

5. Which mobile operating system is most customizable?

a. iOS

b. Android

c. Black Berry OS

d. Windows phone

Answers to Multiple Choice Questions

1. (b); 2. (a); 3. (b); 4. (c); 5. (b)

REFERENCES

1. Adekotujo, A., Odumabo, A., Adedokun, A., & Aiyeniko, O., (2020). A comparative study of operating systems: Case of windows, UNIX, Linux, Mac, Android and iOS. *International Journal of Computer Applications, 176*(39), 16–23.
2. Ahmad, M. S., Musa, N. E., Nadarajah, R., Hassan, R., & Othman, N. E., (2013). Comparison between android and iOS operating system in terms of security. In: *2013 8th International Conference on Information Technology in Asia (CITA)* (Vol. 1, pp. 1–4). IEEE.
3. Ali, A., (2014). Research article a review of different comparative studies on mobile operating system. *Research Journal of Applied Sciences, Engineering and Technology, 7*(12), 2578–2582.
4. Armando, A., Merlo, A., & Verderame, L., (2014). Security considerations related to the use of mobile devices in the operation of critical infrastructures. *International Journal of Critical Infrastructure Protection, 7*(4), 247–256.
5. Bala, K., Sharma, S., & Kaur, G., (2015). A study on smartphone-based operating system. *International Journal of Computer Applications, 121*(1), 4–8.
6. Böhm, S., Adam, F., & Farrell, W. C., (2015). Impact of the mobile operating system on smartphone buying decisions: A conjoint-based empirical analysis. In: *Mobile Web and Intelligent Information Systems: 12th International Conference, MobiWis 2015,*

Rome, Italy, August 24–26, 2015, Proceedings 12 (Vol. 1, pp. 198–210). Springer International Publishing.

7. Delac, G., Silic, M., & Krolo, J., (2011). Emerging security threats for mobile platforms. In: *2011 Proceedings of the 34th International Convention MIPRO* (Vol. 1, pp. 1468–1473). IEEE.
8. Götz, F. M., Stieger, S., & Reips, U. D., (2017). Users of the main smartphone operating systems (iOS, Android) differ only little in personality. *PloS One, 12*(5), 176921.
9. Ivanov, V., Reznik, A., & Succi, G., (2018). Comparing the reliability of software systems: A case study on mobile operating systems. *Information Sciences, 423*(1), 398–411.
10. Jindal, G., & Jain, M., (2012). A comparative study of mobile phone's operating systems. *International Journal of Computer Applications & Information Technology, 1*(3), 10–15.
11. Johansen, D., Van, R. R., & Schneider, F. B., (1995). Operating system support for mobile agents. In: *Proceedings 5th Workshop on Hot Topics in Operating Systems (HotOS-V)* (Vol. 1, pp. 42–45). IEEE.
12. Joseph, J., & ShintoKurian, K., (2013). Mobile OS–comparative study. *Journal of Engineering Computers & Applied Sciences, 2*(10), 10–19.
13. Kamboj, V., & Gupta, H., (2012). Mobile operating systems. *International Journal of Engineering Innovation & Research, 1*(2), 115–120.
14. Khan, J., Abbas, H., & Al-Muhtadi, J., (2015). Survey on mobile user's data privacy threats and defense mechanisms. *Procedia Computer Science, 56*(1), 376–383.
15. Li, M., Xu, G., Lin, P., & Huang, G. Q., (2019). Cloud-based mobile gateway operation system for industrial wearables. *Robotics and Computer-Integrated Manufacturing, 58*, 43–54.
16. Lin, F. X., Wang, Z., & Zhong, L., (2014). K2: A mobile operating system for heterogeneous coherence domains. *ACM SIGPLAN Notices, 49*(4), 285–300.
17. Lin, F., & Ye, W., (2009). Operating system battle in the ecosystem of smartphone industry. In: *2009 International Symposium on Information Engineering and Electronic Commerce* (Vol. 1, pp. 617–621). IEEE.
18. Murmann, T., & Rossnagel, H., (2005). How secure are current mobile operating systems? In: *Communications and Multimedia Security: 8th IFIP TC-6 TC-11 Conference on Communications and Multimedia Security, Sept. 15–18, 2004, Windermere, The Lake District, United Kingdom* (Vol. 1, pp. 47–58). Springer US.
19. Nosrati, M., Karimi, R., & Hasanvand, H. A., (2012). Mobile computing: Principles, devices and operating systems. *World Applied Programming, 2*(7), 399–408.
20. Novac, O. C., Novac, M., Gordan, C., Berczes, T., & Bujdosó, G., (2017). Comparative study of Google Android, Apple iOS and Microsoft windows phone mobile operating systems. In: *2017 14th International Conference on Engineering of Modern Electric Systems (EMES)* (Vol. 1, pp. 154–159). IEEE.

21. Okediran, O. O., Arulogun, O. T., Ganiyu, R. A., & Oyeleye, C. A., (2014). Mobile operating systems and application development platforms: A survey. *International Journal of Advanced Networking and Applications, 6*(1), 2195.
22. Palmieri, M., Singh, I., & Cicchetti, A., (2012). Comparison of cross-platform mobile development tools. In: *2012 16th International Conference on Intelligence in Next Generation Networks* (Vol. 1, pp. 179–186). IEEE.
23. Raggo, M. T., & Hosmer, C., (2012). *Data Hiding: Exposing Concealed Data in Multimedia, Operating Systems, Mobile Devices and Network Protocols* (Vol. 1, pp. 2–5). Newnes.
24. Schilit, B. N., Adams, N., Gold, R., Tso, M. M., & Want, R., (1993). The PARCTAB mobile computing system. In: *Proceedings of IEEE 4th Workshop on Workstation Operating Systems. WWOS-III* (Vol. 1, pp. 34–39). IEEE.
25. Sharma, T. N., Beniwal, M. K., & Sharma, A., (2013). Comparative study of different mobile operating systems. *International Journal of Advancements in Research & Technology, 2*(3), 1–5.
26. Shaw, H., Ellis, D. A., Kendrick, L. R., Ziegler, F., & Wiseman, R., (2016). Predicting smartphone operating system from personality and individual differences. *Cyberpsychology, Behavior, and Social Networking, 19*(12), 727–732.
27. Sheikh, A. A., Ganai, P. T., Malik, N. A., & Dar, K. A., (2013). Smartphone: Android Vs IOS. *The SIJ Transactions on Computer Science Engineering & its Applications (CSEA), 1*(4), 141–148.
28. Tilson, D., Sorensen, C., & Lyytinen, K., (2011). The paradoxes of change and control in digital infrastructures: The mobile operating systems case. In*: 2011 10th International Conference on Mobile Business* (Vol. 1, pp. 26–35). IEEE.
29. Tilson, D., Sorensen, C., & Lyytinen, K., (2012). Change and control paradoxes in mobile infrastructure innovation: The Android and iOS mobile operating systems cases. In*: 2012 45th Hawaii International Conference on System Sciences* (Vol. 1, pp. 1324–1333). IEEE.
30. Weichbroth, P., & Łysik, Ł., (2020). Mobile security: Threats and best practices. *Mobile Information Systems, 1,* 1–15.
31. Wessel, S., Huber, M., Stumpf, F., & Eckert, C., (2015). Improving mobile device security with operating system-level virtualization. *Computers & Security, 52*(1), 207–220.
32. Wu, L., Du, X., & Fu, X., (2014). Security threats to mobile multimedia applications: Camera-based attacks on mobile phones. *IEEE Communications Magazine, 52*(3), 80–87.
33. Wukkadada, B., Nambiar, R., & Nair, A., (2015). Mobile operating system: Analysis and comparison of Android and iOS. *International Journal of Computing and Technology, 2*(7), 273–276.

34. Xuan, X., Wang, Y., & Li, S., (2014). Privacy requirements patterns for mobile operating systems. In: *2014 IEEE 4th International Workshop on Requirements Patterns (RePa)* (Vol. 1, pp. 39–42). IEEE.

35. Ying, K., Ahlawat, A., Alsharifi, B., Jiang, Y., Thavai, P., & Du, W., (2018). Truz-droid: Integrating trustzone with mobile operating system. In: *Proceedings of the 16th Annual International Conference on Mobile Systems, Applications, and Services* (Vol. 1, pp. 14–27).

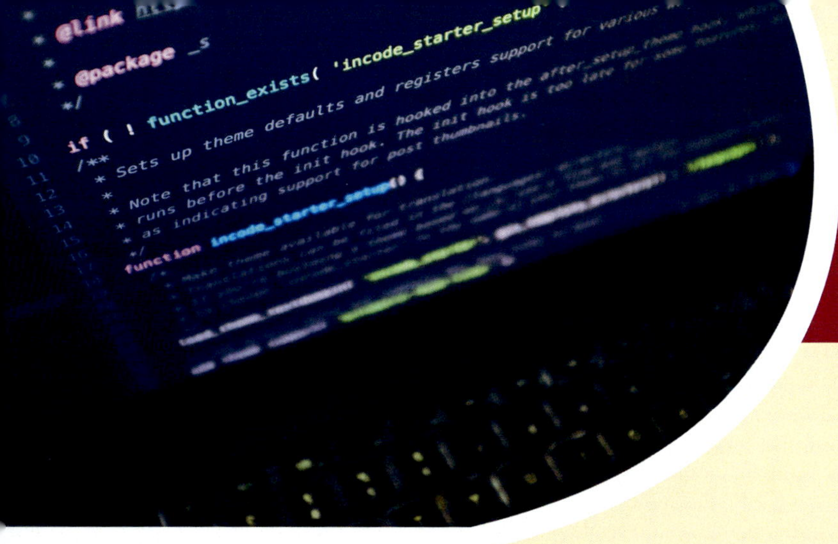

CHAPTER 8

DISTRIBUTED OPERATING SYSTEMS

UNIT INTRODUCTION

A distributed system comprises numerous computer systems connected to a network, each running an operating system (OS) that is distributed and has its clock and memory (Tanenbaum & Van Renesse, 1985). Its main advantages include sharing resources amongst computers, ensuring operation stability through redundant CPUs and resources across systems, and accelerating user applications by running their operations on many machines. Features of four software and hardware components—the network linking them, the distributed OS, and the distributed calculations carried out—are crucial for achieving these advantages (Tanenbaum et al., 1991).

These four elements play the following roles: A distributed system's node is a computer system. Its architecture affects how well it can increase computing speed and operating dependability. To facilitate resource sharing, accelerate computation, and ensure stability, the OS combines the operation of the distributed system's nodes (Tanenbaum & Mullender, 1981). A user uses a distributed computation, in which the activities are carried out over multiple system nodes, to use OS capabilities for accessibility to nonlocal resources and computation speedup. Such a computation uses interprocess communication (IPC) protocols to relay messages among nodes, including data and calculations. Network protocols are used to send these communications over the network (Tanenbaum et al., 1990).

To set the stage for the study of distributed OSes, one will cover key aspects of these four distributed system components in this chapter. Then, discussion on design challenges can occur due to the distributed character of a distributed OS's computing environment (van Renesse et al., 1988).

Learning Objectives

After the chapter, students will be able to understand the following:

- Basic concept of distributed operating systems;
- Learn about the features of distributed operating systems;
- Understanding nodes and their integration operation in distributed operating systems;
- Design issues in distributed operating systems.

Key Terms

- Cluster
- Containers
- Distributed computing
- Fault-tolerance
- Latency
- Network
- Nodes
- Resource sharing
- Scalability

8.1. FEATURES OF DISTRIBUTED OPERATING SYSTEMS (OSS)

A distributed system can comprise multiple or two computers, each with a clock, memory, networking components, and the capacity to carry out part of the OS's control functions (Dasgupta et al., 1991).

As computer hardware prices began to fall and the open system standard was adopted, the utilization of distributed computing systems spread quickly in the 1990s. An open system offers clear, nonproprietary interfaces for interacting with its parts and other systems. Since these interfaces are often created by or certified through a standards body, the computer industry readily accepts them. Their use allows a computer system's progressive evolution by enabling the addition of new parts and subsystems. A great illustration of an open network is the LAN. And can be connected because all computer systems, from supercomputers to low-cost PCs, utilize the same interface. Whenever a distributed network is set up through a local area, network capacity for computing can be gradually increased by adding new computers to the LAN (Jia & Zhou, 2004).

The following software and hardware components are used to achieve the advantages of distributed systems described in Table 8.1:

1. **Hardware Components:** Computers and networking equipment, including cables, connections, and routers (Cachin, 2016).
2. **Software Components:** Operating system (OS) and programming language (PL) characteristics that permit the development of distributed computations, networking software that provides reliable communication, and OS components that handle the creation and planning of dispersed computations and the use of remote resources (Herlihy, 2019).

Did you Know?

The first distributed operating system was developed in the 1970s at the University of Cambridge.

Table 8.1. Benefits of a Distributed System

Feature	Description
Resource exchange	Applications may make use of resources located in various.
Reliability	A distributed system ensures service continuity, or availability, despite errors. Redundancies in the network, resources, and OS services are used to achieve it.
Accelerated computation	An application's execution time can be decreased by having portions of a computation performed in parallel on other computer systems.
Communication	Users or their associated sub-computations are placed in various.
Continual growth	A distributed system may include additional subsystems without replacing or updating current ones, thanks to open system standards. In this manner, the price of improving a distributed system's capabilities corresponds to the required increased capability.

Source: Dhananjay M., Creative Commons License.

A computer system, a distributed system component, is referred to by various names. Referring to computer systems in the following ways: a host is a physical computer system, a node is a system of computers within the sense of logic, and a site is a place in a system that is distributed and houses one host. Processes and resources are examples of local entities, while those located at various locales are examples of remote entities (Belotti et al., 2019).

8.2. NODES OF DISTRIBUTED OPERATING SYSTEMS (OSS)

Different kinds of nodes can exist in a distributed system. A minicomputer node contains one central processing unit (CPU) shared among multiple users to run their applications. Although a workstation node only has one CPU, it supports one or more apps a single user has started. The processor pool node is a node that has many processors. It has several CPUs, possibly more than the number of users whose apps are served simultaneously (Haeberlen et al., 2007).

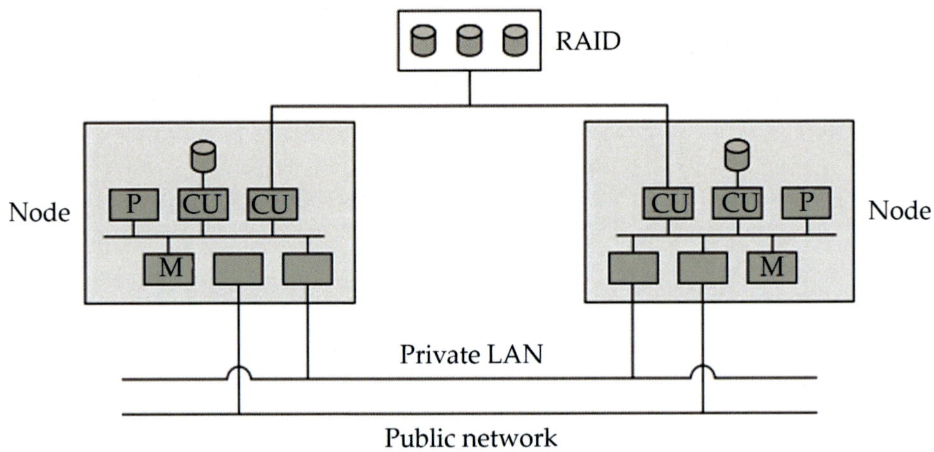

Figure 8.1. Architecture of a cluster.

Source: Stamos, Creative Commons License.

A group of machines is a collection of hosts that collaborate seamlessly. Each server is a node inside the cluster and is one of the distributed system's nodes. A cluster is depicted schematically in Figure 8.1. Two nodes are depicted in the cluster, but additional nodes might be added to clusters to offer incremental growth. Each node is a separate computer system with RAM and I/O hardware (White et al., 2002). The nodes exchange disk storage through storage area networks or multi-host RAIDs, which provide fast transfer rates, great reliability, and incremental growth. Each node has two connections: the individual LAN via which only other nodes within the cluster are linked and a public network via which it may interact with all other nodes throughout the distributed system (Han et al., 2005).

Each node in a cluster is operated by cluster software. It can increase computing performance by allocating jobs from an application to various cluster nodes, and it can increase dependability by utilizing the redundant CPUs and resources in the cluster (Tanenbaum et al., 1991).

8.3. INTEGRATING OPERATION OF NODES OF A DISTRIBUTED SYSTEM

The procedures of an application should be dispersed across different nodes in the system: (i) wherever possible to achieve computation speedup or resource efficiency; and (ii) wherever necessary for providing reliability to reap the advantages from resource sharing, reliability, as well as computation speedup summed up in Table 8.1. It is accomplished by fusing the operation of different system nodes through the interactions between their kernels. The features of some systems are sampled in this part to demonstrate various methods of integrating node activity (White et al., 2002).

Did you Know?

One of the most popular distributed operating system is Apache Hadoop.

OSs for Networks The first type of OS for distributed architectures was a network OS. Its objective is to enable resource sharing across two or more computers that run different OSs. A system OS appears as a layer across the local OS and user processes, as depicted in the schematics of Figure 8.2. The network's OS layer only forwards requests for access to local resources made by processes to the local OS kernel. When accessibility to nonlocal resources is requested, the network OS layer gets in touch with the network OS layer of the node containing the resource. It uses its assistance to implement access to the resource. On top of the OS Unix, other networks OS were created. A well-known network OS created by the University of Tyneside upon Tyne is the Newcastle Connection, commonly known as Unix United. Identical system calls to those used for local files offered access to remote files (Satyanarayanan, 1989).

An incomplete distributed OS is more difficult to develop than a network OS. Local OSs, however, maintain their identities and run separately. Thus, their operations are not merged while their separate identities are accessible to users. Before using the resources of a distant OS, a user in a few networks, and OSs required logging into it. This configuration suggests that to use a resource. A user must be aware of its location. An OS for networks cannot optimize or balance resource usage. This means that certain assets in a node might be fully utilized, while the same resources in different nodes might be poorly utilized or free. A computation utilizes a resource id whenever accessing a resource; as a result, it must be canceled if the resource fails. The network OS can likewise not provide fault tolerance (Mahmud et al., 2018).

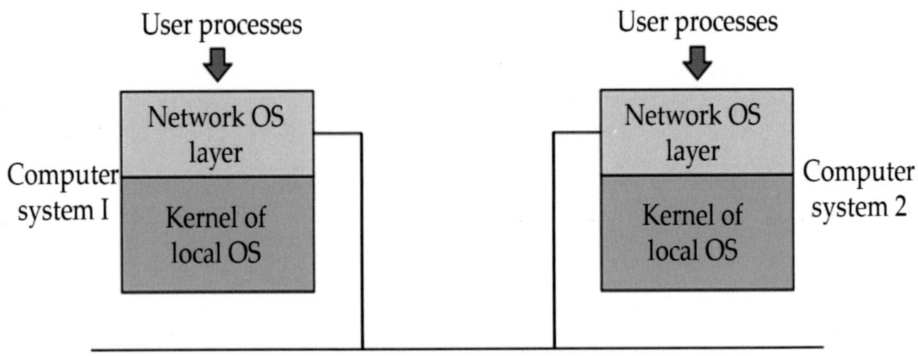

Figure 8.2. Illustration of a network operating system.

Source: Dhananjay M. Dhamdhere, Creative Commons License.

Software for Sun Clusters and Windows Although group software isn't a distributed OS, it has some features present in distributed OSs, like availability through redundant CPUs and I/O devices or computation speedup through multiple CPUs present in the cluster.

Windows cluster servers support fault tolerance in clusters with two or more server nodes. An application must employ a unique application program interface (API) to access cluster services. RAIDs of levels 0, 1, and 5 utilized by each server node provide the bare minimum in failure tolerance. Additionally, the cluster server transfers its duties to an alternative server in case of a problem or server shutdown so that its services are not interrupted (Stoller et al., 2008).

Distributed control methods implemented through actions taken by all nodes control a cluster. This method requires that all nodes have identical lists of nodes within the cluster or a consistent representation of the cluster. The following arrangement meets this condition The node manager frequently communicates with other node managers via heartbeat messages to find node issues. When a fault is found, the node manager broadcasts a message on the private LAN with information about the fault. Each node updates its list of nodes after receiving this message. This is a regroup occurrence (Dupuy et al., 1990).

A resource in a cluster server could be a service, a logical resource, and a physical resource. A resource is defined by offering a DLL interface since it is executed as a dynamic link library (DLL). A resource is a member of a group. A group always belongs to one node within the cluster, but if there is any problem, it can be transferred to another node. Starting and halting a group is the responsibility of the resource management of a node. The resource manager notifies the failover manager if a resource fails and transfers the group holding the resource to ensure that it may be restarted at a different node. All groups found in a node that has a failure are "pulled" across nodes for the resources within them can be accessible. The utilization of a shared disk facilitates this configuration. After failure, the failover manager chooses which groups may be transferred to a restored node. This procedure, known as a failback, protects the system's resource efficiency. Manual performance of the handover and failback operations is also possible (Handigol et al., 2012).

Remember

Distributed operating system can help reduce costs by allowing multiple computers to share resources such as processing power and storage.

The server nodes in a group are divided among themselves via a network load-balancing mechanism. This is how it is done: Although the cluster only has one IP address, its server nodes receive inbound messages. Based on the present load distribution configuration, only one server accepts and processes the message. If a node fails, the burden is split among the remaining nodes, and if another node becomes a member, the load distribution is adjusted to send some incoming traffic to the new node.

The Sun cluster structure combines a cluster of more than one Sun system running the Solaris OS to provide scalable and available services (Zec & Mikuc, 2004).

Availability is given through failover, which involves moving the active services on a failed node to another node. Sharing the load between servers allows for scalability. The distributed file system, networking, and global process management are the three main parts of the Sun Cluster. Global process management generates process ids that are distinct worldwide. This capability is helpful when a process is moved from one node to the next to equalize the computational demands on the various nodes or accelerate processing. A migrated process needs to be able to continue accessing files from a new node utilizing the same path names. This capability is provided via the utilization of a distributed file system. During the 1980s, the Vrije University in the Netherlands created the distributed OS, Amoeba. The main objective of the Amoeba program is to create a transparent distributed computer system that resembles a common time-sharing OS, such as Unix. Creating a testbed for distributive and parallel programming is another objective (Asada et al., 1998).

Three key elements make up the Amoeba system architecture: X terminals, a processing pool, and servers like file and print servers. A bit-mapped terminal linked to a computer, a keyboard, and a mouse makes up the X terminal, a user station. All servers, pool processors, and terminals run the Amoeba microkernel, which carries out the following four tasks:

- Managing threads and processes;
- Supporting low-level memory management;
- Communication; and
- Low-level I/O handling.

Amoeba has two communication protocols in addition to kernel-level threads. Using (RPCs), one protocol offers the client-server communication model, while the other enables group communication. Both these protocols use a (FLIP), a network layer protocol within the ISO protocol stack, as the foundational Internet protocol for real message transfer.

Servers running on the top of the microkernel implement many of the functions carried out by conventional kernels. As a result, servers carry out tasks like process creation, scheduling, and booting. A file server that uses a file in the system is also used. This method reduces the microkernel's size, making it appropriate for various computer systems, from servers to pool processors. The core of Amoeba is the idea of items. Servers manage objects and are safeguarded using capabilities (Chang et al., 2021).

A shell is started on one or more hosts in the system when someone logs in. In other hosts, processes are generated as the user gives commands to perform the tasks. There is no concept of a user's home machine because a user's computation is distributed throughout the hosts within the system. This disregard for device boundaries demonstrates how seamlessly all system resources are interconnected. The system's nodes are modeled after processor pools in Amoeba. The OS allows certain pool processors to execute a command when a user gives it. Pool processors are divided among users as necessary (Shi et al., 2016).

8.4. MODEL OF A DISTRIBUTED SYSTEM

Useful characteristics of a distributed system, such as the effect of errors on its operation and the latency, and the expense of message transfer, are determined using a system model. Typically, a distributed network is modeled as a graph (Charron-Bost & Schiper, 2009).

S = (N, E)

where; N and E, respectively, represent sets of edges and nodes. Each node may stand in for a host, such as a computer system, and each edge may stand in for a connection between two nodes; however, as will be explored afterward, edges and nodes may also have different meanings. The quantity of edges that are connected to a node determines its degree. Each node is believed to have an export list listing local resources available to other nodes and an import list listing nonlocal resources and amenities that the node can use. Leaving out the name server from the system model to keep things simple (Wilkes & Needham, 1980).

There are two different types of distributed system graph models that are practical. The configuration of physical elements in a distributed network is modeled physically. According to this concept, a node represents a computer system, and an edge is an interaction link, with nodes and edges having the consequences that were previously discussed. An abstraction is a logical model. In a logical model, nodes stand for logical entities such as processes and edges for connections between those things. Undirected and directed edges may be used in logical models. An asymmetric relationship, such as two-way IPC, is represented by an undirected edge. An asymmetric relationship, such as a parent-child relationship or one-way IPC, is represented by a directed edge. Remember that in a distributed system, logical model nodes and edges could not correspond exactly to real entities (Fujita et al., 1998).

A model of the system is examined to identify beneficial characteristics of a system, such as those listed in Table 8.2. One crucial characteristic is a system's resilience, or capacity to withstand disruption-free errors. A system that is k-resilient can endure any arrangement of approximately k failures. Fewer faults might be possible to divide a system if n is the lowest level of a node, but at least n faults must happen for a node's isolation to become isolated (Glasser et al., 2004). When a node wants to communicate a piece of information to every other node in the network, it can do so by sending messages to all of its neighbors. Once a neighbor has received one of these messages, it can send identical messages to all of its peers, and so on. This method requires a total of e-messages, whereby e is the total amount of edges in the system (Gärtner, 1999). Each node will get data multiple times as the number of edges connecting it. The system's topology can be used to manage a smaller number of messages because each node only requires a message once. For instance, a simplified protocol whereby only the originating node communicates with its neighbors is an option if the entire network is completely linked. Only one message would be necessary for this process (Dolev et al., 1987).

Table 8.2. System Properties are Determined by Analyzing a System Model

Property	Description
Effect of flaws	A system can be partitioned by a fault, or split into multiple components, to ensure a node in one area can't be accessible from another. A fault may isolate a node from the remainder of the system.
Resiliency	If k is the greatest number of defects a system can sustain without going offline, then the system is considered k-resilient, while k is a constant.
In between-node delay	A communication path's minimal latency depends on the lowest possible latency of every interaction link that makes up the path. The shortest minimum latency over all paths among two nodes is the minimal latency between those two nodes.
Cost of information transmission to each node.	The cost of this operation is determined by the topology of the system and the information-sending method. The cost can be n–1 message in an entirely connected system with n nodes. The cost can be higher if the entire system is not properly connected.

Source: Tanenbaum, Creative Commons License.

The determination of beneficial qualities is performed using both logical and physical models. Evaluating a physical model allows for determining the delay between two nodes. The complexity of the control algorithms utilized in a networked OS is often assessed through analyzes of logical models (Bernstein, 1996).

8.5. DESIGN ISSUES IN DISTRIBUTED OPERATING SYSTEMS (OSS)

The advantages of distributed systems are outlined in Table 8.1, and users of a distribution system expect their OS to deliver both the appearance and feel of a traditional OS. To fulfill these demands, the OS must efficiently distribute data, resources, users, and computations among the system's nodes to take full advantage of each node's capabilities. It results in the following design problems (Lee et al., 2006).

8.5.1. Transparency of Resources and Services

Transparency implies that resource and service names are independent of location inside a system. And makes it possible for applications to use local and remote resources interchangeably (Bertot et al., 2010). Additionally, as a change in location has no impact on the resource's name and therefore has no impact on the apps that use the resource, it allows an OS to modify the precise location of a resource freely. The OS can use transparency to migrate data to accelerate programs, lessen network traffic, or make the most use of disk space. Because the calculation can continue to use migrated sources, transparency also helps with migrating computations (Joshi, 2013).

8.5.2. Distribution of Control Functions

The kernel provides control functions to manage the system's resources and processes, including scheduling, managing deadlocks, and resource allocation (Farivar et al., 2013).

In a distributed system, centralized control functions encounter two issues: The centralized function might not be able to make the right judgments due to network latency, which makes it impossible to get consistent data on the current status of resources and processes in all system nodes. A centralized function could be the system's singular failure and performance bottleneck point. To address these issues, a distributed OS provides a control function using a dispersed control algorithm, whose operations are carried out in several system nodes in a coordinated fashion (Jeon et al., 2010).

8.5.3. System Performance

In addition to the methods used by traditional OSs, the distributed OS employs two fresh methods: data migration and computation migration. Data migration speeds up process response times and lowers network latency. Computation migrations are used to ensure that each of the CPUs within the system receives nearly equal amounts of computational demand. This process is known as load balancing (Åström, 2000).

Adding nodes and users often causes a distributed system to expand over time. Because of the increased pressure on the OS's resources and services and the increased overhead of its control operations, process response times may worsen as a system gets larger.

The performance of a distributed system should be scalable to prevent this degradation from preventing system growth, i.e., the amount of data transferred should rise as the system capacity grows while the delays and response times shouldn't deteriorate. Utilizing a self-sufficient cluster of hosts is a crucial scaling approach to prevent network traffic from increasing when additional clusters are brought into the system (Bobrow et al., 1986).

8.5.4. Reliability

When problems occur, fault tolerance mechanisms ensure that resources are available and that system operations continue. By offering redundant resources and communication channels, link and node errors are tolerated. An application can utilize a different network path to reach the resource or a different one if there is a problem with the resource itself or the network path. In this manner, a resource is only inaccessible when unanticipated faults happen (David et al., 2008).

Data consistency becomes a problem when it is copied or distributed. A fault shouldn't cause the system to be in a situation where some distributed data parts are updated, but others haven't when several parts of the distributed data are changed. To prevent this, a distributed OS uses a two-phase commit procedure (Swift et al., 2005).

Distinct system nodes may conduct distinct computer parts. Imagine that a node and link fault occur while doing such a computation. The system should then carefully return most of its sub-computations to earlier states saved in backups after evaluating the damage the fault has caused. This strategy is known as recuperation. Additionally, the system must manage ambiguities regarding a fault's root cause (Georget et al., 2017).

8.5.5. Security

Since interprocess messages may transit through a computer system known as communication processors, which may function independently underneath its own OS, security takes on a new dimension in distributed systems. A hacker may take over this computer system and alter the communications that are sent via it or use them for impersonating. Such attacks are stopped by unique message authentication, and security measures are used (Ullman, 1983).

ACTIVITY 8.1:

i. Build a simple distributed operating system using virtual machines or containers.
ii. Compare the features, advantages, and disadvantages of different distributed operating systems.

8.6. SUMMARY

The main advantages of distributed systems are resource sharing, dependability, and calculation speedup. These advantages are attained via a distributed OS, which integrates the operation of various computer systems, guarantees dependable network connectivity, and efficiently supports the execution of distributed computations. This chapter looked at relevant distributed OS strategies. A distributed system is made up of nodes connected to a network. In contrast, a node can be a single computer system or a cluster, a collection of computers cooperating and sharing resources. Within a node, a cluster can increase processing speed and reliability (Santini et al., 2016).

A graph models a distributed system. In a logical model, they represent processes and connections between processes; in a physical model, edges, and nodes of the graph are links and nodes of a distributed system, respectively. Graph models of the system are utilized to assess a system's reliability characteristics or to develop the algorithms that make up a distributed OS. Providing resource sharing, dependability, and performance within distributed context presents new design challenges for OS developers (Mourad et al., 1987).

REVIEW QUESTIONS

1. What is distributed operating system and explain some of its features?
2. What is transparency and how does it improve the user experience in distributed operating systems?
3. What is a node and how does it differ from a traditional computer or device?
4. What are some of the key considerations when deploying nodes in a distributed operating system?
5. What are some of the key design issues that need to be addressed in distributed operating systems?

MULTIPLE CHOICE QUESTIONS

1. Which of the following is not a feature of distributed operating systems?

a. Resource sharing
b. Fault tolerance
c. Complexity reduction
d. Scalability

2. Which of the following is a key design issue in distributed operating systems?

a. Device compatibility
b. Resource allocation

c. Operating system speed

d. Screen resolution

3. What is a key challenge associated with communication between nodes in a distributed operating system?

a. Latency

b. Screen resolution

c. Processor speed

d. Memory capacity

4. What is a node in a distributed operating system?

a. A central computer that manages the network

b. A mobile device that connects to the network

c. A computer or device that is a part of the distributed operating system network

d. None of the above

Answers to Multiple Choice Questions

1. (c); 2. (b); 3. (a); 4. (c)

REFERENCES

1. Asada, G., Dong, M., Lin, T. S., Newberg, F., Pottie, G., Kaiser, W. J., & Marcy, H. O., (1998). Wireless integrated network sensors: Low power systems on a chip. In: *Proceedings of the 24th European Solid-State Circuits Conference* 1, pp. 9–16. IEEE.
2. Åström, K. J., (2000). Limitations on control system performance. *European Journal of Control, 6*(1), 2–20.
3. Belotti, M., Božić, N., Pujolle, G., & Secci, S., (2019). A vademecum on blockchain technologies: When, which, and how. *IEEE Communications Surveys & Tutorials, 21*(4), 3796–3838.
4. Ben-Or, M., & Ron, D., (1996). Agreement in the presence of faults, on networks of bounded degree. *Information Processing Letters, 57*(6), 329–334.
5. Bernstein, P. A., (1996). Middleware: A model for distributed system services. *Communications of the ACM, 39*(2), 86–98.
6. Bertot, J. C., Jaeger, P. T., Munson, S., & Glaisyer, T., (2010). Social media technology and government transparency. *Computer, 43*(11), 53–59.
7. Bobrow, D. G., Mittal, S., & Stefik, M. J., (1986). Expert systems: Perils and promise. *Communications of the ACM, 29*(9), 880–894.
8. Cachin, C., (2016). Architecture of the Hyperledger blockchain fabric. In: *Workshop on Distributed Cryptocurrencies and Consensus Ledgers* (Vol. 310, No. 4, pp. 1–4).

9. Castro, M., Costa, M., Martin, J. P., Peinado, M., Akritidis, P., Donnelly, A., & Black, R., (2009). Fast byte-granularity software fault isolation. In: *Proceedings of the ACM SIGOPS 22nd Symposium on Operating Systems Principles* 11(1), pp. 45–58.
10. Chang, Z., Liu, S., Xiong, X., Cai, Z., & Tu, G., (2021). A survey of recent advances in edge-computing-powered artificial intelligence of things. *IEEE Internet of Things Journal, 8*(18), 13849–13875.
11. Charron-Bost, B., & Schiper, A., (2009). The heard-of model: Computing in distributed systems with benign faults. *Distributed Computing*, *22*(1), 49–71.
12. Dasgupta, P., LeBlanc, R. J., Ahamad, M., & Ramachandran, U., (1991). The clouds distributed operating system. *Computer, 24*(11), 34–44.
13. David, F. M., Chan, E., Carlyle, J. C., & Campbell, R. H., (2008). CuriOS: Improving reliability through operating system structure. In: *OSDI* (Vol. 8, pp. 59–72).
14. Depoutovitch, A., & Stumm, M., (2010). Otherworld: Giving applications a chance to survive OS kernel crashes. In: *Proceedings of the 5th European Conference on Computer Systems* 1, pp. 181–194.
15. Dolev, D., Dwork, C., & Stockmeyer, L., (1987). On the minimal synchronism needed for distributed consensus. *Journal of the ACM (JACM), 34*(1), 77–97.
16. Dupuy, A., Schwartz, J., Yemini, Y., & Bacon, D., (1990). NEST: A network simulation and prototyping testbed. *Communications of the ACM, 33*(10), 63–74.
17. Dwork, C., Peleg, D., Pippenger, N., & Upfal, E., (1986). Fault tolerance in networks of bounded degree. In: *Proceedings of the 18th Annual ACM Symposium on Theory of Computing* 11, pp. 370–379.
18. Farivar, M., Chen, L., & Low, S., (2013). Equilibrium and dynamics of local voltage control in distribution systems. In: *52nd IEEE Conference on Decision and Control* (Vol. 1, pp. 4329–4334).
19. Fujita, S., Hara, H., Sugawara, K., Kinoshita, T., & Shiratori, N., (1998). Agent-based design model of adaptive distributed systems. *Applied Intelligence, 9*(1), 57–70.
20. Gärtner, F. C., (1999). Fundamentals of fault-tolerant distributed computing in asynchronous environments. *ACM Computing Surveys (CSUR), 31*(1), 1–26.
21. Georget, L., Jaume, M., Tronel, F., Piolle, G., & Tong, V. V. T., (2017). Verifying the reliability of operating system-level information flow control systems in Linux. In: *2017 IEEE/ACM 5th International FME Workshop on Formal Methods in Software Engineering (FormaliSE).* 1, pp. 10–16.
22. Glasser, U., Gurevich, Y., & Veanes, M., (2004). Abstract communication model for distributed systems. *IEEE Transactions on Software Engineering, 30*(7), 458–472.
23. Hadzilacos, V., (1987). Connectivity requirements for byzantine agreement under restricted types of failures. *Distributed Computing, 2*(2), 95–103.
24. Haeberlen, A., Kouznetsov, P., & Druschel, P., (2007). PeerReview: Practical accountability for distributed systems. *ACM SIGOPS Operating Systems Review, 41*(6), 175–188.

25. Han, C. C., Kumar, R., Shea, R., Kohler, E., & Srivastava, M., (2005). A dynamic operating system for sensor nodes. In: *Proceedings of the 3rd International Conference on Mobile Systems, Applications, and Services* (Vol. 1, pp. 163–176).
26. Handigol, N., Heller, B., Jeyakumar, V., Lantz, B., & McKeown, N., (2012). Reproducible network experiments using container-based emulation. In: *Proceedings of the 8th International Conference on Emerging Networking Experiments and Technologies* 5(2), pp. 253–264.
27. Herlihy, M., (2019). Blockchains from a distributed computing perspective. *Communications of the ACM, 62*(2), 78–85.
28. Iyer, R. K., & Rossetti, D. J., (1985). Effect of system workload on operating system reliability: A study on IBM 3081. *IEEE Transactions on Software Engineering*, (12), 1438–1448.
29. Jeon, J. H., Kim, J. Y., Kim, H. M., Kim, S. K., Cho, C., Kim, J. M., & Nam, K. Y., (2010). Development of hardware in-the-loop simulation system for testing operation and control functions of microgrid. *IEEE Transactions on Power Electronics, 25*(12), 2919–2929.
30. Jia, W., & Zhou, W., (2004). *Distributed Network Systems: From Concepts to Implementations* (Vol. 15, p. 19). Springer science & business media.
31. Johnson, A. M., (1971). The microdiagnostics for the IBM system 360 model 30. *IEEE Transactions on Computers, 100*(7), 798–803.
32. Joshi, A., (2013). Assessing the impact of transparency and accountability initiatives in service delivery. *Development Policy Review, 31*, s29–s48.
33. Lee, F. C., Xu, M., Wang, S., & Lu, B., (2006). Design challenges for distributed power systems. In: *2006 CES/IEEE 5th International Power Electronics and Motion Control Conference* (Vol. 1, pp. 1–15).
34. Mahmud, R., Koch, F. L., & Buyya, R., (2018). Cloud-fog interoperability in IoT-enabled healthcare solutions. In: *Proceedings of the 19th International Conference on Distributed Computing and Networking* 19(2), pp. 1–10.
35. Mourad, S., & Andrews, D., (1987). On the reliability of the IBM MVS/XA operating system. *IEEE Transactions on Software Engineering*, (10), 1135–1139.
36. Santini, T., Carro, L., Wagner, F. R., & Rech, P., (2015). Reliability analysis of operating systems for embedded SoC. In: *2015 15th European Conference on Radiation and Its Effects on Components and Systems (RADECS)* (pp. 1–5).
37. Santini, T., Carro, L., Wagner, F. R., & Rech, P., (2016). Reliability analysis of operating systems and software stack for embedded systems. *IEEE Transactions on Nuclear Science, 63*(4), 2225–2232.
38. Santoro, N., & Widmayer, P., (2007). Agreement in synchronous networks with ubiquitous faults. *Theoretical Computer Science, 384*(2, 3), 232–249.
39. Satyanarayanan, M., (1989). Integrating security in a large distributed system. *ACM Transactions on Computer Systems (TOCS), 7*(3), 247–280.

40. Shi, W., Cao, J., Zhang, Q., Li, Y., & Xu, L., (2016). Edge computing: Vision and challenges. *IEEE Internet of Things Journal, 3*(5), 637–646.

41. Stoller, M. H. R. R. L., Duerig, J., Guruprasad, S., Stack, T., Webb, K., & Lepreau, J., (2008). Large-scale virtualization in the emulab network testbed. In: *USENIX Annual Technical Conference, Boston, MA* (pp. 255–270).

42. Swift, M. M., Bershad, B. N., & Levy, H. M., (2005). Improving the reliability of commodity operating systems. *ACM Transactions on Computer Systems (TOCS), 23*(1), 77–110.

43. Swift, M. M., Martin, S., Levy, H. M., & Eggers, S. J., (2002). Nooks: An architecture for reliable device drivers. In: *Proceedings of the 10th Workshop on ACM SIGOPS European Workshop* 1, pp. 102–107.

44. Tanenbaum, A. S., & Mullender, S. J., (1981). An overview of the amoeba distributed operating system. *ACM SIGOPS Operating Systems Review, 15*(3), 51–64.

45. Tanenbaum, A. S., & VanRenesse, R., (1985). Distributed operating systems. *ACM Computing Surveys (CSUR), 17*(4), 419–470.

46. Tanenbaum, A. S., Kaashoek, M. F., Van, R. R., & Bal, H. E., (1991). The amoeba distributed operating system—A status report. *Computer Communications, 14*(6), 324–335.

47. Tanenbaum, A. S., Van, R. R., Van, S. H., Sharp, G. J., & Mullender, S. J., (1990). Experiences with the amoeba distributed operating system. *Communications of the ACM, 33*(12), 46–63.

48. Ullman, R. H., (1983). Redefining security. *International Security*, *8*(1), 129–153.

49. Van, R. R., Van, S. H., & Tanenbaum, A. S., (1988). Performance of the world's fastest distributed operating system. *ACM SIGOPS Operating Systems Review, 22*(4), 25–34.

50. Velaardi, P., & Iyer, R. K., (1984). A study of software failures and recovery in the MVS operating system. *IEEE Transactions on Computers, 33*(06), 564–568.

51. White, B., Lepreau, J., Stoller, L., Ricci, R., Guruprasad, S., Newbold, M., & Joglekar, A., (2002). An integrated experimental environment for distributed systems and networks. *ACM SIGOPS Operating Systems Review, 36*(SI), 255–270.

52. Wilkes, M. V., & Needham, R. M., (1980). The Cambridge model distributed system. *ACM SIGOPS Operating Systems Review, 14*(1), 21–29.

53. Zec, M., & Mikuc, M., (2004). Operating system support for integrated network emulation in IMUNES. In: *1st Workshop on Operating System and Architectural Support for the on-Demand IT InfraStructure (OASIS)* 11(1), pp. 3–12.

INDEX

S

T

U